HAVANA

History and Architecture of a Romantic City

HAVANA

History and Architecture of a Romantic City

MARÍA LUISA LOBO MONTALVO

With the collaboration of Zoila Lapique Becali and Alicia García Santana
Translated by Lorna Scott Fox

Prologue by Hugh Thomas

On December 14, 1982, UNESCO's Intergovernmental Committee for the Protection of the World's Cultural and Natural Heritage declared Old Havana, along with its system of fortifications, to be a World Heritage Site.

THE MONACELLI PRESS

I dedicate this book to my parents,
Julio Lobo Olavarría and María Esperanza Montalvo y Lasa,
and to all that is Cuban.

First published in the United States of America in 2000 by
The Monacelli Press, Inc.
10 East 92nd Street, New York, New York 10128

Library of Congress
Catalog Card Number: 00-106279
ISBN: 1-58093-052-2

Printed and bound in Italy

Designed by Jay Anning with Roberto de Alba

ACKNOWLEDGMENTS

We, the author's children, along with the collaborators, Zoila Lapique Becali and Alicia García Santana, are deeply grateful for the support we have received over the years from a great many individuals and institutions, foreign and Cuban, inside and outside, without frontiers. We regret if any persons have been omitted or, rather, left anonymously concealed within the institutions mentioned below. It is impossible to enumerate them all, but we hereby acknowledge our debt to their quiet, committed efforts to disseminate the culture of Cuba: to each and every one of you, our thanks.

We would especially like to thank John J. Ryan III, whose constant help and support have been invaluable.

We are particularly appreciative of the assistance provided by Florida International University and its Cuban Research Institute: Lisandro Pérez, Uva de Aragón, and Ana Sippon; in equal measure we are indebted to the Biblioteca Nacional José Martí in Cuba, to its director Marta Terry, and to the Colección Cubana department. Without the unconditional support of all of the above, this book would not have been possible.

We have received further invaluable help from other institutions and offices, including the Cuban Ministry of Culture, the Museo Histórico de la Ciudad de La Habana, and the City Historians Office: Eusebio Leal, Rayda Mara Suárez, and Diana Barreras. The Archive and Special Collections section in the Otto G. Richter Library at the University of Miami allowed us full access to its data. For this, many thanks its director Esperanza de Varona.

We are grateful for the special efforts made on our behalf by Carmen Palmieri and Jorge González of the Miami Dade Public Library and its Foreign Language Department, and to everyone at the Key Biscayne branch. Unstinting support also came from Miami Dade Community College and its director Eduardo Padrón, and from the University of Miami School of Architecture, where we thank Elizabeth Plater-Zyberk.

Several Cuban museums and their learned specialists came generously to our assistance: the Museo Colonial and its director Margarita Suárez; the Museo Nacional de Bellas Artes, the Museo Nacional de Artes Decorativas, the Museo de Arte Sacro in the Basilica of San Francisco de Asís, and the Museo de la Platería; the compact Museo Municipal in El Cerro, and that of Música Cubana under the direction of María Teresa Linares.

Libraries and institutions in other countries, including the British Museum and the Royal Geographic Society in London and the Biblioteca Nacional in Madrid, supplied us with invaluable information.

We are also indebted to the Casa de las Américas and its sub-director Marcia Leiseca; to the Centro Nacional Cubano de Restauración y Museología; to the Instituto Cubano de Artes e Industrías Cinematográficas and its directors Alfredo Guevara and Moraima González, as well as to the Fondo de Bienes Culturales under Nisia Agüero.

Thanks to Havana University and to Meche Arche in particular, and to the Wolfsonian Foundation, especially to Mickey J. Wolfson.

Religious institutions in Cuba were most helpful, especially the Seminario de San Carlos y San Ambrosio and the churches of La Merced, el Espíritu Santo, Santa Catalina in Havana, and Nuestra Señora de la Asunción de Baracoa in Oriente province, where we were privileged to meet Father Valentín, who accompanied us through that region as both photographer and guide.

The Cuban National Heritage Foundation, with our enthusiastic friend Alberto Sánchez de Bustamante, who supported us throughout.

A special mention must go to Vicente Echerri for his tireless editorial help and continued support.

We also wish to extend our deepest appreciation to a number of professionals and friends for all their help and advice, including Pedro Menocal, Margarita Cano, the architects Raúl Rodríguez, Nicolás Quintana, and Beatriz Masú, and the writer Eloísa Lizama Lima. We shall never forget the moral and material support given by Mercedes de la Torre, Marquesa de Arcos.

Special mention goes to Jorge Viera of Northern Trust Bank, and to María D. Castillo and María E. Healey of Beta Capital Management, for their patience and unwavering support.

We cannot overlook two companions who provided decisive encouragement and inspiration for this project, though they are no longer with us: the Cuban poet Eliseo Diego, and the scholar and art critic Giulio Blanc.

Architects Pablo Hernández Villalón, who also supplied us with images, Andrés and Douglas Duany, Daniel Taboada, Charles Dunn, Raúl García, Manuel Gutiérrez, Frank Martínez, Ricardo Porro, and Raúl Lastra.

Photographers Grandal, Piero Paolo Gasparini, Pedro Jiménez, Korda, Eduardo dos Santos Araujo, Miguel Angel Báez, and others.

We would especially like to thank Roberto de Alba, without whose input and creativity we would not have been able to realize our mother's visions.

Our deepest thanks to the below mentioned, who also contributed to this book: Rosita Abella, Salomé Agüero, Agustín Batista, Baron and Baroness Lodovico Blanc, Margherita Blanc, Willy Borroto, Flavia Campilli, Claudio Castillo, Monsignor Carlos Manuel de Céspedes, Olga Connor, Father José Conrado, Emilio Cueto, Josefina Diego, Loli Espino, Fina García Marruz, Monsignor Angel Gaztelú, Gustavo Godoy, Pedro Herrera, Fico Maciá, Narciso Menocal, Andrés Oppenheimer, Lydia Pedreria, Umberto Pena, Marifeli and Eliseo Pérez Stable, Enrique Pineda Barnet, Mirna Quiñones, Leandro Romero, Gustavo Sed Nieves, Dolores Smithies and Elena González del Valle, Andrés Solares, Ana and Frank Soler, Frank Steinhart, Brian Stone, Carmen Suárez León, Fernando Uría, Nelson Valdés, Lesbia de Varona, Olga Vega, Juan Veranes, Marquesa de Villalta, Cintio Vitier. And special thanks to Ingrid Yac for her patience and unwavering hard work.

Contents

The Foremost City in Spanish America   *118*

The City of Columns   *150*

The Garden City   *184*

Tradition and Modernity 258

Beyond Havana 286

Epilogue 303

Notes 306

Bibliography 312

Maps 316

Index 318

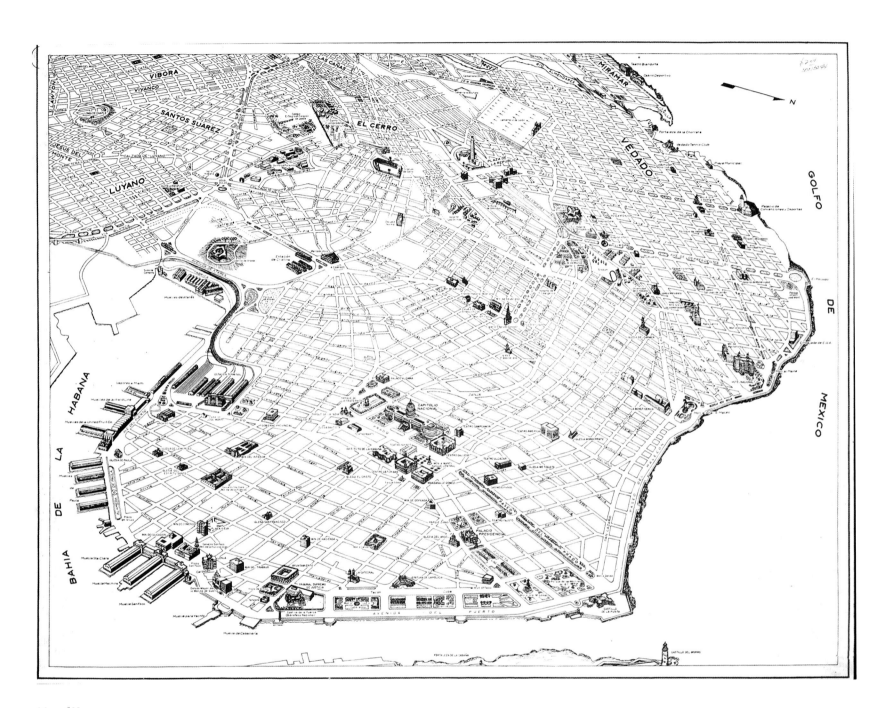

Map of Havana

Prologue

Cuba has a most eccentric place in the five-hundred-year history of America since 1492. After acting as a springboard for the Spanish conquest of Mexico, the island sank into neglect. But its capital, Havana, was used by the Spanish empire as a place of rendezvous for two treasure fleets—one from Veracruz, bearing the silver of Mexico, and the other from Portobelo and Cartagena, carrying the silver of Peru. The large-scale development of the sugar trade in Cuba in the nineteenth century enabled Spain to accept the loss of the continental empire with serenity.

During the Victorian era, Cuba became one of the richest colonies in the world, with railways antedating those of Spain and a sugar technology that was outstanding. But in the first half of the twentieth century Cuba exchanged her dependence on Spain for a similar if more indirect subjection to the United States, followed by an even more surprising relation with the Soviet Union during the last thirty years of its existence. From the menu of political experience, Cuba has chosen, at one time or another, almost every dish. Her future is unpredictable, but it is worth noting that now, for the first time in her long history, for good or for evil, Cuba is alone, subject to no foreign power or influence.

But if no one knows what may occur on the island in the days to come, the capital, Havana, will remain one of the pearls of the Americas. It is one of the more surreal contradictions in Cuba's history that revolutionary Cuba has shown how to keep the best of the past in some ways more successfully than nations that see themselves as conservative. Havana today is one of the few cities in which surviving buildings allow the historian, the casual tourist, and the artist to experience a new sense of the past. I understand that this is in great part due to the achievements of Eusebio Leal, to whom all those interested in the history of Cuba will be eternally grateful. On Obispo Street is a lovely late-sixteenth-century private home, as well as several remarkable ecclesiastical buildings of the seventeenth century. The palaces of eighteenth-century noblemen remind us that in the Spanish Caribbean the owners of sugar plantations lived on the premises, in contrast to their English counterparts, who stayed in Jamaica only as long as necessary to make a fortune and then retired to a fine stone mansion in England worthy of a character in a Charlotte Brontë work. The magnificent house of that giant of commerce and the nobility, Santiago Cuesta y Manzanal, first Count of Reunión, still stands today, in testimony to the fortunes amassed through the slave trade in Havana in the nineteenth century. Likewise, a hundred lavish palaces of the twentieth century commemorate the "dance of the sugar millions" of the 1920s.

Havana is not an antique shop, for, though some of the best of these buildings are museums, it is a city still lived in intensely and, if the political scene has changed, the sunsets are still there to recall that both the conquistador and the Communist, saw, and see, the same dramatic reds at dusk. Such cities are not, of course, unknown in North America. Newport, Rhode Island, for example, has a brilliant past constantly on show, and even the successful Boston of the late twentieth century has a solid eighteenth-century foundation that informs the way most people see the city. But Havana is on an altogether nobler scale.

To show us this remarkable city a good guide is essential. María Luisa Lobo is the ideal person. She was born to the task, being a daughter of Julio Lobo—one of the last great men of Havana before the revolution of 1959—as well as of María Esperanza Montalvo, descended from one of the most remarkable colonial families of old Cuba. Both her parents were powerful influences in equipping her for writing this book. Her father—so proud of his houses in Havana and of his great sugar plantations in the country, so learned about so much in Cuba—was a descendant on one side of Sephardic Jews based for generations in Curaçao, and on the other of great Venezuelan entrepreneurs. His daughter tells us in her moving, beautifully written introduction several anecdotes that serve to fix that remarkable father in our imaginations. But the Montalvo side must not be discounted. The founding father of the clan, Lorenzo Montalvo, came to Cuba from Medina del Campo in Spain in 1734, became commissar of the navy, and built a great hacienda at Macuriges in the province of Matanzas, to the east of Havana. Here he made himself one of the first Cuban sugar kings—a Julio Lobo, it might be said, of the late eighteenth century. Other Montalvos became pioneers in the sugar trade or statesmen in the new Cuba of the 1900s.

The Lobos were Sephardic Jews from Spain. They were expelled from Spain in 1492 and their journey to the New World led them through Lisbon, Amsterdam, London, Curaçao, and finally to Caracas, Venezuela. Julio Lobo y Olavarría was born in Caracas in 1898 to Heriberto Lobo and Virginia Olavarría, a Catholic from a prominent Venezuelan family. Heriberto had established himself in Caracas as a successful banker. He was forced to flee into exile when Cipriano Castro seized power in the early 1900s. The Lobos settled in Cuba.

Lobo was said to have swum across the Mississippi and fought a duel in his youth. He graduated from Columbia University at the age of sixteen and obtained a master's degree in chemical engineering from Louisiana State University. He made and lost several fortunes before he was thirty. In middle age, he survived several heart attacks and an assassin's bullet, which lodged deep in his brain. In the years before the Castro revolution, Julio Lobo became the preeminent sugar producer and trader in Cuba, and was a known figure on the world financial stage. He owned fifteen sugar mills and some 500,000 acres of cane land and was by far the most prosperous *hacendado* of Cuba. He was known as the single largest producer of sugar in the world: not only did he grow sugarcane and produce sugar from his many mills, but he also sold, traded, and speculated in sugar through his trading company. He was one of the few "vertically integrated" sugar producers of his day and he was said to have "cornered" the world sugar market at the height of his career. He also owned a merchant fleet, a wireless company, and was the controlling shareholder of Banco Financiero and Galbán Lobo, the family trading firm. Although he was a first-generation immigrant, he was nationalistic and patriotic. In 1958, when he acquired the Hershey, Rosario, and San Antonio sugar mills, he was fond of saying that as of that point onward the majority of mills were in the hands of Cubans. So great was his credibility in the sugar world that, even after his properties had been confiscated, he was apparently offered the post of minister of sugar by Che Guevara.

Lobo knew people from all walks of life. Scientists and academics would attend his gatherings, mixing with local personalities and Hollywood actors and entertainers. He especially enjoyed meeting people with eccentric passions and strange hobbies. Despite being a sophisticated and social man, Lobo loved the simple things in life. He would delight in taking his daughters fishing on one of his tugboats rather than a fancy yacht. But above all

he loved the Cuban countryside, especially his beloved cane fields, and he reveled in the smell of the mills in the harvest season. He was often seen far away from Havana on his plantations, constantly searching for ways to make the production of sugar more efficient. Tinguaro was his favorite plantation, and he used its *casa de vivienda* as his country home. He had affection for his workers and viewed them with a sense of paternity. Lobo was a pioneer in bringing modern health and sanitation to the Cuban countryside. María Luisa inherited that passion and was placed in charge of health and sanitation at her father's plantations.

Lobo was also a philanthropist and promoter of the arts, and he created a foundation to assist gifted students to attain higher education. His chief passions, however, were for his Napoleonic collection and his art collection (which included early German primitives, Dutch Masters, Italian Renaissance and Impressionist paintings, and more than three hundred oils). The paintings, which he lent to the Museo Nacional in 1955, formed the nucleus of that museum's permanent collection. The Napoleonic collection, however, was the most celebrated of his collections and was considered the most important outside of France. It included personal effects that had belonged to the emperor as well as to the imperial family, furniture and decorative arts commissioned by them, paintings of the family, military equipment and dress from the campaigns, weapons and armor, and a valuable collection of Napoleonic documents, including personal correspondence from the emperor to members of his family and to the field marshals and ministers of the empire. His own empire, including both his business and his personal objects, vanished with the revolution.

But it is not mere ancestry that allows María Luisa Lobo to serve so well as guide to the modern traveler in Havana. Throughout *Havana* runs a profound knowledge of the life of the extraordinary sugar plantations from which her father's fortune derived. She lived for many years in Thurloe Square, London, where she entertained both lavishly and imaginatively. Later she was to be found in Miami, where she acted as a focus for those Cuban intelligentsia who still loved their country, even if they could not or would not go there. María Luisa Lobo possessed an idiosyncratic curiosity and unpredictable energy. Above all, she had a passionate affection for what she saw and found out in Cuba. After her death, a journalist described her sitting for hours at a table in Havana's Biblioteca Nacional in search of *le temps perdu*. But that journalist could not have known how vividly she would write about the Havana she knew. For beginning in the early 1970s she made numerous journeys to Havana, and elsewhere in Cuba, in order to revive her memory of those unique sights. I defy anyone to read the introduction to this book—with its graphic portrayals of summer journeys to El Wajay or to the sugar plantation, its evocation of long-lost sounds and scents of the Lobo homes in Havana—without wishing that María Luisa had written more about the life she knew.

Yet this book is only intermittently about María Luisa. It concerns Havana and its houses, churches, convents, fortresses, and institutions. María Luisa treats each part as a labor of love, although it is not difficult to see that it is the eighteenth and nineteenth centuries that move her most. All the same, she seems to feel at home in the evocation of the mood in which the first fortresses of Havana were built in the sixteenth century. As she discusses La Fuerza, the first of Havana's many forts, she recalls an earlier building on the site. She imagines the state of mind of Isabel de Bobadilla, the wife Hernando de Sota left behind. It was at that place that Isabel waited, looking northward and hoping in vain for a sail that might signal the return of her husband, one of several conquistadors who died in Florida. Alas, she was only the first of many women who looked north in vain.

But it is Havana's eighteenth-century life that will most command our attention. The descriptions of such houses as that of the Conde de San Juan Jaruco or of the Marqués de Aguas Claras bring us in contact with people whose lives we can only imagine. The Andalusian and Mediterranean stylistic roots of these buildings cause us to reflect on that great international undertaking—the Spanish empire, of which Havana was for a long time the brilliant Carribean outpost. We know where we are when we see *rejas*, balconies, and patios; we know the ancestry of these calm interiors. We may not recognize the coats of arms over the great doors, perhaps because they have been rubbed away, but we know that we are in the unchanging world of Spanish self-assertion, so eternally and effortlessly challenging to Anglo-Saxon pretensions. In public buildings, such as the Palacio de los Capitanes Generales or the Havana Cathedral, the Colegio of Belén or the Church of La Merced, we know ourselves to be in the thrall of powerful political figures or the princes of a great international church. But the relatively small size of even the Palacio de los Capitanes Generales reminds us that government in those days was on a small scale in comparison with what it has now become in all countries in the twentieth century. That point is made strongly when we observe the size of the Casa de Mateo Pedroso in Calle Cuba. In the twentieth century no private citizen in any given country has a residence as large as the building housing that country's center of administration. But Mateo Pedroso was not, I think, making that point when building his vast palace. He was building as a Pedroso, as a member of an ancient family deeply engaged in local politics as well as the economy of the island, one who knew that he was helping to preside over a great change in the business of the manufacture of sugar begun at the time of the British capture of Havana.

When the author writes of the nineteenth century, she identifies with the Condesa de Merlín, daughter of the Conde de Jaruco, who pioneered the use of the steam engine in the Cuban sugar business. The Condesa was related to the author through her mother's side, and was also an exile. She lived for a long time in Paris, married to a French general. She returned in the 1840s to write one of the best accounts of contemporary Cuba. In a very moving chapter she describes her reconnection with the women who played with her as a child in the palace of the Conde de Jaruco.

María Luisa does not end her work with her recounting of the golden age of sugar. She passes through the sumptuous houses of those whose turn-of-the-century gardens were designed by Jean-Claude Nicolas Forestier, who served as curator of parks in Paris, and proceeds to take the story right into the mid-twentieth century. She tells us of great houses designed in the 1940s by such architects as Mario Romañach and Silverio Bosch. She goes on to write of Vedado and El Cerro and other new suburbs that were honeycombed with fine modern structures after the 1930s depression. Finally, interior decoration takes its bow, and even bathrooms are designed imaginatively. The author dwells for a page or two on post-1959 buildings, such as the Escuela de Artes Plásticas on the grounds of what used to be the Havana Country Club.

Winston Churchill, in a 1940 speech in the House of Commons, on the occasion of the death of Neville Chamberlain, described how "history with its flickering lamp stumbles along the trail of the past, trying to reconstruct its scenes, revive its echoes and kindle with pale gleams the passion of former days." In the re-creation of the Cuba of the future, the recovery of the history of this fascinating country will play a very important role.

María Luisa Lobo Montalvo's brilliant work, so beautifully illustrated with her own photographs, is a major contribution to such an effort. New generations of readers will learn that Cuban history did not begin in 1953 or 1959 with Batista and Castro, but will recall 1511 and Diego Velázquez, 1790 and the Conde de Jaruco, the Pedrosos, and of course the Montalvos. Perhaps Pico Turquino in the Sierra Maestra will again be remembered primarily for its black orchid. What a tragedy it is that María Luisa will not be with us in person to see for herself how it all evolves. For she died in 1998, in Miami, just after putting the final touches to her work. Nevertheless, within this book she is eternally present.

HUGH THOMAS
London
1999

INTRODUCTION
My Faraway, Lost World

It is not by chance that we are born in one place and not another, but in order to testify. I have attended as intensely as I was able to what God has bequeathed me; the colors and shadows of my homeland, the customs of the family, the manner of expressing things, and the things themselves: dark sometimes, and sometimes light. These ways of looking, listening, smiling will disappear along with me, because they are unique in every man; and as none of our works is eternal, or even perfect, I know that I leave behind, at best, a warning to you, an invitation to be attentive. To be, more so than ever I have been, in what God has bequeathed us.

—Eliseo Diego, Por los extraños pueblos,
in his dedication to his children, Havana, 1958

I could never say to you: this was a dream, and this was my life.
But it was not always that way. At the beginning, the table really was laid, and my father did fold his hands on the tablecloth, and the water sanctified my throat.
And I will name the things, so slowly
     that when I lose the Paradise of my street
and my forgettings make it a dream,
     I can summon them suddenly with the dawn

—Eliseo Diego, En la calzada de
Jesús del Monte*, 1949*

Havana: History and Architecture of a Romantic City was an intensely personal labor of love for me. That is why the present remarks will be not so much a formal introduction as a testimonial, reliving childhood years spent on the island of my birth. I have always marveled at our Cuban world: my own, with all its peculiarities, and the essences of an everlasting, immortal Cuba. Now, as I recall it in this way, I shall recapture memories.

I remember the trips to El Wajay on the outskirts of Havana. There my grandparents' wonderful summer home was hidden among ancient fruit trees. We would travel—my sister and I, cousins, nannies (the days of fearsome governesses had not yet dawned)—in an enormous Chrysler custom built for our grandparents, with folding seats, a convertible roof that saved them from having to stoop to get in, and special holders for our thermoses of orange juice and crushed ice. We always stopped off at La Ciénaga—the swampy domain of the Abreu family, where they had built a folly, a French

medieval castle, on some high ground in the middle of a tropical wood—to buy vegetables from the Chinese. The Chinese cultivated tidy allotments in rows and lived in spotless *yagua* (palm-bark) shacks. These polite people, speaking in a mixture of Spanish and Chinese that we could barely follow, were mired in a world that seemed miserable and alien to me. Even years later, I could not comprehend how it could be part of "my" city, for I was still more arrogant than compassionate. We would happily journey on, with half of the little ones chanting a singsong "Que llueva, que llueva, la Virgen de la Cueva" and the other half pitching in with "San Isidro Labrador, quita el agua y pon el sol." With these contradictory incantations to the weather, I used to wonder how they decided who to listen to up there.

It was in El Wajay that I first heard railway trains, "full of fame and power,"[1] as they rushed through the night with whistles that tore at the silence pulsing with crickets. Wherever I may be, the throatiness of a cock crow takes me straight back to the enchanted world of my childhood—to El Wajay, to Finca Leonor, with its great soughing trees with enormous fronds and wiry little ones—covered with sour cherries for making jelly, with peonies for nuns' rosaries, with gourds, one for each grandchild, engraved with his name and birthday by the *guajiro* Manuel, forever dressed in gaiters and *yarey* hat, a machete in his belt.

I remember the aroma of freshly roasted and ground coffee drifting through the house. The scent of my bath, the odor of the moss sprouting between the mosaics, the smell of our earth. I have searched for that smell in vain around the world: the coarse fragrance wafting up from the soil seconds before a downpour, as though it were opening up to receive the rain, the "smell of woman, of gravesoil and bedclothes, of kissing and foliage."[2]

*The Tinguaro sugar plantation, in a lithograph issued by
French artist Édouard Laplante in 1855.*

Landscape, *oil painting by René Portocarrero (1912–1985).*

We used to ride bareback through the village, past the neoclassical church and pretty porticos, where it often poured on one side of the street and not the other. I remember how the rain used to pursue us like a flying curtain, and our mad race to stay ahead of it. Those first years, a universe of grandparents and tenderness, full of astonishment and wonder, were not exempt from pain. Innocence is soon ended. Paradise is lost early on; I had seen those children with swollen bellies, dirt-encrusted eyes, bare feet. Besides, this was the 1940s, a lawless time of gangsterism, and my father[3] himself was machine-gunned, leaving him partially paralyzed.

I remember the names of Havana shops: "La Época," "La Filosofía," "Fin de Siglo," or "El Fénix," lofty names that had perplexed visitors since the last century, since they bore no relation to the goods on sale within. And I recall the thrilling names of the towns on the way down the main highway: Hoyo Colorado, Caimito del Guayabal, Gyanajay, Artemisa, Perico, Ceiba Mocha, names as lulling as our landscape, as the towns themselves.

The villages to the west around Pinar del Río: what a dizzying variety of columns on every block! What an outpouring of fantasy! Even the jaunty *bohío* huts sported columns on the porch, hugged by braids of bougainvillea and showers of laburnum and jasmine that formed glorious mantles over the humble thatch of palm fronds. Sensual, feminine Cuba—rounded like a breast, as Columbus well noted. Rounded too are the bumps of the *mogotes*, looking as artificial as pieces on an undulating game board. The great water-jars are bulbous, as are the pregnant squashes and the royal palms with their little love-handles and curving headdresses. Rounded are the provincial columns, mirroring the palms whose sharp frond-tips—virtually the only pointed thing in the landscape—may be the perch for a tiny bird, miraculously poised like a brooch pinned to the infinite sky.

Then, the country backyards. In the soporific peace of the corral, the animals skid suddenly in fright at the crash of a palm leaf. And the unforgettable smell of pigs wallowing in wet earth as they gnaw contentedly on *palmiche* berries, the odor of a ripe guava, split open where it dropped to the ground, the irreplaceable smells of our land. Sweet mandarins, frayed mangoes, *mameys*, sapotas, avocados, star apples. The perfumes of all these mingling with those of the animals and with their sounds. Chickens, ducks, doves, and the occasional foolish turkey all together in the steamy, odorous shade. Each minding its own business, pecking here and there, while the satiated pig snores.

Oh, those Cuban suckling pigs! In Pilón they used to roast them on guava-branch spits; in Tánamo the piglets were baked underground, wrapped in banana leaves. The Escambray method was to sauté or "drown" them in huge pans full of oil, but everywhere they were flavored with a paste of garlic, oregano, and sour orange. In town as in the country, no household could do without its little criollo lime or bitter-orange bush for seasoning. Who could ever forget the midnight banquet of ham hocks and pickles in the village of Cuatro Caminos, or the spicy sausages of El Congo[4] in Catalina de Güines!

I remember an outlandish train station, covered in mosaics, that saw us off to Escambray—on journeys that were more romantic, in my eyes, than any adventure on the Orient Express. Alone with our father, unencumbered by nannies or governesses, we pulled away at nightfall, snuggled up in our bunks, and at daybreak the train mysteriously stopped by the banks of the

Above: Mogote *hill in Valle de Viñales.*

Left: Slender royal palms.

Agabama, out of sight of any houses or bridges, in the middle of a canefield. People were waiting for us with horses, and we forded the river with our bags held high, coming out into the little *batey* of modest wooden houses. Sam, the cheery Jamaican factotum, called my pony Sunshine; I never liked the name, but it stuck.

Together with the batey urchins we spent all day frolicking in the river, daring each other to see who could get closest to the waterfall without actually being carried off in its appalling thunder. I remember Pikín and the other boys with whom we galloped through the hills of Escambray—the country girls were prissier, less tomboyish than us. All our father said was, "Just don't lose sight of the chimney-smoke at home." We scuffled between the hooves of the zebu cattle, played hide-and-seek among the mills and boilers and evaporators of the plant, and launched ourselves down mountains of golden-sugar sacks on improvised toboggans of *yagua* strips. Later by the same means we would whizz down the marble stairs of our grandparents' town house in El Vedado.

And we were left just as free in the other plantations: Tinguaro, Tánamo, Pilón . . . the Sierra Maestra and Sierra del Cristal, with their streams and pools embroidered with buds of rose apple and butterfly lily—*mariposa blanca*, our fragrant national flower[5]—and their trees invaded by orchids, air plants, and creepers. The ascent to Pico Turquino, on the trail of the black orchid said to thrive there mysteriously, on the highest summit in Cuba. The tree ferns, arcane and prehistoric, the hermaphroditic, vivid tree snails,[6] and the marine fossils of the Sierra Maestra. "Look," said my father. "We must have been

The Tinguaro sugar plantation.

underwater when the Maya were at their peak. Otherwise they'd have come over from Yucatán and left traces on the island. Could we have been Atlantis?" and he laughed. I think of the bashful poppy that could not be touched without gathering its trembling petals together, and of the dancing Carolina flower, which twirled more gaily than anything. I remember the hedges of flowering immortelles, spray after spray of tumbling pink froth. I remember nights and places where it seemed that the phosphorescent stars could be netted from the sea, bright sparkles over the keys of Tánamo and Pilón.

So many marvels! In the house in Vedado where I was born there was an enchanted patio, the "Courtyard of Riddles," with high walls spilling jasmine and a bubbling fountain, where my father used to play the magician at our children's parties. How often I heard him say that the rare charm of a Moorish garden was due to the three elements of privacy, fragrance, and the sound of cascading water. Our patio had all these things, plus a floor of Seville mosiacs swirled into castles, people, animals, and fruit. In the evenings we used to dine there with our parents, and, after coffee, the sister who had behaved best that day was rewarded with the honor, the very great honor, of lighting my father's cigar, and pressing the gold cigar-band around her finger like a ring. After this ritual, we put our hands over our eyes and he'd call out "Castle!" or "Eagle!" or something else, and we'd race to put our foot on the right mosaic figure. Then the cool music of the fountain would have to calm our excitement until we were sent, protesting, to bed. And my father, who liked to give things their own names, christened it the Courtyard of Riddles.

After that we moved to Quinta Avenida in Miramar, near the big marble urn on Forty-second Street. This was a modern house with huge gardens, Californian colonial style. My father woke us before dawn to watch the cactus flowers open with what he insisted was a "pop"—we never managed to hear it. With him we pedaled on bicycles down to the mangroves, where we saw the sun come up as we swam; then we'd rush home to change, and Father would personally take us to school, with our pigtails still wet.

In the late afternoons, my father and I tried to paint landscapes and sunsets onto the pungent lids of cigar boxes. He challenged me: "Let's see now, Mani, if we can do it without being vulgar. These sunsets are damned difficult! Chartrand[7] was so right! Cuban light *is* full of lilac and mauve—look how well they go for the caimito and the trees, but be careful—it's not the same light in Havana as it is in Varadero, or in the country . . ."

Varadero—what can I say about that marvelous seaside place of so many games and sorrows—about the fresh, cool wooden houses, fretted with carved lace before Kawama existed? Kawama houses were of sand-colored stone, roomy and comfortable, with wide porches, and free of the Frenchified pretension and fuss of the mansions built in the 1950s, at the beginning of the end. On the irridescent turquoise shore, ladies in big straw hats paddled with their guests, gossiping amiably with their backs to the ocean, smoking or sucking *mamoncillos* and squishy Filipino mangoes. Even today, *habaneros* who are regulars along the Malecón will sit on the wall with their backs to the sea, to attract the girls and soak up the breeze that blows from land or water according to the hour.

In Varadero we were never attacked by barracuda or sharks. In that time so long past that is so present to me, it seems we were blessed with some

The butterfly lily, Cuba's national flower since 1938.

The tree snail, famous for the vivid patterning of its shell.

magical protection. We children, happy and carefree, used to accompany our grandparents to their properties in Punta de Hicacos, nearly at the end of the peninsula, passing by the enormous estate of Eleuthère Irenée DuPont, with its iguanas and golf course. We gathered coco plums to make into jelly with sugar, cloves, and cinnamon on coal-fired stoves—"much better than those newfangled electric things," Leticia, the cook, declared. We poured the confection into a big glass bowl and put it on the sideboard in the dining room, beside the other jars of guava, grapefruit, papaya, or sour-orange preserve. These would be added to the many desserts served at home, such as the custard apple, and *mamey* ices prepared by the Chinese on the beach. And on the porch there were more enticing glass bowls, full of banana and *malanga* snacks, always fresh and crunchy for the enjoyment of friends who dropped in on foot or by boat, with that informality so typical of Varadero.

Some nights we fished for blue crab in the Kawama lagoon—before it became a marina—while telling each other spine-chilling tales of mystery and terror. "How scary, how scary!" we would sigh blissfully. Then Leticia would cook up the crab with corn flour in a clay pot, nearly as delicious as the steamed tamales we had at my Montalvo grandmother Yiya's house.

Games and more games, kids' games, adolescent games. Poker with the grown-ups, gossip like the grown-ups, grown-up heartaches. What happened to the innocence of the fireflies and the *guisaso* grasses, the stubbornly hidden hermit crabs, the scorpions, the giant *cobo* snails[8] and the land snails? What became of the Chinese-grocer figures made of mother-of-pearl, tiny

replicas of those men and women who later formed part of the great exile? It was the second for them—if there ever can be more than that first and total displacement, however often suitcases are packed from then on. In New York I saw those men and women once, on a bitterly cold and snowy night, working in a Sino-Cuban restaurant in yet another ghetto, doubly alienated in that icy weather that froze the soul.

Fishing expeditions were occasions for giggling and guitar-strumming, scaring away the red snapper and infuriating the more earnest fishermen on nearby yachts. Baked red snapper, *cabrillas* Colbert, fried *rabirrubias*, Cárdenas lobsters, and oysters from the mangrove swamps. But best of all would always be fresh-caught *cabrillas*, fried on board and washed down with some of our fabulous ice-cold beer.

At dusk we toasted *mamoncillo* seeds around a bonfire on a white stretch of sand, singing and playing. And at dawn, we might hunt for turtle eggs—like dented ping-pong balls that had been secretly, painstakingly buried on the beach by the lumbering loggerhead turtles. We placed the eggs in wooden crates, well protected and covered with sand but in full sunlight for forty days; then when the babies hatched, we'd return them carefully to the sea.

I remember the murmur of our gentle waves, and the wind whispering plaintively through the gray Australian pines, which were so lugubrious and out of place. The song of the breeze as it ruffled palms, wild cane, coconut, and banana trees, each to a different tune; and listening to *danzón* music while crossing the Yumurí river. The notes of the flute were as sweet as the valley, music and landscape merging into one.

The marble urn located on 5th Avenue and 42nd Street in Miramar.

A landscape by Esteban Chartrand (1840–1883), suffused with the golden light so beloved of this Cuban romantic painter.

The Varadero home of Elena Lobo Olavarría. It is built from quarrystone and precious timbers, like many such beach houses of the 1940s and 1950s.

In the remoteness of memory, I hear the *guajiro* encourage his team of oxen—"Siboneeeey! Azabacheeee! Perla Finaaaa!" I breathe the intense, overpowering smell of the cane harvest, of its liquor, syrup, and *cachaza* brew. I again enjoy that regular nocturnal stroll through the *bateys*, among wooden houses with elaborate valences over their verandas, like the buildings of a spa. I hear the plantation noises, the strange braying of pistons, so relentless, potent and assured, and the creaking of crushers over the cane stems. We wandered in and out of the buildings and watched the ovens devouring the steaming fibers, watched the men laboring half-naked in the muggy, asphyxiating heat.

During the 1950s, my father commissioned Guido Cantelli[9] to compose a symphony about the sugar harvest. It was to begin with the chant of the ploughman as he furrowed the earth, and conclude with the pandemonium of the wharves and the sound of ships' foghorns receding in the distance. I wonder now how Cantelli would have dealt with this world in musical terms had he not been killed in a plane crash in 1957. Could he have captured that era as well as Hipólito de Caviedes[10] did in the medium of paint—in a series of murals around the inner patio of my father's office, deep in Old Havana?

The Yumurí valley at dawn, in an oil painting by the nineteenth-century Belgian artist Henri Cleenewerck.

Detail of a mosaic mural depicting the sugar harvest. The work was designed by the Spanish artist Hipólito Hidalgo de Caviedes.

The colonial courtyard of the Galbán-Lobo offices, on San Ignacio Street in Old Havana.

Postcard of O'Reilly Street in Old Havana.

Postcard of El Vedado.

That office was on San Ignacio Street, between Obispo and O'Reilly, a stone's throw from both the Plaza de Armas and the Plaza de la Catedral, in one of the most traditional sections of the old town. I remember that colonial patio, lost in the entrails of the building but lovingly respected during the modernization. It had a water-tank and an ancient statue of Saint Ignatius embedded in one wall. From the office, down O'Reilly Street, you could see the boats sliding lazily through the still waters of the bay.

I can remember the smell of the coffee stalls on Obispo Street, three cents a cup, a smell that clung to the narrow, crowded street and caused noisy bottlenecks when, in a demonstration of criollo casualness, drivers would hop out of their cars to savor the strong, black, heavily sweetened brew. And I recall the ritual visit with my Lobo grandparents to Mendis's small shop for some honey candies. We'd scramble out of the car with Secundino, the chauffeur, while Tití and Yeyo waited patiently for us, along with the rest of the traffic on O'Reilly.

The Havana of the first decades of this century seems naive to us now, when we look at yellowing old photographs or postcards. The broad sweep of Línea Street in Vedado was lined with eclectic mansions in every style, bristling with towers. There were smaller houses too, with neat gardens and shady porches. There were parks with pergolas and bandstands, and columned corner warehouses. The rumbling progress of tramways, full of powdered matrons—white, mulatto, black—placidly fanning themselves on their wicker seats, in spite of the breeze; the horse-drawn buses or *guaguas*, lottery vendors and peanut hawkers pestering the passengers with "Jackpot tomorrow! Winners sold here!" or "*Manííí, maní tostado*, buy your roasted peanuts, sugared peanuts!" In the street, it was "Piiineapples, fresh pineapples" and "*Pican, no pican*, spicy or sweet" from the tamale seller, mixed with the cries of the knife-sharpener, the bottle man, the flower man. . . . From dawn to dusk, the cooing and fluttering and wheeling of countless pigeons animated the roofs and towers of Vedado. With grandfather Yeyo we listened to radio serials: *Tamakún, the Wandering Avenger; Manuel García, King of the Fields; The Three Villalobos; Right to Be Born; Impatience of the Heart,* and *Tarzan,* heralded by his terrific yell. After lunch, with Yeyo's permission, we would assume our positions behind our chairs and let out bloodcurdling sounds, to the horror of any unwary guests. Then the click-clack of domino pieces as Yeyo and his friends played on the porch surrounding the big house on Fourth Street, high on its ridge, the house that later passed to my father.

I shall never forget the view from my windows: the sea and the sky were the backdrop, while to the west rose the slender tower of Saint George's School, with glowing mosaics and a cupola that belonged in Istanbul; the art deco building designed by my great-uncle Arturo Lobo, surmounted with rhythmic pinnacles cut out against the blue sky; the tops of the palm trees whose gentle swishing caressed my rooms and terrace. To the east was the white Sarrá mansion, with its gardens and chapel, and behind this were stacked roofs, towers, and more gardens. In the distance, the curve of the Malecón roadway and promenade tracing the seashore and finally the rugged outline of El Morro, looming over the horizon.

Years later I dreamed of someday building a house that would encapsulate our Cuban essentials along modern lines. I had already outgrown my hack-

A shady gazebo on 5th Avenue between 24th and 26th Streets, in Miramar.

neyed passion for the various Louis, and had begun to collect colonial furniture and contemporary Cuban painting. I used to crisscross the countryside in the Hershey truck looking out for those distant clumps of great trees that meant groves of ancient, spreading bay-rum trees, *mamoncillos, mameys,* oranges . . . all so exuberant, so carelessly extravagant, so unlike those practical little shrubs that anyone can grow or consume. Were our ancestors perhaps more refined in spirit and more intimate with nature than ourselves, to have always brought back exotic seeds and sprouts from their travels? Beneath the fragrant shade of such giants there would be some grand old house, often in ruins, with cedar or mahogany wardrobes left outside in all weather for the doves. I used to buy up dilapidated furniture, bits of ironwork, marble, and mosaic, even stained glass, haul it all back to our warehouse and leave it, dreaming of the beautiful, happy home where each piece would find a place someday. Sadly, it was not to be. Which may, in part, explain this book.

I smell Guerlain's Eau de Cologne Impériale, which all the men in my family used; and my mother's jasmine-scented Joy. Later, the tenuous fragrance of the elegant, worldly "Catalina Lasa," a rose named for the translucent flush, almost like *mamoncillo,* of my great-aunt's complexion. On gala nights I would wear this rose instead of the habitual orchid corsage. And I see the drill suits and tuxes the planters wore, and the fine linen pleats of

Right: Cupola of Saint George's College, on the corner of Linea and 6th Streets in El Vedado. In the foreground are the art deco pinnacles of the Lobo building.

Below: View of the bay of Havana.

their *guayabera* shirts, and I get a fresh whiff of Eau Impériale . . . and very near the end, there were lavish, perfumed sprays of "Black Prince" in the opaline vases of the Salón Napoleónico.

Fragrances again: that of night jasmine (which I sought high and low until I came across a sad, dejected specimen at the Chelsea Flower Show in London); of magnolia and *picuala*, of ilang-ilang and frangipani; of the lone Arabian jasmine of municipal parks and Sunday concerts; of the modest rosebushes of rural schools in little yards presided over by the inevitable bust of José Martí. What an indescribable, tormenting tenderness is aroused in me by all this!

My vital Havana, the boisterous Havana of the republic, committed to its ideals and to the pleasure of its spaces. . . . Nights always refreshed by the wind, open-air cafés in El Prado with all-women orchestras, leisurely walks through the streets, concerts in the parks, and the shoulder of the Malecón in a strong north wind, battered by the waves. As I explored its plazas, houses, and periphery once more, trying to seize, to pin down the image, I found what had almost ebbed away: a past that continues to be present in the city's ancient and venerable stones, in its *intermezzo* spaces, and, sometimes, in its modern ones.

My romantic vision of Cuba, and of Havana in particular, is marked by memory, by the distance that separated us for many years, by the yearning for childhood and youth and, of course, the nostalgia that clings to any world so abruptly abolished. I salute the Cuba of my forefathers, who helped to make it; the warm-hearted people who call one another *mi vida* or *mi cielo*, and all its people. I am homesick for my childhood and for a far-away world, lost in the distance.

Julio Lobo's Salón Napoleónico.

Romantic Origins

The place was called Gan-Eden, the Garden of Delight, and it belonged to the Caliph Haroun Al-Raschid, who, when his heart was contracted, used to come to that garden and sit there; so his heart became dilated, and his anxiety ceased.

—*William H. Hurlbut, "Noureddin and the Fair Persian,"*
Pictures of Cuba*, 1855*

It is the romantic vision of our American world that interests me here, as a way of uncovering one of the definitive secrets of my city. As part of a certain cultural legacy, this vision embraces the existence of the Isles of Earthly Paradise, the Garden of Eden, the Fountain of Eternal Youth, the lands roamed by Amazons and the people of Atlantis—unknown, exotic worlds that were predestined, promised, and awaited.

One of the most widely read books of the Middle Ages was the tale of Marco Polo's journeys, in which the Venetian merchant described his stay at the fabulous court of China. When he returned to Venice after an absence of twenty-four years, the story caused a great stir among his contemporaries, especially in sailing and cartographic circles. Ancient scholars such as Pliny and Herodotus had also passed down the names of legendary islands, peopled by sirens who were half woman, half bird or fish. Isidore of Seville went so far as to maintain that Paradise would be found in the first place to appear east of the known world, while Saint Brendan believed that it lay to the west, in a luxuriant island full of flowers and fruit.

In 1477 a young Genoese mariner arrived in Lisbon. His name was Christopher Columbus, and he was consumed by the longing to find distant islands abounding in gold, pearls, and precious stones; this obsession ruled his life and is evoked in all of his writings. Driven by the fever of discovery that held Europe in its grip between 1470 and 1480, Columbus sought in the golden cities of the Great Khan the key to a shorter sea route between Portugal and Asia. In 1492 he was led to discover a New World, waiting on the other side of a mysterious ocean that had scarcely been explored before.

Fanciful speculation was now enriched by the reality of this New World, so utterly different from Europe, with its outlandish plants and beasts and strange peoples who went naked, like Adam and Eve in the Garden; people who spoke in unknown tongues and traded their gold for baubles. This magical, fresh world that so bewitched Columbus and his men when they first set foot on Cuban soil on October 28, 1492, was to become uneasily entwined with the Spanish universe, confined at that time to a severe Castilian monastery under men of the Gospel who had shaped this powerful culture into extremes of intolerance and permissiveness, bigotry and mockery, indigence and ecclesiastical opulence. The consistency of Spanish identity becomes apparent in these paradoxical dualities, and the two faces of the coin are always united by a streak of obscure, dynamic passion. But along Spain's southern shores a Mediterranean grace permeated the popular lode of wisdom, and this was the founding knowledge that would be bequeathed to the American world. Here were men with courtly ideals, shaped by religious literature and novels of chivalry, who found a natural field of adventure in the expanses of the New World. Their exalted sensibility, courtly ideals, and propensity toward war and mystery compose one element in the construction of American romanticism. Alejo Carpentier expressed this when he undertook to define the *real maravillos* in Spanish America:

> Here the unusual is commonplace, and it has always been so. Courtly novels were penned in Europe, but lived out in America; and while the adventures of Amadis de Gaule were written in Europe, it was Bernal Díaz del Castillo who gave us the first true-life book of chivalry, in his *History of the Conquest of New Spain*.[1]

Detail of a map of Cuba by José M. de la Torre, 1853

Top: In Old World legend, mariners and missionaries sailing through uncharted waters were waylaid by seductive mermaids.

Bottom: Saint Brendan.

Right: Medieval circular map of the world.

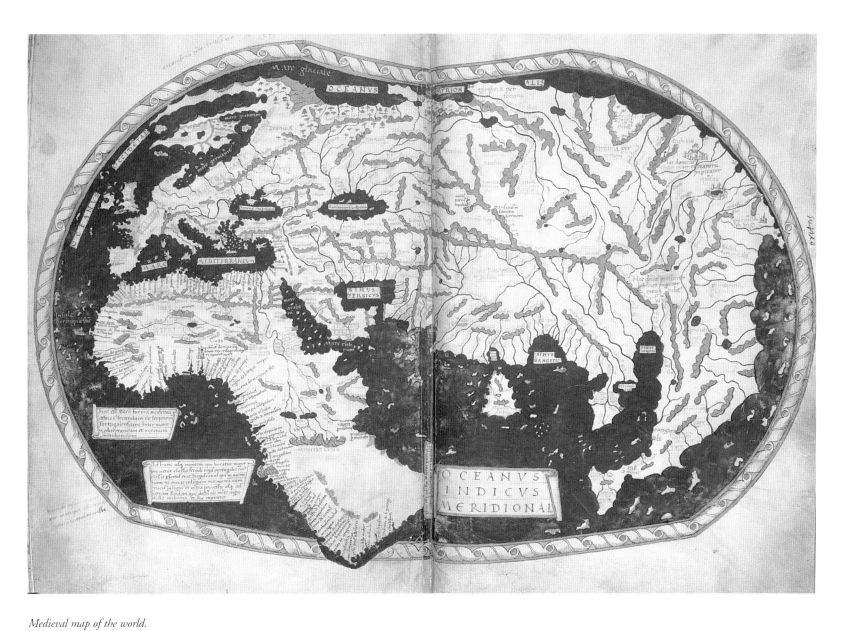

Medieval map of the world.

It is in that book that Bernal Díaz tells us how greatly Cuba was missed, how captivated the Spaniards were by the island:

> And I also must mention the curses spat by Narváez's men against Cortés, and the words they spoke, to wit, that they wanted nothing more to do with him or his land, and the same went for Diego Velázquez, who had sent them hither, for they had lived peacefully enough in their Cuban homes, enraptured and without a care.[12]

Thus was born an idyllic perception of the island that was to endure over hundreds of years. In the nineteenth century, despite the infamy of African enslavement, the English traveler William H. Hurlbut summarized his impressions of Cuba in his book *Pictures of Cuba*, when he made reference to the *Thousand and One Nights*: "The place was called Gan-Eden, the Garden of Delight . . ."[13] However, the utopian thinking that was kindled among Europeans by a dream of paradise regained, in the lands that had been "discovered" across the Atlantic, was equally responsible for encouraging a treacherous belief in regimented, ideal societies from which a "new man" might emerge. The invention of the American myth proved a failure in the colonies founded by the Spanish, the French, and the Portuguese on this continent. Cuba (the largest, wealthiest, and most paradisiacal island of the New World) was destined to be the stage on which the utopia of a new society was played out to its final consequences in our own time.

The city of Havana in communion with the sea, in its dawns and dusks, tempests and rains, with the sensuality of its breezes and its backdrop of crumbling stones, has always offered a haven for feeling, in whose shelter the imagination takes flight. Havana is the site of emotional extravagance; its history is one of pirates, of fleets laden with gold, precious gems, and exotic feathers, dropping anchor in a fortified harbor. Havana is the antiquity of stone and the sinuousness of the Cuban gait; it is the villas of El Cerro and the mansions of Vedado, the vital life of the villages. Her mellow, undulating landscape found men able to interpret it with the fidelity of a Bautista Antonelli, the architect who made the fortress sprout from rock like sculpture. Havana is a city of rivers and palms, majestic twilights open to the sea and to the gulf on a long meandering strip of shore, tracing the outline of a shell. I was never able to break Havana's spell and have never forgotten the charm of my city. That is the reason for this book.

Map of Cuba by the Venetian cosmographer Coronelli, sixteenth century.

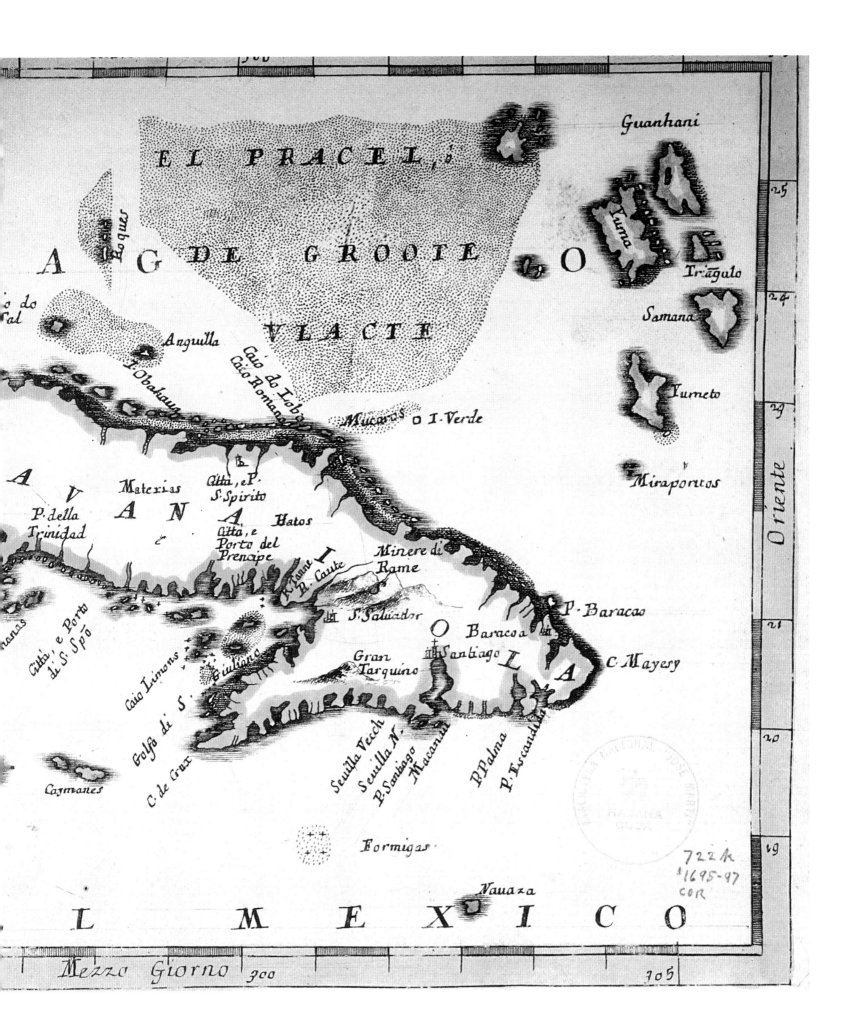

Above: Sixteenth-century allegorical representation of the New World.

Right: The Almendares river separating El Vedado from Marianao.

A Villa *Is Born*

*The north coast has some fine ports, and the best and most excellent among them
is that once known as Carenas and now called La Habana, which has the
capacity for many galleons, and there are few such in Spain or indeed in many
other places of the world that might equal it.*

—*Bartolomé de las Casas,* History of the Indies

The *villa* or borough of San Cristóbal de La Habana was named after Saint Christopher, patron saint of travelers, followed by the adaptation of an indigenous word, part toponym and part the name of a local chieftain, Habaguanex. As time went by, the Christian name fell into disuse, leaving only the indigenous name. The last but one of the first seven Cuban boroughs, Havana was founded in 1514 by Pánfilo de Narváez, lieutenant to governor Diego Velázquez, on the south coast at the mouth of the Onicaxinal, today's Mayabeque River. By that date the magnificent port of Carenas on the north coast was already well known, having been discovered by Sebastián de Ocampo in 1509 when he was exploring the island. From then on, every ship put in at Carenas before setting sail on its long and hazardous journey.

Due to the insalubrious conditions of Cuba's southern coast, the conquistadors began to take an interest in the northern area; this, in conjunction with other events and circumstances, encouraged Havana's wholesale displacement to a new site. In 1517 the intrepid pilot Antón de Alaminos discovered the current of the Gulf of Mexico, which henceforth would become the obligatory route home to Spain. And the conquest of Mexico by Hernán Cortés in 1519 would turn Carenas into the chief point of connection and operational center for the mainland territories.

The small population was initially relocated to the banks of the Chorrera (later Almendares) River, in a place that was subsequently called Puentes Grandes. Shortly afterward, it moved up to the mouth of the river. Finally, in 1519, it settled in the great bay of what was still known as the port of Carenas, strategically positioned opposite the Florida Straits and the Old Bahamas Canal, on the new communications route between the New World and the ports of Seville and Cadiz. Tradition has adopted November 16 as the date of foundation—when the first town council took its seat, and the first mass was celebrated under a silk-cotton tree, on the spot that would become the Plaza de Armas or parade ground.[14]

This spot on the island had found at last, with natural majesty, its allotted people and city. First there had been the warm waters of the gulf, the green, rounded hills and lush vegetation. The brilliant luminosity of the Caribbean tropics and the starry night of deepest blue and violet were waiting, like a gorgeous but empty ring, for the gem of the city that would match it; the city that would thrive on a fantastic traffic of gold, silver, and exotic goods, besieged in violent reality by storybook pirates and *corsaires* (the latter being legitimately licensed to attack enemy shipping), perpetually destroyed and rebuilt by tenacious, obsessive men whom a whim of fate had dispatched to this crossroads of the world. The city of Havana was the stuff of legend from the start, and its one rule was always to break the rules. During council sessions, when royal orders were approved by the aldermen present, the following ritual was observed: "Each one of them of his own accord took the said provision in his hands and kissed it, then placed it atop his head, saying that he obeyed it and was disposed to comply with it." But on some occasions, this process had an extra proviso: "We take notice but do not comply."[15]

Initially confined to the area surrounding the Plaza de Armas, the town spread along the western edge of the bay in a narrow strip. A church was built, and the religious orders, the town council, and the customs office were also housed here; none of the edifices survive today. Lining these crooked early streets were small *bohíos* or indigenous shacks roofed with palm fronds;

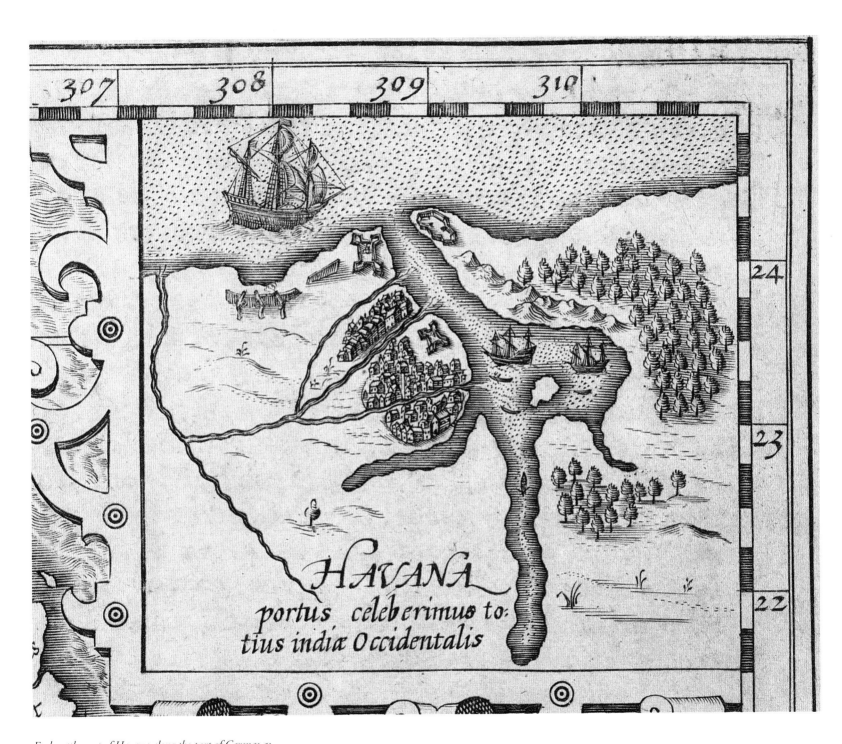

307   308   309   310

24

23

22

HAVANA
portus celeberimus to:
tius indiæ Occidentalis

*Early settlement of Havana along the port of Carenas as
depicted in a sixteenth-century map.*

Top: The Almendares river, with shady overhanging curtains of creepers filtering the light.

Middle: The classic bohío *hut, which is still built in the countryside from various parts of the useful royal palm.*

Bottom: Bohío *on stilts.*

they had fenced yards for growing fruit and vegetables and keeping domestic animals. The city came slowly into being at the foot of the hills.

The Spaniards took up the building techniques of the natives. According to Bartolomé de las Casas in his *History of the Indies*, Columbus was favorably impressed by the local *bohío*, which he describes as follows: "The houses are made of very long, thin strips of wood and straw, shaped like a bell in that they are narrow at the top and broad at the base, well able to accommodate numerous people, with a space left open at the top for the smoke to escape, covered with a finely worked and proportioned cap or crown."[16] Another indigenous dwelling was the round structure known as the *caney*, reserved for prominent members of the community.

The chroniclers also record the existence of houses on stilts, amphibious creations erected by the Indians in the lagoons. In other buildings, the pitched roofs woven from branches and thatched with palm rested directly on the ground. This type of structure was adopted by Cuban campesinos, who dubbed it *vara en tierra* (rod in the ground); it is still used today, among other things for storing fruit and tubers.

The Spaniards doubtless appreciated the *bohío* because it was adapted to the climate, easy and quick to construct, and required no material other than the wood and fronds of the palm tree—a plant that grew in such abundance that it became the Cuban national symbol. This indigenous dwelling still persists in the countryside, after undergoing minor adaptations during the sixteenth century to the habits and needs of Europeans. It has survived despite the fact that the authorities promptly made efforts to ban it, not only because of the frequency with which it was apt to catch fire; more importantly, the indiscriminate felling of palm trees, which were communally owned, deprived farmers of the *palmiche* fruit on which they relied to feed their livestock. For this reason the colonists were urged to build their homes in stone.

I rediscovered the *bohío* many years later, when I was exploring Cuba to collect graphic evidence of my roots. Of course, the extreme simplicity of this dwelling reflects the poverty of its inhabitants; nevertheless, it blends into the landscape with a harmony that has not escaped the attention of painters, writers, and composers over the last two hundred years. With its leafy roof and walls of boards or *yagua* strips, it suggests an outgrowth of the royal palm itself, a prolongation of the island forest.[17]

Early Havana soon included homes built of stones and tiles, by order of a royal edict dated March 4, 1539, and aimed at those residents who had benefited from "the distribution of Indians."[18] When the town was sacked and burned by French pirate Jacques de Sores in 1555, however, none of its buildings withstood the onslaught except for the occasional masonry house, such as that belonging to Juan de Rojas.

The Laws for the Indies, promulgated by Philip II in 1573, instructed that future settlements should be founded on elevated ground, so as to benefit from both northern and southern winds. In coastal towns, the distance of the principal square to the harbor was to be calculated as a function of the number of householders, taking account of projected growth. In Havana, the corners of the square led into four main streets, oriented toward the four winds. The streets were narrow in order to protect the houses from the relentless sun.

Bohío *in a valley at the foot of a hill.*

Top: *"Rod in the ground" structure, a rustic barn for storing agricultural produce that doubles as an emergency cyclone refuge.*

Middle: Bohío *by the beach.*

Bottom: *Framework and thatching of a* bohío *roof.*

Partial view of the Riberos de Vasconcelos house, on Obrapía and San Ignacio.

The ordinances also stipulated that houses should be made with solid foundations and walls of adobe and planks, in the interests of rapid and thrifty construction. Once the ground floor was complete and the patio areas had been allocated, each settler was to erect a fence of wood and branches, and contribute to a continuous defensive line of palisades and trenches to keep out pirates. Horses and other animals were permitted in patios and corrals, which had to be spacious for reasons of hygiene. There is nothing left today of these sixteenth-century buildings, but surviving records may give us an idea of the higher-ranking ones: they were typically two stories high, with the upper level reserved for habitation and the lower for commercial activities. By the end of that century, a desirable home was worth the considerable sum of one thousand ducats.[19]

Between 1558 and 1588, there were fifty-seven artisans established in the town. These masons, stonecutters, carpenters, blacksmiths, and silver-smiths worked on the most outstanding projects of the time, including fortresses, churches, monasteries, government buildings, and the residences of the elite. In 1579 construction of the Franciscan monastery out of ashlars or bricks was proposed, with ceilings of carved wood and tiled roofs; one year earlier, the Dominican temple and monastery had been founded. On that occasion, Governor Francisco Carreño ordered the mayors and alder-men to measure out the plots of land adjoining the monastery "in accor-dance with the plan or grid that this borough has been assigned."[20]

The furnishing of the earliest Havana homes during the sixteenth century tended to be rustic and improvised, not even attempting a rudimentary imi-tation of Spanish models. Just as the first colonists adopted, for strictly prac-tical reasons, the native style of housing, so they went on to copy the local furniture of plain benches and tables, for there was plenty of timber, especially palm wood. Once the colony was established it began to import furniture from Spain, which was soon being reproduced by local craftsmen; these pieces exhibited the Mudejar influence that was fashionable at the time. They included "friars' armchairs" (*sillón frailero*), massive embossed leather chests, many-drawered *bargueño* desks, and a dais, the largest item in the family home, serving as a work area by day and a sleeping couch by night.

The urbanization of what was then known as the Plaza Nueva dates from 1587: here the market would be pitched, and festivals were celebrated. An important feast day was Corpus Christi, marked by dances, sacramental and secular drama, comedies and storytelling; the revelry was accompanied by jesters and musicians, and even enfranchised or freed slaves were welcome. Bulls were let loose, people rode out in fancy dress, and games of chance were played. We should recall that the Laws for the Indies had insisted since 1573 that recreational areas should be made available "in such ample mea-sure that though the population continue to grow, there shall always be suf-ficient space for all the people to go out and amuse themselves."[21]

From its foundation, one of the major problems for Havana was the shortage of drinking water. Toward 1592, the Italian engineer Juan Bautista Antonelli temporarily solved this issue by building the Royal Channel, an artificial river seven kilometers long. It terminated in the Plaza de la Ciénaga, later called Plaza de la Catedral. This ditch irrigated the lands on either side with water from the Almendares River, giving life to the inhabi-tants and to the Indian Fleet, as well as supplying the haciendas, farms, and sugar plantations along its path.

In the last year of the sixteenth century, fifteen prominent residents of Havana were granted a loan from the king to start new and better-equipped sugarcane plantations; this event is regarded as the foundation of the island's sugar industry, one whose future crucial importance for Cuba no one could then have foreseen. Much later, my own family was to play a large part in its development: my mother's forebears, the Montalvos, were noted landowners during the nineteenth century, and my father was one of the leading sugar industrialists of this century.

The year 1592 was when San Cristóbal de La Habana received its coat of arms, by decree of Philip II. The shield displayed a sea, three castles (La Fuerza, El Morro, and La Punta), and a golden key. And at last, a Royal Letters Patent issued on December 20 of the same year raised it to the rank of City. "Now chaos was slowly turning into the profundity of a cosmos . . . the emergence and triumph of the city could already be discerned, against the jungle, against the formless."[22]

The Key to the New World

I hereby declare that it is my will and desire that henceforth and for all time said borough should go by the name of the City of San Cristóbal de la Habana, of the said island of Cuba, and likewise I ordain that its people shall be granted all the privileges, franchises, and graces that the householders . . . of like cities must and do enjoy.

—Philip II of Spain, Royal Letters Patent of December 20, 1592

Old Havana holds a special fascination. The Palacio de los Capitanes Generales,[23] near the Plaza de Armas, was in the first half of the twentieth century an area where the august nobility of the buildings presided over the hustle and bustle of the city's financial heart. One can wander for hours through the old zone, discovering the loveliness of a facade, the filigree of an unusual railing, or the grandeur of an ancient doorway behind which the customs and manners of a long-lost past still seem possible.

At the corner of O'Reilly and Avenida del Puerto, to one side of the Plaza de Armas, stands the Castillo de la Real Fuerza, the oldest fortress in Cuba. It is a stout sixteenth-century block in the middle of a little fenced park, and in the days of my childhood it housed the National Library. La Fuerza had not yet been built in 1539 when Hernando de Soto, then governor of Cuba, was seized by the desire to explore and conquer Florida. Soto left his wife Isabel de Bobadilla in charge, ensconced in the great Fuerza Vieja; but I always imagined doña Isabel on the ramparts of the smaller castle, scanning the horizon for some sign of the husband who never came back. The tragic fate of that valiant woman—who gave up all the comforts of civilization to follow an adventurer, only for him to desert her in the midst of a hostile, unknown world—moved me with an inexplicable poignancy.

La Fuerza was the first bulwark to be constructed in Havana, reflecting the *villa*'s growing importance as the pivot of trade between Spain and its colonies. The vast wealth accrued by the port sealed its destiny, and on February 14, 1553, it was designated as the island's capital by a Royal Provision that also authorized the governors to reside there.

On December 9, 1556, Philip II, now lord of a territory extending from the Netherlands to the great silver mines of Potosí in the Peruvian Andes, issued a decree designating Havana as the "foremost port of the Indies, at which ships in provenance from Portobelo, as from New Spain, or any other place on their way to my Kingdom will break their journey."[24] In 1561, the system of the Indian Fleet was officially established under the direction of Pedro Menéndez de Avilés (1519–1574), who governed Cuba from 1568 to 1573.[25]

Whenever the fleet docked, hundreds of men of different origins and nationalities streamed down the gangways to shore, and the town became a lively hubbub of activity and exchange. Sailors caroused in the many taverns and inns that resounded to the shouts of card-players and dice-throwers, mixed with the strains of Spanish music and the thud of African dancing. From this musical fusion emerged the mulatto genres that traveled in the feet of soldiers and sailors back to Spain: the *folie*, the chaconne, the saraband, the *sarambecca*, and other dances "of the Indies." Brothels thrived and crime soared. Yet alongside this violent, dissipated, sensuous port culture, which soon became synonymous with decadence, there existed another Havana, faithful to its customs in tranquil domestic interiors and the cloistered peace of churches and monasteries.

Havana's increasing importance and wealth also determined its fortification, and it became the first stronghold on the trade route between Spain and the Americas. The Fleet of New Spain anchored in Veracruz to collect, in addition to the gold and silver of Mexico, goods from across the Pacific that had been carried overland from Acapulco: the spices, porcelain, and silk of the Philippines, China, and the Moluccas. After wintering in the colonies, the ships put in at Havana for supplies and readied themselves for the perilous Atlantic crossing, which they made under escort by a convoy of heavily armed warships.

The tower of La Chorrera in a painting by
Esteban Chartraud, 1882

The Castillo de la Real Fuerza, sculpted by Jerónimo Martín Pinzón. Behind it is the Palacio del Segundo Cabo.

Far right: La Giraldilla, the bronze figure crowning the Castillo de la Real Fuerza.

Few places in the world were as suitable for such a purpose as Havana was in those days. The city was surrounded by flatlands punctuated by heights, three of which were eventually crowned with imposing fortresses as part of a maritime defense system on a continental scale.

The symmetrical design of those early castles corresponded to the Renaissance ideal of the time, with a regular pattern that influenced later structures, becoming standard both in Havana and elsewhere on the continent. The square, pentagonal, or hexagonal model with bulwarks attached to the vertices proved to have superb defensive capacity, while it was easily adaptable to any geographical setting. The fortresses punctuating the shoreline were not only built on top of limestone promontories but were also made of that stone. Coral reefs, shells, and marine fossils testify to the ancient bond between the city and the sea that caresses it. In Cuba these are called *piedras conchíferas*, shell-bearing rocks, and they are too porous to lend themselves to clean carving. But the water cisterns inside the fortresses were hacked deep into this rock, enabling seawater to be filtered through the stone until it was drinkable.

Later, under the direction of Italian engineers—the best military builders of the day—a more open composition was adopted, oriented in several directions. Renaissance techniques and designs continued to be employed, but these later fortresses recalled a classic medieval solution in which the fortress was built on a site that was in itself inaccessible.

The integral structure of such buildings (inspired by Vauban's principles of an interrelated, overlapping defense) was ultimately to supersede the intrinsic value previously ascribed to the thickness of the walls. In fortifications such as La Cabaña, El Príncipe, and Atarés, we observe a more complex internal organization; however, these examples fall short of the creative versatility of El Morro, being little more than faithful reproductions of contemporary tenets.

All these bastions were conceived and designed by Italian and Spanish military engineers, assisted by master-builders and officials of the same nationalities. But what of the anonymous workmen who lifted up such monuments—who were the craftsmen, the masons, the foremen, carpenters, and ironsmiths? All of them must have been specialized in works of fortification and would have earned respectable wages in ducats, *reals*, or *maravedíes*. Under them toiled a legion of convicts and slaves.

Simultaneously conspicuous and blended into the landscape, the necklace of fortifications is an important element of Havana's unique atmosphere. The German scholar Alexander von Humboldt set them within the whole impression he had of Havana when he stopped here in the early nineteenth century. He took back with him a vivid memory and account of "those fortresses crowning the rocks to the east of the port, that inner harbor of sea fringed with hamlets and farms, those prodigiously high palm trees, and that city half-hidden by a forest of masts and sails."[26]

Top: The tower of La Chorrera, built in the seventeenth century by order of Governor Francisco Riaño, at the mouth of the Almendares river.

Above: Detail of a wall of La Chorrera tower, showing the shell-bearing or Jaimanitas stone.

Left: Turret of El Castillito near the mouth of the Almendares river.

Castillo de la Real Fuerza

After Havana was destroyed in 1555 by the French pirate Jacques de Sores, the Spanish Crown decided to build a more solid fortress to replace the original, ineffectual tower known as La Fuerza Vieja. In 1558 therefore, Spanish master-builder Bartolomé Sánchez began work on the Castillo de la Real Fuerza, using plans drawn by Ochoa de Luyando. The works were placed under the direction of Francisco de Calona in 1562 and completed by him in 1577.

The new fortress's location was less than ideal, however, being placed well inside the mouth of the bay, on flat and unprotected ground at one of the corners of the square that fittingly came to be known as the Plaza de Armas, or parade ground. The building is notable for the moat that surrounds it and the drawbridge leading to the main entrance. La Fuerza was intended to house the local garrison and stow the gold and silver cargoes of the Indian Fleet, while serving as the governor's residence.

The small cylindrical watchtower was built in 1632 under the aegis of Governor Juan Bitrián de Viamonte. It was crowned by a bronze weathervane in the shape of a woman, known as La Giraldilla, the work of Jerónimo Martín Pinzón Solís (1607–1649). From her turret overlooking the city, La Giraldilla signalled the entrance to the port and read the weather for seamen and townspeople alike. This figure has endured through the centuries as one of the quintessential symbols of Havana.

Under the Republic, the castle contained the National Library until it was moved to its present location during the 1950s. In 1963, the building underwent a restoration directed by Francisco Prat Puig and from that time on has been used as a museum.

Castillo de la Real Fuerza, main gate and moat.

Left: View of the entrance to the bay with two of Havana's landmarks, La Giraldilla and El Morro in the distance.

Below: Castillo de la Real Fuerza seen with part of the moat and the Palacio del Segundo Cabo.

Castillo del Morro and Castillo de la Punta

Greedy for America's riches, England was so relentlessly harassing Spanish fleets that Philip II had to embark upon an ambitious program of fortification throughout his far-flung dominions in the New World, from Florida to the Magellan Straits. To this end he hired Italian engineer Juan Bautista Antonelli, who was assisted by various colleagues and subordinates, including his son, Juan Bautista "El Mozo," and his nephew Cristóbal de Roda. Antonelli's legacy still arouses amazement in regard to its vast geographical dispersion and the monumentality of these fortresses, which were raised in Portobelo, Cartagena de Indias, Veracruz, Puerto Rico, Santo Domingo, Venezuela, and Havana, all in less than fifty years.

Antonelli made a study of Havana's geographical characteristics before planning the construction of two castles, El Morro and La Punta, on either side of the entrance to the bay. They were situated such that the crossfire between the two would make Havana virtually impregnable. Ever since the sixteenth century, the steep crag of El Morro had been used as a lookout post for pirate and *corsaire* ships; La Punta was an observation point at the entrance to the port.

The construction of the castle, whose full name was Los Tres Reyes del Morro, was undertaken in 1589. Eventually, in 1594, the work passed into the hands of Cristóbal de Roda, who completed it in 1630. The efficiency of this stronghold and its harmonious blending with the natural promontory earned it high praise from the start. A lighthouse was added during the eighteenth century and replaced in 1844 by a slimmer, more functional example that soars forty-two yards above the peak. The rocky outcrop of El Morro, with castle and tower rising in one line from stone to sky, is another unforgettable landmark of Havana.

San Salvador de la Punta, a trapezoidal structure surrounded by bulwarks, was finished in 1600. The tradition of closing off the bay by stretching a heavy chain across, in this case from El Morro to La Punta, was begun in 1597. Contrary to what we might expect, this chain was made of "cedarwood beams, some of which are most convenient for such a purpose, with very stout iron links, quite suitable for what is intended, affixed beneath the arquebusery and the musketry of El Morro and La Punta."[27]

At the time of the Republic, La Punta became the seat of the Admiralty High Command, and after the triumph of the revolution, it acted as the militia training school and housed some state administrative offices. It is currently undergoing repairs in preparation for becoming a naval museum.

Above: El Morro, one of the emblems of the city, guarding the narrow entrance to Havana bay.

Right: The lighthouse of El Morro, with a corner of the Castillo de la Punta in the foreground.

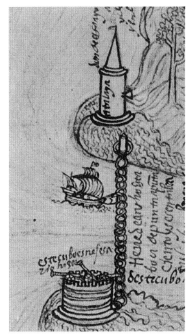

Top: El Morro silhouetted against the sea.

Top right: Contemporary sketch (1603) of the wooden chain that joined El Morro and
La Punta, by Cristóbal de Roda.

Bottom: El Morro at evening.

Fortaleza de San Carlos de la Cabaña

According to legend, it was Juan Bautista Antonelli who foretold that whoever was "master of the position of La Cabaña shall be master of the city also."[28] This prophecy was fulfilled in 1762, when the English were able to take Havana by seizing the high ground of La Cabaña, the vantage point from which they decisively bombarded El Morro and the city itself. After eleven months of British rule on the island, Spain repossessed Havana in exchange for the territory of Florida, and the town's defenses were rapidly amplified and modernized in line with recent advances in military techniques. El Morro was rebuilt and new castles erected: La Cabaña, Atarés on the

bluff of De Soto, at the back of the bay, and last El Príncipe, on a hill known as De Aróstegui.

The fortress of La Cabaña, built between 1763 and 1774 at a cost of 14 million pesos, was unquestionably the largest of all those undertaken by Spain in the Americas. It was seven hundred meters long and occupied a total of ten hectares. The project was drawn up by a French engineer, M. de Vallière, and executed by his famous colleague Silvestre Abarca. Its plan demonstrates the complexity attained by the military techniques of the day, which called for a large garrison. The structure consists of an irregular, highly fragmented polygon with walls protected by bul-

warks, ravelins, and fortified towers. The spacious barracks, storerooms, cisterns, chapel, and other services for the troops, planned on a scale that would enable them to resist a lengthy siege, were laid out inside a fortified enclosure independent of the outer wall. La Cabaña boasts an impressive moat dug out of the rock and a monumental main door, attributed to the master-carpenter from Cadiz, Pedro de Medina. The complex was a citadel in itself. La Cabaña was used as a jail and a place of execution as well as an army barracks from colonial times until 1990, when it was converted into a museum.

Above: Crest on the doorway of La Cabaña.

Left: Main entrance to the fortress of La Cabaña, with a doorway attributed to the Spanish engineer Pedro de Medina (1738–1796), from Cadiz.

Opposite page: The fortress of La Cabaña, view from Old Havana.

Above: *Facade of the chapel of La Cabaña.*

Left: *Inside La Cabaña.*

The Antechamber of the Indies

It is founded on a wondrous plain on the shore of a deep lake, or finger of sea, curving inland; it forms the site of a populous city, which is abundantly supplied with meat, fish, turtles, freshwater tortoises, maize, and yucca, and flours that are ordinarily shipped from New Spain, as well as quantities of fruits yielded by the earth, for while the clime is hot, it affords clear skies and wholesome breezes.

—*Antonio Vázquez de Espinosa,* Compendio y descripción de las Indias Occidentales, *1622*

The Italian traveler Giovanni Francesco Gemelli Careri in 1699 described Havana, not entirely accurately, as "a small township of half a league around, on a plain, at the latitude of 23 degrees and 27 minutes. It is rounded in form and its landward walls are small and low, the other flank being protected by the canal. It numbers some four thousand souls, including Spaniards, mulattoes, and negroes, lodged in houses one story high. The women are exceedingly handsome, and the menfolk of pleasant mien."[29] Centuries later hardly a trace remains of that small township, its vestiges only barely discernable among the buildings of Old Havana.

In 1605 the king was informed that the population of the city numbered nearly three thousand inhabitants.[30] In 1612 Governor Ruiz de Pereda considered that "this city has much increased, since in the space of four years, more than two hundred houses have been raised."[31] From the beginnings of the seventeenth century, well-to-do householders with masonry homes were required to place a lantern at their door, to be lit between dusk and midnight unless the moon was shining. The sugar economy was growing and tobacco was attracting keen interest in European countries other than Spain. Naval construction lent ever greater splendor to the burgeoning town—traffic in the port was intense.

Continually beset by pirates and *corsaires*, epidemics, and hurricanes, this was a society that seldom bothered with its fiscal obligations and engaged in as much contraband as legal trade. Both these forms of commerce brought in merchandise and luxury goods by land and sea; in exchange the prizes of molasses, tobacco, hides, salt meat, and precious hardwoods were borne away. Official exports to Spain were exclusively conducted via Seville, but Havana was also a reexportation center for goods originating in other parts of America and Europe. Its citizens were thus fairly prosperous, despite their pleas of poverty in many documents addressed to the local government and the Crown.

Other archives record the rhythms of pious and profane holidays, celebrated annually with the utmost pomp, as well as occasional feasts to mark a royal wedding, the birth of a prince, or the accession of a new monarch to the throne. During such fiestas, the capital shook to the boom of cannon and bursts of musket-fire from the ramparts of all three castles. Streets and houses were decked in lights, and religious processions wound along from early in the morning to late afternoon, when they closed with mass and a sermon. On lay holidays the participants threw themselves into games and diversions of every kind, some traditional from the previous century, others an exciting novelty. In both religious and secular festivals, black freedwomen, whether single or married, were obliged to join in balls and dances on pain of being fined, according to a 1626 complaint presented by enfranchised slaves to the governor and passed in turn to the king.

In subsequent decades, the Church sought to outlaw the dancing and music that had been customary during religious holidays, on grounds of indecency. The Diocesan Synod held in Santiago de Cuba in 1680 ruled that such displays should be banned from holy precincts and private homes alike. The forbidden canticles were based on religious couplets of the kind so common in Spanish folklore; these stanzas were incorporated into the fiestas of Andalusian origin that are still celebrated today in certain rural areas of Cuba.

Allegory of the city of Havana on a José Morales cigar-box label.

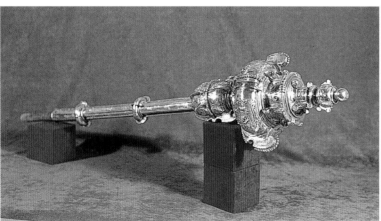

Top: Silver filigree cross, seventeenth-century Havana School, from the monastery of San Francisco.

Bottom: Silver mace from Havana City Hall crafted by silversmith Andrés Díaz.

The same synod forbade any processions after dark during Lent and Holy Week, ruling against the participation of women in all of them, "whether in their own garb or in Nazarene attire."[32] The only late-night processions allowed were those of the True Cross and Jesus the Nazarene on Holy Thursday, but without the presence of women; in 1792 Bishop Tres Palacios revoked even this license. It was also forbidden to stage bullfights on feast days. Only the July 25 feast of Saint Christopher, the city's patron saint and "head of its church," was spared. There were yet further prohibitions aimed at the involvement of blacks and mulattoes in the festivities, reflecting fears about alien religions and the syncretic blending of these with Catholic practices. Nevertheless, nearly twenty years later Gemelli Careri described the sight of blacks and mulattoes on the eve of Carnival "in picturesque attire, gathering in a great congregation for the entertainments," an early reference to what would evolve into the Day of the Kings festival, and eventually into the masked parades or *comparsas*.

Despite its steady development and riotous fiestas, licit or otherwise, the streets of Havana were still unpaved, clogged with evil-smelling mud or choked with dust according to the season. Yet in the midst of this, some aspects of life were positively sybaritic. The elaborate clothing, even that of less prosperous citizens, was startling:

> Men's clothing consisted of outfits of French linen, silk, and velvet, in gaudy colors. These were offset by gold chains and rings, as well as swords and daggers, often studded with precious jewels. In comparison to the men, the women must have looked almost drab, even when they were arrayed in the best gowns they possessed.[33]

Contemporary testimonies written by Havana residents mention luxury items as part of household inventories, including oil paintings large and small of Flemish landscapes or Christian scenes, either of local or foreign origin. We also hear of carved statues of saints, mirrors in ebony or gilded frames, ebony holy urns, and images of beaten silver.

From the late sixteenth century on, the work of Havana's *retablo* and altarpiece makers, stonecutters, and silversmiths began to gain renown. These artisans were employed chiefly by the church, the shipyards, and the more affluent private citizens. Ships built here were lavishly adorned with carvings and other rich decorations.

By the end of the seventeenth century, many churches in Havana had amassed quantities of *retablos*, paintings, filigree crosses, chandeliers, reliquaries, tabernacles, and other silver treasures made in the city to sharpen the impact of religious images. Among the many outstanding silversmiths, some names have come down through history: Juan Díaz engraved the silver maces presented by Governor Juan Bitrián de Viamonte to the town council of Havana in 1631; Jerónimo de Espellosa[34] carved a filigree crucifix intended for the Church of San Marcos de Icod de los Vinos, in the town of Tenerife in the Canary Islands, a gift from the dean of Havana, Nicolás Estévez Borges.

Slowly but surely, criollo culture came into being during the course of the seventeenth century. That intimate dialogue between the native woods and the men who worked them began, a dialogue that molded the beams of the solid frame roofs, the wooden doors, windows, balconies, and lathed balustrades of houses, churches, and other buildings, as it shaped the furniture within. Two items became standard all over the island during the early seventeenth century: the paneled wardrobe and the *taburete*, a rustic, no-frills chair made of Cuban hardwood with a leather seat and back-rest—like a simplified version of the Spanish armchair, without benefit of the latter's upholstered leather and elegantly shaped legs. The paneled wardrobe reproduced the decorative geometric motifs that were commonly applied to the doors, windows, and roofs of the day. As a rule, these closets were supported on flattened ball feet. The *taburete* has outlasted the march of the centuries to become an indispensable piece of Cuban furniture, whose finish varies according to the owner's economic standing without altering the chair's fundamental characteristics.

Seventeenth-century Cuban tables were reproductions of Spanish ones but were carved from the valuable hardwoods of the island, preferably mahogany. In noble households it was customary to hang a cloth on the wall behind the main hall table, displaying the family titles and coat of arms. By this period, precious hardwood chests known as *cajas habaneras* were already being exported from Havana. As described by the Venezuelan historian Carlos F. Duarte, these chests were smooth-sided and held together with wide bands of wrought iron made to various elaborate designs. The beds, by contrast, were little more than wooden frameworks ornamented with grooves, covered in rich fabrics that were the real focus of attention. Also in use was the four-poster with lathed posts that looked like bobbins, a decorative element equally popular on windows. However, simple cots lined with fabric remained the preferred sleeping arrangement until well into the nineteenth century.

In the early days, the woods surrounding the city were cut down to provide fuel and the material for making small domestic objects, as well as to clear land for sugarcane. But once Philip II had opted to build the library and the monastery choir of his palace, El Escorial, out of precious woods from Cuba, this resource rapidly gained in market value. From the seventeenth century onward, the timbers whose quality or texture earmarked them for more prestigious purposes came under protection. In 1604, Governor Valdés set a boundary of up to five leagues for the logging of the forests around the city, with the exception of wood destined for building houses or ships. He must have also recognized that the forests were one of Havana's best defenses against pirates, in that they made access to the town considerably more difficult.

At some point during this century a new type of house was introduced in Havana: the patio house, which was to be the starting point for the city's traditional domestic architecture. This kind of design was reminiscent of the ancient Mediterranean traditions, both Christian and Moorish, and was ideally adaptable to the tropical island climate. The Cuban home's peculiar identity was forged through a long process of evolution, in which a wide range of factors converged, shaped by the *cotidiano*.

In her prologue to the countess of Merlín's book *Viaje a La Habana*, Gertrudis Gómez de Avellaneda defines such an identity in the simplest terms: "There are bonds between those who began life under the same sky . . . the same habits . . . a single way of seeing and feeling."[35] This is the sense of community that unites people, wherever they may be; this is what sets us apart from others, the source of what is called *lo cubano*.

Trussed ceiling.

Wardrobe in the style of Luis de las Casas, late eighteenth century.

Wooden chest with inlaid carvings.

Typical Cuban taburete chair, seventeenth century.

The tradition of the Granadan house, with its Moorish influences, took root in Havana. How this came about, no one knows. Did some of the persecuted Moslem converts manage to flee to Cuba, or was this development a result of the strength and scope of the Hispano-Moorish building tradition, the common heritage of a good deal of popular Spanish architecture? And when did this pattern first appear? It is hard to say for sure, but by the seventeenth century these exotic styles were undoubtedly here to stay. Strangely enough, Havana contains seventeenth-century buildings of medieval origin, built at a time when the baroque was spreading across Europe. This was perhaps the first of Cuban anachronisms, those disconcerting anomalies that gave rise in the long term to what might be regarded as Cuban architectural models.

It was in Havana, of course, at the point of confluence of the Americas, that the first buildings of genuine constructive distinction were erected. This word "constructive," rather than "architectural," refers to houses created by master-builders who were the heirs to an immemorial tradition passed down from generation to generation, indifferent to the concerns of official architecture and its aesthetic canons. The absence of cultured European styles is not, therefore, to be wondered at.[36]

These early houses were simple in the extreme: one- or two-story structures organized around a small rectangular patio, with arched galleries along the shorter sides. Houses on two levels sported balcony-type galleries upstairs, complete with wooden balustrades and posts; they ringed the entire patio to make it the intimate heart of the house and its principal focus. Corner buildings of one story often added an upstairs corner room (*cuarto esquinero*) in a way that evokes the Moorish mirador tower;

such rooms had higher ceilings than the rest. The lower part of the house would be used for retail, storage, and *accesoría* rooms that could be rented out. All these houses also functioned as giant funnels, channeling rainwater down the sloping tiled roofs to be collected in a tank in the patio.[37]

But in a land blessed by the miracle of light, in want of cooling drafts to mitigate the intense heat, the house diverges from the Mudejar model: it turns toward the street, projecting balconies outward like apertures to the outside world. What was the origin of this sociable balcony that was to remain a feature throughout the colonial period and much of the Republican era—the Canary Islands? Was it a tropical mutation of the *solana*, the sun-trap beloved of northern Spain, or a kind of criollo offspring of the Arab ambulatory? Or was it, as archaeologist Francisco Prat maintains, a transposition to the exterior of the galleries around the inner patio?[38] Many such balconies, regrettably, have been lost.

In these buildings, some of the most splendid features are the trefoil and mixtilinear arches. The simplest examples of the first type take a trilobate form, and the finest are enriched with prominent moldings, alluding to the Islamic arch. The second type, however, is the arch par excellence of this period and is created by a combination of convex and concave lines, surmounted by a semicircle. Sometimes by reducing the breadth and raising the height of this semicircle, an ogee arch is formed. Such early houses present striking color contrasts between whitewashed walls and the burnt sienna of the roof, parrot-feather-green paneled doors and the reddish hue of clay paving tiles. They are venerable architectural ancestors that have left a lasting imprint on Cuban domestic architecture. Whatever influences were absorbed thereafter, the building traditions of the early days have unfailingly

Right: Upper gallery of the Casa del Árabe.

Opposite page, left: View of the patio in the Casa del Árabe.

Opposite page, right: House with a typical corner balcony and downstairs shop.

continued to define the character of the Cuban house.

Such housing maintained a presence within the city up to the first decades of the eighteenth century, when it was blended with new approaches to house construction. It shared its overall characteristics, materials, and techniques with the religious architecture that so effectively broke up the urban perspective by means of massive perimeter walls and sharp-rising steeples. The most primitive churches were laid out on the basilica model, which provides for a single nave with the chancel at the back and a tower attached to the side; monasteries, on the other hand, were planned around classic cloisters, with the church abutting the longest wall. In any of these constructions, it is the trussed ceilings that are the most arresting feature, since these achieved, notably in the ecclesiastical examples, an unusual degree of elaborate perfection. The beauty of early Cuban ceilings, hewn from the valuable hardwoods that enabled such consummate carving, is the finest testimony to early Cuban architecture.

Surviving examples that answer to these characteristics can still be found scattered around a relatively wide radius within the boundaries of Old Havana. At the time they were built, they stood out in contrast to a town made up overwhelmingly of one-story buildings. In the days of Governor Francisco Dávila Orejón (1664–1670) there still existed a large number of *bohíos* in the capital's center and larger avenues, although most were located in what were then the outer suburbs, districts such as Campeche, Egido, or Peña Pobre.

The city wall represented the physical limits to the growth of Havana, as the town moved away from its original place on the lip of the bay. It put out feelers to the west, with the urbanization of the Plaza del Cristo, straight on from the Plaza Vieja along the street of Teniente Rey. To the south, it grew in the direction of its shanties, where some of the chief religious complexes were located. By the late seventeenth century, many of these were already established, including the churches of Parroquial Mayor and Espíritu Santo and the monasteries of the Dominican, Franciscan, and Augustinian orders, as well as the San Juan de Dios Hospital. The counterparts were of Santa Clara and Santa Catalina de Siena. In addition there were the hermitages of Santo Cristo del Buen Viaje, San Francisco de Paula, El Santo Angel Custodio, and Nuestra Señora del Monserrate, plus the oratory of San Felipe Neri.

Havana's system of defenses, reinforced by the determination of its inhabitants, preserved it throughout the sixteenth and seventeenth centuries from falling into enemy hands. The boldness of the criollo corsairs kept the many foes prowling around Cuba's coastlines at bay and even chased them well out to sea. But this resolve was not enough to deter England from its ambition to take possession of the country. In 1665 Commander Smith expressed the advantages of an English Cuba as follows:

> The Spaniards are fearful of all comers, and they give credence to an old prophecy according to which the English will soon be strolling the streets of Havana as freely as do they. Havana might come to be as valuable to us as Gibraltar, and were we to rule both, then the Spaniards would have to grant us the liberty to trade in America, instead of forcing us to pay, as now, a high price for it.[39]

This ancient and much-dreaded prophecy was to be fulfilled in the next century.

117–119 Obispo Street

Completed in the late sixteenth century, the house at 117–119 Obispo Street, next to the Plaza de Armas, is one of the oldest residences still standing in Cuba. In 1648 it was the property of Captain Antonio Hocés Carrillo, a native of Córdoba in Spain.

This house reveals the assimilation of Hispano-Moorish patterns in its techniques of construction, its roofs, and its arrangement around a central patio. The facade is original, despite having undergone substantial modifications. The walls are smooth, as was customary for early dwellings in Havana, with *tejaroz* eaves over projecting balconies supported on brackets. It retains its paneled doors, as well as an ox-eye window in the center of the facade. The left side is raised high, like a typical Moorish mirador. Inside, the stunning trussed ceilings display ties decorated in the purest Mudejar tradition, while the octagonal wooden posts of the upper galleries, the flat-roofed lean-tos where the cooking was generally performed, and the low elevation all confirm the venerable antiquity of this house. It is currently used as a museum and the office of the city historian.

House on Obispo 117–119, present office of the city historian. The house was built around 1648, though its facade was subsequently altered. The Mudejar ceiling is one of the best preserved in the city.

Obrapía Corner with San Ignacio

In 1637 Gaspar Riberos de Vasconcelos married Beatriz de Faria, who had inherited from her parents a house located on Obrapía and San Ignacio. The property passed after their death to Juan de Castilla Núnez del Castillo, Marquis of San Felipe y Santiago, the first of his line to settle in Cuba, who earned his title by founding the village of San Felipe y Santiago del Bejucal in his hacienda of El Bejucal, outside Havana. During the second half of the eighteenth century, Juan Francisco Núñez del Castillo y Sucre inherited all his properties and the title of Third Marquis. His wife, the Havana-born Juana María Molina, added on to the house, giving it the aspect we see today.

This corner house displays a street-level shop, a mezzanine, and a top floor with corner balcony, supported by brackets and sheltered by a tiled roof. This feature, recently restored, was originally added by Riberos de Vasconcelos, who was also responsible for the doorway and the heraldic shield with his family coat of arms. The interior is laid out around a typical patio, tucked nearer the back of the property and flanked by galleries of plain wooden posts. The wood ceiling of the mirador features the motif of the Franciscan rope belt. The far aisle, arched on two levels, and the baroque carving on the doors date from the additions made to the house during the eighteenth century.

House of Riberos de Vasconcelos, on Obrapía Street, taken from an angle that excludes the covered balcony.

12 Tacón Street

Located on a most desirable site, to the back of the Castillo de la Fuerza and overlooking the sweep of the bay, stands the house at 12 Tacón Street, between Empedrado and O'Reilly. It constitutes an excellent example of the advances made by Cuban domestic architecture in the early eighteenth century. The house was built by a mulatto freedwoman, Juana Carvajal, who had been granted emancipation—and an inheritance—by her mistress Lorenza de Carvajal in 1698. According to a deed of March 22, 1725, Juana Carvajal added to this "high and low house, outer walls and roofing tiles that she has ordered to be made new."[40] The same date appears carved into one of the arches of the upper level. In 1748 the house was purchased by the Havana lawyer, mayor, and council alderman Pedro José Calvo de la Puerta, who after three years connected it with number 8, next door. Married to Catalina O'Farrill, he was made Count of Buena Vista in 1766. His son, Nicolás Calvo de la Puerta O'Farrill, inherited the house in 1781.

According to José Agustín Caballero, Nicolás Calvo was adept at drawing, painting, and playing the clavichord. He knew Latin, Greek, Italian, English, and French; enjoyed advanced mathematics; and when at home was always to be found poring over the *camera obscura,* some novel electric or pneumatic machine, or his celestial and terrestrial spheres. He owned a superb chemistry laboratory, an exceptional botanical collection, a microscope, a telescope, and various other instruments that were less than common in Cuba at that time.[41]

This dwelling contains very old traces of mural decorations. In one room a set of paintings depicting European cities and palmy tropical landscapes was found, apparently dating from the second half of the eighteenth century. The images betray the hand of a popular artist with a knack for reproducing the themes of contemporary European prints. Their handling of architectural and natural elements in these murals expresses an ingenuous sense of time and place. Today, the house is the premises of the Archaeology Department of the City Historian's Office.

Top left: Tacón 12, detail of tiled roofs and tejaroz *eaves formed by rows of superimposed, whitewashed tiles.*

Left: Tacón 12, abutment of second-floor arch.

Bottom left: Tacón 12, interior ceiling detail.

Above: Tacón 12, viewed from the Castillo de la Real Fuerza.

Opposite page: House on Tacón 12, seventeenth century.

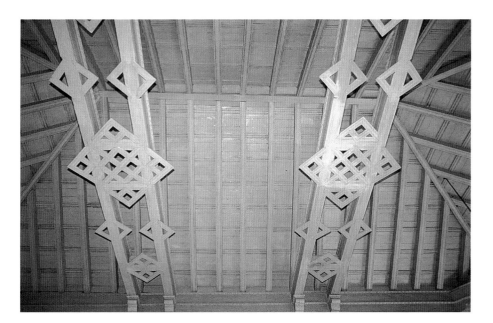

Convent of Santa Clara

Steps began to be taken as early as 1607 to found a women's convent, aimed at the maidens of Havana who had failed to make a suitable marriage and were thus considered to be at risk of losing their "honor and reputation." The building was erected between 1638 and 1644.

The convent occupied an area of two blocks, interrupting the continuity of Aguiar Street. It was equipped with three large cloisters and an adjoining piece of land originally intended for the vegetable garden. The main cloister is a lovely square court brimming with greenery and surrounded on the lower level by galleries formed by arches over columns. On the upper level the arcade is marked by simple, straight wooden shafts; the interaction between the two conveys an impression of lightness and grace.

The campanile tower of the church, the oldest of those preserved in Old Havana, soars up at the intersection of Cuba and Sol Streets. It was built in 1698 by a master from the Canary Islands, Pedro Hernández de Santiago. The most noteworthy feature of the Convent of Santa Clara is the Moorish trussed ceilings of the interior, the finest example extant in all of Cuba. The roof of the choir is especially fine; it bears the inscription of its completion date, 1643, and the name of the master carpenter, Juan de Salas Argüello.[42]

The convent has been kept in an adequate state of repair, except for the third cloister, which is in ruins. It is now the headquarters of the Centro Nacional de Conservación, Restauración, y Museología.

Right: Convent of Santa Clara, upper-story gallery with wooden posts and braces.

Opposit page, top left: Convent of Santa Clara, carved ceiling by carpenter Salas Argüello.

Opposite page, top right: Convent of Santa Clara, internal gallery.

Opposite page, bottom: Detail of trussed ceiling, showing a variety of carvings.

Church of Espíritu Santo

Toward 1638 a simple church was raised on Cuba and Acosta Streets, in what was then called the Campeche neighborhood. It was destined for the devotions of the freed blacks and mulattoes who had contributed both money and labor to build it. The original single nave underwent a series of additions during the eighteenth and nineteenth centuries. The lateral tower, another work by the master-builder Hernández de Santiago, was finished in 1706. In 1725, Bishop Jerónimo Valdés commissioned at his own expense a striking Gothic chancel vault, the only one of its kind in Havana. Valdés himself, who was much beloved by the Cuban people, is buried in this church. In the mid-eighteenth century, under Bishop Pedro Agustín Morell de Santa Cruz, the temple was widened by building a new aisle along its left side. In 1848, on the occasion of some wholesale repairs, the facade was also altered to accommodate the neoclassical pediment seen today. During the same century catacombs and burial crypts were discovered below, as well as the grave of Bishop Valdés. In 1773 this church became the only place of worship in Havana with the right to offer sanctuary to fugitives from the authorities.

More recently, thanks to the efforts of Monsignor Ángel Gaztelu—the poet and writer who was also a member of the literary group Orígenes—the church was restored (1960–1961), with the help of many prominent artists who responded to his appeal. This restoration, under the supervision of Eugenio Batista with assistance from Francisco Prat, uncovered an original ox-eye window. Antique windows complete with stained glass, room dividers (a favorite device of the period, resembling saloon doors), and fanlights were recovered from ruined buildings in Old Havana and put to use. Bishop Valdés's gravestone and his recumbent statue are the work of sculptor Alfredo Lozano, who also contributed two reliefs: one of the Annunciation, in *capellanía* stone, and the other of the baptism of Christ, in bronze. The courtyard was reconstructed in the colonial style and endowed with a great iron gate salvaged from an old house in the neighborhood.

Left: The church of Espíritu Santo, one of the oldest in Havana, begun during the seventeenth century and remarkably restored in the early 1960s at the instigation of Monsignor Angel Gaztelu, with material salvaged from buildings in Old Havana.

Above: Espíritu Santo, view of eighteenth-century rib vault.

Above: Espíritu Santo, window surmounted by mediopunto *or fanlight.*

Left: Espíritu Santo, color from the stained glass splashes the nave.

The City of Palaces

Save for a few, the streets are perfectly straight. The houses are of two or three stories, of masonried stone, and almost all with wooden balconies; their terrace roofs appear as cheerful as those of certain towns of the Spanish peninsula . . .

—*Villiet d'Arignon,* Voyage du S . . . à la Havane,
la Vera-Cruz et le Mexique, *1740*

During the first half of the eighteenth century, Havana—crossroads of the Indies—ceased to be a mere hub of American commerce, and became a thriving city, exporting the bounty of the tropics: tobacco (despite the state monopoly decreed in 1717), sugar, salted meat, hides, livestock, and hardwoods. It was an expensive city, where wages were higher than in Spain or Holland. And as Hugh Thomas observes, the cosmopolitan character of this port town infected the country at large.

Around this port, shipyards became established and renowned, growing into one of the major economic resources of the town. Cedar, mahogany, *sabicu,* and other precious timbers felled in the island's woods were prodigally used in the industry and hewn into majestic, shapely galleons, destined for the various Spanish armadas. The *San Juan,* with 60 cannons, was the first great rig to be produced in Havana, in 1724, by the famed shipbuilder Juan de Acosta. Then came the 112-gun *San Carlos,* and the *Santísima Trinidad.* The latter was built in 1769 by Mateo and Ignacio Mullán with Juan de Acosta, and was of towering size, equipped with 136 guns and reputed to be the largest in the world at that time. It was the most notorious ship in all the Spanish Armada.[43]

Not until the eighteenth century did Cuba gain, for the first time, a status of its own as Spain began to appreciate the income derived from such an economic engine. This development profited the criollos of Havana, to the detriment of most producers elsewhere in the country. They amassed more and more wealth as the years went by, and did especially good business during the brief spell of English domination in the city, leading them to chafe against the restrictions imposed by the state monopolies from which they had initially benefited. One way or another, the most blatant smuggling

continued merrily on. The Marquis of La Ensenada received an anonymous letter in Madrid, dated December 8, 1753, denouncing the lawless state of affairs in Havana:

> And we find in this City . . . an utter wantonness regarding the introduction of garments . . . with such a lack of moderation or circumspection, that by way of ports, coasts, and rivers, through the bay, the Customs houses and the landward gates of the city, these articles flow in reckless abundance, so much so that there are different markets to sell them to traders and customers, while more are hawked through the streets in handcarts, prices being as cheap as their purchase must allow, when there are no duties to pay nor risks to incur.[44]

During that century the city extended the list of amusements to be allowed during the religious feasts, which in fact for some time had been enlivened with music and dancing. Bullfights lasted for three days. In midcentury it was still common to wheel out huge puppets known as "Greeks" or "giants," just as people had done a hundred years before.[45]

Charles III mounted the throne of Spain in 1759. He promptly found himself drawn into the Seven Years' War (1756–1763), on the side of France against England. This conflict, fought on every sea and continent, proved catastrophic for the allied powers. It was part of England's overall plan to strike against the capital of Cuba, and on June 6, 1762, the English fleet dropped anchor outside the port of Havana. Taken by surprise, the city hastened to man its defenses, while some of the more eminent citizens, under a hail of cannonfire, to remove their belongings to the safety of the hinterlands.

The 112-gun ship Santísima Trinidad, *built in Havana in 1769*.

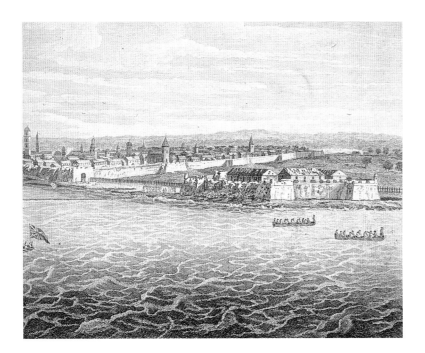

Top: View of Havana from the sea (1762) by the marine artist Dominique Serres. Plate #14 of a series engraved in London.

Bottom: The bombardment of Havana from the sea, during the English siege. A drawing by Dominique Serres engraved by Maison, giving us a glimpse of the port as it was in 1762. Plate #10 of the series.

After more than sixty days' siege the English entered Havana, although they were never to control the whole of the island. The ensuing months of occupation deepened the rift between criollos and Spaniards, as the *habaneros* angrily condemned the mistakes committed by the representatives of the colonial government. In a letter addressed to the king, a group of Havana women deplored the lack of courage and resolve exhibited by the authorities responsible for defending the town. The document was signed by one hundred titled ladies, led by Teresa Beltrán de Santa Cruz, Second Countess of Jaruco, and Beatriz Agustina de Jústiz, Marquise of Jústiz de Santa Ana.[46]

The English invaders had to devise a persuasive campaign to win over the recalcitrant population of Havana. The free trade they brought, though restricted to commerce with English ships and ports, opened both the pockets and the eyes of the local merchants; it can be argued that the brief change of master in Havana speeded an economic process in the region that might otherwise have taken years to develop. As a further consequence of these events, Havana became better known to the outside world through the vehicles of literature and, especially, engraving.

When Bishop José Agustín Morrell de Santa Cruz was banished to Florida on account of the resistance he showed the British, he was instantly glorified in a wave of verses and couplets that were chanted around town. An impoverished, obscure engraver, Francisco Javier Báez, captured for posterity the moment at which the bishop was carried away by the English soldiers, still seated on the stool on which he had been taking his breakfast.[47]

It was not long (1763) before the Spanish government was restored in Cuba, but now a fierce struggle was waged by its citizens to achieve economic autonomy. The concession of free trade with Spanish ports, obtained in 1778, was the first step toward the achievement of wholesale commercial freedom. Until that time the island's trade had been controlled by the ports of Cadiz and Seville, cities that had therefore exerted a marked influence upon eighteenth-century architecture in Havana.

The economic upswing consolidated a new social class that took an unprecedented interest in the capital, its streets and services, and its places of public revelry. These *habaneros* also cared intensely about the prestige of their homes, the lineage of their families, the rituals of domestic life, the refinements of dress, the comforts of furniture, and the excellence of food; they were equally alive to innovations in literature, history, or the sciences. They defended their community of faith and the dignity of its temples, while feeling intimately committed to the world they lived in, the world into which one projects oneself to be simultaneously reflected back; and this refraction of feeling is sensed throughout the Cuban house.

Thus the last third of the century saw the emergence of much that was new in Havana. The first periodical, *La gazeta de La Habana*, appeared in 1764; a printing press was founded by Esteban José Boloña in 1766; the San Carlos y San Ambrosio Seminary undertook the reform of its curriculum in 1773. Antonio Parra's book on Cuban fish—the first Cuban science book, with etchings by his son Manuel Antonio Romualdo—came out in 1787; another journal, *El papel periódico de La Habana*, began publication in 1790. Two years later, Francisco de Arango y Parreño wrote his celebrated treatise on agriculture, *Discurso sobre el fomento de la agricultura en La*

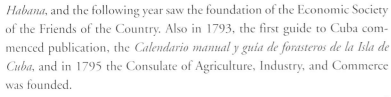

Portrait of José Montalvo, who was regarded as one of the most important businessmen of the day. Oil painting by Juan del Río (1748–1819).

Portrait of a Young Lady by Cuban painter Vicente Escobar y Flores (1762–1834). She cuddles a lapdog of the breed known as Bichón Habanero.

Habana, and the following year saw the foundation of the Economic Society of the Friends of the Country. Also in 1793, the first guide to Cuba commenced publication, the *Calendario manual y guía de forasteros de la Isla de Cuba*, and in 1795 the Consulate of Agriculture, Industry, and Commerce was founded.

The economic bonanza kindled a new interest in artistic creation and encouraged the development of high culture. In the absence of good schools where young people with talent and vocation could specialize in their chosen discipline, many opted to travel to Europe or Mexico. Alternatively, budding artists or craftsmen could serve as apprentices in the studios and workshops of European practitioners resident in Cuba, or copy the prints and religious images, whether painted or carved, that were so plentiful in Havana's churches and private houses. The Church played an important role by commissioning works from painters and sculptors, and there was also a constant demand for such skills in the shipyards. Many order-books survive, giving precise descriptions of the job required: for instance, to sculpt and paint massive mythological figures amid leaping dolphins, or highly colored caryatids to support the poop deck or provide

a figurehead for the prow. Artisans were not only called upon to decorate the outside of ships; they also crafted cherubs or saints for the staterooms below. Along with this output, of course, easel painting also thrived, and there was a keen market among the Havana elite for portraits signed by artists of repute.

On July 29, 1792, *El papel periódico de La Habana* extolled the "progress" that could be appreciated in every domain of life in the capital, with particular reference to the arts:

> None can deny that in the realms of naval carpentry, sculpture, carving, painting, gilding, engraving and even architecture, there exist artificers of exceeding ingenuity and taste, as is proven by the several works that have been deemed worthy of praise, not only by our countrymen but also by foreign judges, and this with the precise circumstance that their makers are native to Havana.[48]

The article goes on to name the leading architects, artists, and artisans in Havana, and emphasizes the social significance of the works carried out by them throughout the city. Among the architects, Lorenzo Camacho and

The Lombillo house, next to that of the Marquis of Arcos, built during the first half of the eighteenth century.

Ignacio Balcoa y Arcés are mentioned. The painters include José Nicolás de la Escalera and several others who have since been forgotten, like Joseph Veloso, Joseph Ignacio Valentín y Jáuregui, and Arcila, even though their works were, according to *El papel periódico*, gracing the walls of Casa de Gobierno, public buildings, and private homes.

Juan de Salas y Argüello was a painter of saints' images and altarpieces who worked for the nuns of Santa Clara along with his brother Rodrigo, a master joiner. Pedro de Acosta y de los Santos, born in Havana in 1794, worked on the decoration of the Coliseo Theater. In 1799, the Capitulary Acts of the Havana Town Council recorded that *maestro* Salvador Sánchez had painted and decorated a fresco for the theater of the Casa de los Baños, in the cathedral square. Also in 1799, an Italian painter named José Perovani landed in Cuba; he was to contribute some adornments to the Coliseo Theater, and to work on the Cathedral. However, the most outstanding figure of the late eighteenth and early nineteenth centuries was Vicente Escobar y Flores (1757–1834). This painter—mulatto by birth, white on paper—is surely the supreme "bridge" figure of the two centuries, thanks to his long life and prolific output.

By the close of the century, music and dance had also attained a high degree of sophistication. There was a passion for the balls, both private and public, that were held in people's own houses, so that dancing became an almost casual extravagance; one witness reckoned that around fifty such parties were given every night. The chronicler Buenaventura Pascual y Ferrer tells us that "in the Plaza Mayor, stands an open house which can be attended by subscription. The most distinguished families in town can be spied there, and there are various rooms set aside for dancing, refreshments, gaming, and so on."[49] The smarter set, notes Pascual, danced in the French manner: the event "kicked off" with a minuet that was followed by a lively contredanse. In the case of blacks and mulattoes, the dancing was driven by one or two guitars and a hollow gourd with slashed sides. The singing and dancing were noisy and gay, and the orchestras that played at all these events were composed of black and mulatto musicians.[50] The activity of such artists meant that African religious rhythms were gradually woven into the European cadences, a process that culminated with the birth of a genuinely Cuban music. Not only the musicians, but also most of the non-European craftspeople were of African descent, since whites nursed a lamentable contempt for any trade they considered demeaning.

At the high end of the social scale, important changes were taking place: the upper-class abode had discarded its modest anonymity, becoming identified with the surname or title of its wealthy proprietors. One referred now to the mansions of the Count of Jaruco or the Count of Casa Lombillo, the houses of the Marquis of Arcos or the Marquis of Aguas Claras—or to the homes of the Pedroso, Aróstegui, Bassave, Chacón, and Montalvo families. As Arrate commented in 1760, "And such exquisite care is not confined to the outer ornament of persons, but is also applied to the inner arrangement of their homes, whose furnishings and garnitures are proportionately grand . . ."[51]

This kind of luxury was the norm on the periphery of Havana, where planters and other grandees had splendid manors, not only in the villages but also on sugar plantations, coffee estates, and other properties. The testimony of Major Joseph Gorman of the Massachusetts regiment, an officer of the English occupation who was visiting the environs of the capital to negotiate with the landowners, describes this sumptuous way of life:

> We were received with the utmost ceremony and pomp in the various villages by the magistrates and principals who had retired to the countryside during the siege . . . the gentlemen's residences are more akin to palaces, with ten or twelve rooms to every floor. The better class of persons is courteous and affable enough, yet seemingly indolent, lovers of furniture and opulent, gaudy attire . . .[52]

But we also know of more rustic abodes, built of branches and palm in the vicinity of some country river, where the wealthy went to have fun. In San Antonio de los Baños, Güines, Arroyo Naranjo, and other hamlets concentrated around a plantation or estate, many families gathered in the aftermath of Holy Week, not so much to bathe as to dance, play bowls, watch and perform comedies and masques, and run with young bulls.

At this time, Havana had a population of 30,000 people. The new mansions stood out in conspicuous contrast to the majority of more modest, single-story housing. By the estimate of Bishop Morell de Santa Cruz, in 1754 the city numbered 3,497 houses that strayed from the norm "in that every man builds according to his lights and his purse. Some are indeed so handsomely constructed, that the most populous City would not balk at counting them among its own grandest. . . ."[53]

The houses of Havana's magnates were, in effect, on the way to becoming small palaces; they gave rise to a new style that progressively took over, endowing Old Havana with its singular, unmistakable atmosphere. This was a type of construction born of the Renaissance and internationally disseminated by the baroque, characterized above all by the presence of an arcaded courtyard. What had been a rectangular patio became an ample central square, enclosed by rows of arches on columns and penetrated via a monumental vestibule doubling as a carriage entrance. The doorway, which often displayed a family crest, was now set into the middle of the facade. This approach discarded the side-entrance of earlier styles, adopting a strict bilateral symmetry; only a handful of buildings, such as those we see on the Plaza Vieja, kept their main entrance to one side of the facade. The overall height was also raised to accommodate a mezzanine, projected toward the street and serving as offices (or, some say, as slave dormitories). The ground floor was used as a storeroom or shop. The top level was reserved for living-space proper, symbolically cut off from downstairs by a lattice gate placed across the landing. Such was the Cuban storehouse-home, qualified as *señorial* or "stately."

The first examples of this design appeared fringing the plazas, behind ample arcades that would give rise to the noble porticos that still enhance some of Havana's squares. The Plaza Vieja is especially remarkable for the coherence and unity of its covered colonnades, which march uninterrupted around all four sides. Is this the transposition to public space of the patio gallery? Or does the patio constitute a kind of private plaza? We can only affirm that both patterns were deployed in unison: the court overlooked by arched galleries, the plaza hemmed by unbroken arcades.

Inside the houses, the persistence of tradition enables us to witness the peculiar dialogue—so very criollo—between stone walls, Florentine arches, and baroque porches with neo-Mauresque timber ceilings. The panels of the

doors have grown larger and occasionally feature baroque carvings, in which sinuosity is stretched, by the close of the century, to the point of rococo.

Outside, the traditional *tejaroz* eaves were gradually giving way to cornices, and there may already have appeared a parapet or two around the top of some mansions of that period. Wooden balconies coursed from end to end of the facade, marked on the sides by elegant curves. Their columns were losing the octagonal shape and began to acquire a lathed, rounded look; windows were fronted by balusters to match the balconies. However, very few buildings still conserve these wooden features, which were mostly replaced by ironwork during the nineteenth century.

In large houses of the eighteenth century, the primary focus of interest on the facade was the doorway, large enough for a carriage to pass. Wicket gates were fitted into the "Spanish-style" doors, a legacy of the previous century, so as to enable entrance on a more human scale. The moldings of the doors acquired a rococo flavor in the last third of the century, with a type of jamb used in the port towns of southern Spain, especially Cadiz; it was adapted in a version dubbed *jamba habanera*, whose popularity is ascribed to the influence of Pedro de Medina, assistant to the great engineer Silvestre Abarca. Medina was involved in the construction of the Segundo Cabo and Capitanes Generales palaces, besides working on the Havana Cathedral, thus leaving his mark on the three buildings hailed as the "golden triptych" of baroque Havana.

But the baroque came into its own in religious buildings above all, with a level of achievements that would never be exceeded. Among other novelties it brought the *fachada-retablo*, or facade blocked out in the manner of an altarpiece; the transept, the cupola, and the vaulted ceiling. There were still cases, however, in which the domestic model was followed, combining stone walls with criollo-Mudejar ceilings.

Eighteenth-century churches were placed at the top of small or large plazas, each of which formed one of various "centers." In contrast to other Hispanic cities, which radiated out from a single nucleus, Havana associated each of its chief public spaces with a specific function: the Plaza de Armas was the political-administrative center, the Plaza Vieja held the market, and the Cathedral Square was the seat of religious authority. By 1778, Havana contained five large plazas, eleven small ones, eight churches, seven convents, three monasteries, six hospitals, and two educational institutions. The population had grown to 51,561 inhabitants, of which 40,737 lived within the city walls in a total of 5,172 houses.[54] The island capital was reputed to be one of the most populous of America.

This demographic and building boom was the result of a steady increase in economic activity. Pursuing a policy of enlightened despotism, Spain appointed only the ablest governors and administrators to serve in Cuba, suspended its monopoly on trade, and reorganized the public revenue system under two new bureaus, the Office of the Exchequer and the Court of Accounts. The Spanish administration also began, for the first time, to invest in the city's physical allure and public services. Thanks to Governor José de Ezpeleta (1788), Havana was provided with bathhouses, and glass-encased street lamps in areas of importance; these were not extended to the whole town until the arrival of Governor Luis de las Casas (1790–1796).

Under the governorship of Ambrosio Funes de Villalpando, Count of Ricla (1763–1765), the city underwent its first division into districts. Streets were named and houses numbered. The next governor, Antonio María de Bucarely (1766–1771), supervised the completion of the fortresses that were erected in the wake of the English assault. Felipe Fondesviela, Marquis of La Torre (1771–1776) was responsible for the first works of urban infrastructure.

De la Torre ordered the construction of two major bridges (Puentes Grandes) and several smaller ones, with a view to facilitating communications between the town and its periphery; he also had the main streets paved and equipped with sidewalks. A further measure was to eliminate all the dwellings that still had palm roofs from within city walls, and it was forbidden thereafter to build *bohíos*—the obsession of all Havana's governors since the first stone was laid. A devastating fire that had consumed many homes was the Marquis's pretext on this occasion, although his decree was not invariably obeyed. A later ballad on the subject humorously recalls the incident, roughly as follows:

> The Marquis of La Torre
> Destroyed palm-roofs with ire
> For this he's not sorry:
> It starved out the fire.
>
> His order proclaimed
> That he who retained
> Untiled houses must axe them or sell;
> With this he earned fame
> For curbing the flames
> And quashing the fiery hell.
>
> And thus fair Havana
> Was freed from the bane
> That cruel overran her
> And caused so much pain.
>
> Now she is secure
> And has little to fear
> For if by a sorrowful chance
> A house catches fire
> It alone feeds the pyre
> And nobody else takes offence.

De la Torre also undertook to refurbish the Plaza de Armas, as part of an ambitious program for a spate of large public and private projects. Only two buildings came to fruition: the Palacio del Segundo Cabo, and the Palacio de los Capitanes Generales. Both were ultimate examples of the palatial tendency, and in tandem with the nearby monastery of Santo Domingo (which was converted into the seat of Havana University during the eighteenth century), they constitute one of the most beautiful environments of the city. During the 1950s, the monastery was torn down despite the protests of many citizens, and a modern building erected in its place.

The Marquis's administration also laid out the two first public promenades in Havana: the Paseo de Paula and a boulevard outside the walls, later christened Paseo del Prado. Both spaces, landscaped according to the French school, were remarkable for their open nature, the first giving on the sea and the second on the countryside; they differed in this from the profoundly

View over the Plaza Vieja through a window in the Jaruco house.

Above: Arcades and murals of the Cárdenas house.

Above right: Upper balcony. of the Cárdenas house, facing the Plaza Vieja.

Right: Studio-house belonging to the Venezuelan painter Montilla, opposite the Basilica of San Francisco de Asís built in the eighteenth century.

Hispanic, cloistered feel of the plazas. These avenues were to become the mecca of social life during the nineteenth century. In the words of the governor, the Alameda de Paula set out to be

> . . . the jewel and relief of the city. There is no pleasanter station in all the town, due to its positioning and vistas; exposed to fresh breezes, encompassing the whole bay and placed in the best and foremost of precincts, it achieves a public arena within the walls, in place of what was formerly a midden. It is the most recommendable spot for recreation in so scorching a climate as ours, and was surely destined for this very purpose since the foundation of the city.[55]

At one end of this boulevard, the Coliseo Theater was built in 1775. Here the people of Havana flocked to see operas, zarzuelas, recitals, comedies, ballets, and pantomimes.

Broadly speaking, the urban developments in Havana at that time testified to a plentiful supply of first-rate artisans. Nevertheless, the persistence of characteristic elements of the Hispano-Mauresque tradition, the spontaneous choice of building sites, the simplicity of architectural resources, and the homogeneity of a population that was not yet layered into social classes, all reflected a city in the process of formation. Its definitive countenance was to emerge in the following century, when Cuba attained worldwide preeminence in the sugar trade.

Portrait of Governor Luis de las Casas, who presided over the arrival of the Enlightenment in Cuba.

The O'Donnell Column with its military insignia, including the arms of Havana and the Spanish lion, erected on the Alameda de Paula in Old Havana.

Casa de la Obrapía

The Obrapía owes its name to a testament left by Captain Martín Calvo de la Puerta in 1669, which provided for an annual donation or "pious work" in benefit of five young girls who had no dowry; this provision lasted until well into the twentieth century. In 1648 the house was equipped with two upper rooms, a mezzanine, warehouses, shops, a mirador, and a terrace roof. It was enlarged in 1659. Since Calvo's son, Nicolás, died before his father, leaving no heir, Martín Calvo appointed the Chief Standard-Bearer, Nicolás Castellón (1628–1686), to be the first patron of the Obrapía.

The main door displays a carved crest that has provoked heated discussion among experts, for some attribute it to the Calvo family and others to the Castellóns. However, it is no secret that Castellón's will, signed in 1685, mentions the order of a "carved doorway fitted to the dimensions of my dwelling [that] stands in Cadiz awaiting the first opportunity to be delivered."[56]

During the second half of the eighteenth century, this house became known as the Palace of the Marquis of Cárdenas,[57] because it had descended to Agustín de Cárdenas, Castellón's grandson. Agustín was awarded the title of Marquis of Cárdenas and Monte Hermoso in 1765, for services rendered to the Crown during the English siege of Havana. In 1771, his widow Bárbara Beltrán de Santa Cruz inherited the property and the trust. During the time of the Second Marquis of Cárdenas, who also founded San Antonio Abad de los Baños in the hinterlands of Havana, the house was redesigned, acquiring the appearance it has today as a venue for exhibitions and conferences.

The Obrapía house.

Above: Obrapía house, upstairs gallery.

Above right: Obrapía house, lower colonnade around the patio.

Right: Obrapía house, inner patio.

Top: Obrapía house, bay with
mixtilinear arch.

Bottom: Obrapía house, decorated
door with trefoil arch.

Left: Obrapía house, staircase to
the upper level.

Casa del Conde de San Juan Jaruco

Located on the Plaza Vieja, at the corner with La Muralla street, the well-known Casa del Conde de San Juan Jaruco is a quintessential example of the new breed of stately home favored in the city since the first decades of the eighteenth century. The main entrance has an emblazoned doorway, and the vestibule opens onto a square courtyard surrounded by imposing arched columns. The facade presents an arcade with columns and arches that echo those of the interior and are reiterated around the loggia of the top floor. Throughout the loggia and on the facade are what may be the most spectacular fanlights in the city.

Gabriel de Santa Cruz, father of the future Count of Jaruco, hired Diego de Salazar on June 5, 1732, to build a "high and low [dwelling] on the corner of the new square."[58] Thanks to the same document, we know that the house was built following an anonymous plan. The following year, Santa Cruz applied for permission to build arcades, "being that I am among the leading personages of this city and that my forebears and myself have faithfully served Your Majesty in all things . . . I beg you grant me license."[59] This suggests that the possession of an arcade was a token of social prestige. The house was completed around 1737, and remained in the family of the Counts of San Juan de Jaruco y de Mopox until the mid-nineteenth century. It has recently been refurbished for use as a gallery and art shop.

The Plaza Vieja facade of the house of the Counts of San Juan de Jaruco.

Left: Jaruco house, painted mural friezes.

Above: Jaruco house, upper gallery seen from inside the house.

Jaruco house, view of the upper gallery around the central court.

Above left: Jaruco house, stained-glass fanlight set into the round arch of a window.

Above right: Mediopunto *fanlight and slatted French shutters facing the Plaza Vieja.*

Left: Mediopunto *fanlight and slatted shutters reflected on the piano.*

Casa del Marqués de Arcos

The conspicuous mansion of the Marquis of Arcos, on Mercaderes between Empedrado and O'Reilly, is outwardly quite similar to that of the Counts of Jaruco, although its composition is somewhat less successful, due to the limitations of the site. Halfway through the eighteenth century, Diego Peñalver-Angulo purchased a single-story building that had been in existence since May 1707.[60]

The property was overhauled toward 1746, providing it with two additional floors "and furthermore with permission to build an arcade along the square."[61] To make room for this addition Peñalver bought some houses on the adjoining alleyway that then connected the plaza with Mercaderes Street—unleashing a prolonged dispute with his neighbors, the Chacón family, who were opposed to the destruction of the alley.

The house is notable for its elegant balcony rails, among the first in Havana to introduce Louis XV motifs. This was installed at the end of the eighteenth century when the building was being modified by Don Diego's son, Ignacio de Peñalver y Cárdenas, treasurer-general of the army and the royal exchequer, and first Marquis of Arcos by a royal dispatch of 1792.

Above: To the left, the arcade of the Marquis of Arcos's house, close to the house of don Luis de Chacón, both in Cathedral Square.

Opposite page, top left: Arcos house, facade on Cathedral Square.

Opposite page, top right: Arcos house, upper facade. Note the balcony rail and attic room.

Opposite page, bottom: Arcos house, view from the square.

Casa del Marqués de Aguas Claras

Located on the corner of San Ignacio and Empedrado Streets, this residence merges to the west with the overall structure of the Plaza de la Catedral. In the opinion of some researchers, its construction was initiated by Sebastián Peñalver in 1751 and finished in 1775, by which date it already belonged to Antonio Ponce de León, first Marquis of Aguas Claras. Others maintain that the Marquis did not occupy the place until the early nineteenth century. Whatever the case may be, the residence took his name, and he made significant architectural alterations to it, as did his prominent mulatto descendant Francisco Filomeno Ponce de León (1822–1884).

An unusual feature of this building is the way one proceeds directly through the portico into the corridors lining the central courtyard. Like the other houses in this square, except for the Chacón home and the bathhouse, its front arcade is composed of four round arches, two on either side of a basket arch in the middle.

The galleries that surround the patio on the upper level are protected by French slatted shutters, and round arches blocked by stained glass—the famous Cuban *mediopunto*. The upstairs bays are fitted with the same shutters, with rectangular fanlights resembling gathered drapes. To the rear of the terrace roof we find the servants' quarters.

A well-known restaurant has occupied these premises for many years.

Right: The Aguas Claras house with its mirador room. To the left, the former Baños house.

Below: The residence of the Marquis of Aguas Claras in Cathedral Square.

Top left: Aguas Claras house, view of the inner court, with neighboring towers and roofs.

Top right: Upstairs gallery in the Aguas Claras house.

Right: Aguas Claras house, shuttered upstairs gallery.

Above: Havana Cathedral, from the balcony of the Aguas Claras house.

Palacio de Correos (Palacio del Segundo Cabo)

The Palacio de Correos is on O'Reilly and Tacón Streets, on the Plaza de Armas. It is also known as the Intendencia, or the Palacio del Segundo Cabo, but by whatever name, this is one of the loveliest buildings in Havana. Designed by Silvestre Abarca, the project further benefited from the contributions of Works Director Antonio Fernández de Trevejos, citizen of Havana, and from that of Pedro de Medina of Cadiz, Abarca's right-hand man and a "proven master in the art of cutting stone."[62]

The structure is a poem of elegance and grace. It was begun in the winter of 1770 and was completed by 1772. Its facade has a portico supported on complex pillars, accented by classical pilasters that are intermittently repeated on the upper floor. The top level is crowned by a continuous parapet, of the kind that was to be very popular in the nineteenth century, and the windows and the balcony supports are, with similar anticipation, made of iron. Curved lines predominate in the triangular pinnacles, the ornamentation of the bays, the admirable arch of the entrance hall, and the convolutions of the frieze. This duality, between a waning baroque and a nascent neoclassicism, informs every aspect of the building. The tower, somewhat out of sight, possesses traits that are purely classical. "The mirador that rises on one corner of the post office recalls those of Cadiz houses, and its purpose was obviously the same: to sight approaching ships, or mailboats in this case."[63]

Within, the atmosphere is serene and light: the design repeats the familiar layout of stately homes, with a central patio lined with corridors behind arches on columns, with high pedestals and considerable elevation in order to make room for the mezzanine, a common feature of the period.

Several publishing houses now operate inside the palace.

Top left: Side view of the Palacio del Segundo Cabo, alongside the moat of the Castillo de la Real Fuerza.

Top right: Facade of the Palacio del Segundo Cabo.

Bottom left: Palacio del Segundo Cabo, wrought-iron gate leading to the inner court.

Bottom right: Pilaster on the flat roof of the Palacio del Segundo Cabo.

Left: Entrance to Havana bay seen from the roof of the Palacio del Segundo Cabo.

Bottom left: View of the gallery, with the glow of a fanlight on the back wall.

Below: Upper gallery blocked by slatted shutters and stained-glass mediopuntos.

Palacio de los Capitanes Generales

The Palacio de los Capitanes Generales, on Tacón Street between Obispo and O'Reilly on the Plaza de Armas, was duty-bound—in the words of the Marquis de la Torre—to be "commensurate with the numerous population and the magnificent edifices being built by private citizens."[64] It has been attributed to Antonio Fernández de Trevejos and to Pedro de Medina, but there is no firm evidence for either hypothesis. Angulo Íñiguez believes it may be by the same architect as the Palacio de Correos, in view of their similarities; María Sánchez Agustí reckons that the plans were drawn up by Abarca himself but does not dismiss the possibility of Trevejos, "who might merely have taken his cue from the plans drawn for the postal building."[65]

Due to its resolute horizontality, this building sacrifices in grace what it gains in majesty. The frontal arches maintain the pillar theme, but here they are accented with semicolumns. The bays are brought out by molded *jambas habaneras* of varied design, and the main hall leads into a colossal courtyard lined by two levels of galleries, making it one of the most beautiful in Havana. To the left side of the front arcade, a majestic white marble staircase rises to the mezzanine and upper gallery.

The palace was built between 1776 and 1791. In the beginning the town jail was situated to the back of it, but in 1835 this institution was moved to new premises at one end of the Paseo de Isabel II, and the area it had occupied was absorbed into the Capitanes Generales by an enlargement of the patio. A statue of Christopher Columbus by J. Cucchiari was installed in the middle of this courtyard; giving the impression of being alien to its surroundings, its sleekly polished lines and volumes are in stark contrast to the rough walls and overwhelming baroque presence of the edifice. During the 1930s, the building underwent a final alteration, recovering the vegetation that was typical of colonial patios and baring the stonework. This last intervention meant stripping the whitewash from the walls to expose the masonry, in pursuit of some ill-thought-out "beauty of the stone."

In 1938, the writer and historian Emilio Roig de Leuschenring founded the City Historian's Office in a part of this building, which was being used for Havana City Hall. Today, the palace is the site of the Museo de la Ciudad de La Habana, founded by Eusebio Leal.

Above: The Spanish coat of arms, surmounting the monumental marble doorway of the Palacio de los Capitanes Generales.

Right: The Palacio de los Capitanes Generales, seen from the roof of the Palacio del Segundo Cabo.

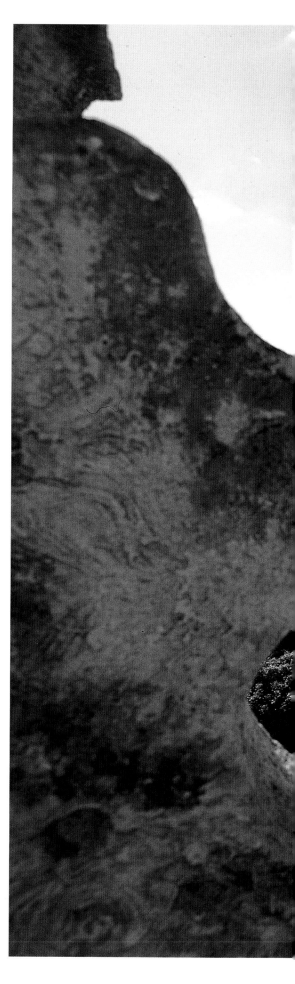

Top: Palacio de los Capitanes Generales, close-up of the springing point of the arches.

Above: Palacio de los Capitanes Generales, partial view of the patio.

Right: Palacio de los Capitanes Generales, central court and galleries.

Above: Palacio de los Capitanes Generales, the White Room.

Left: Palacio de los Capitanes Generales, the Mirror Room.

Casa de Mateo Pedroso

The Pedroso house, on Cuba Street between Peña Pobre and Cuarteles, dates from 1780. It was commissioned by Mateo Pedroso y Florencia (1719–1800), a Permanent Alderman and Ordinary Mayor of Havana and one of its most influential citizens. Despite its huge, spreading facade it is a harmonious creation, owing no doubt to the continuous balcony with turned wooden railings, overhung by a tiled roof that runs parallel from end to end in the front. Curves prevail in the mixtilinear vestibule arch and the baroque patterns on the doors. The ample corridors overlooking the patio are closed off by slatted shutters; the largest of these galleries was used as a dining room, as we know from the memoirs of the Countess of Merlín, who came to Havana in 1842 to stay with her uncle Juan Montalvo in this very mansion. "We take our meals in one of these galleries, because to have indoor dining rooms is unthinkable here, due to the heat."[66]

As time went by the Cuban elite began to imitate the French notion of enclosed dining rooms, but these were little used, since the galleries were irresistibly open to the tropical breezes and sheltered from the sun. Often lined with friezes in colorful patterns, they were brightened by potted plants clustered around the floor and swaying from the beams, while the painted columns were smothered in flowering, fragrant creepers. Canaries trilled in their bamboo cages, and sometimes one might hear a parrot squawk.

This fine house is presently the Palacio de la Artesania. It was restored in 1938 by architect Joaquín Weiss, assisted by Francisco Prat, on behalf of María Teresa Rojas, who inherited it from her stepsisters.

The Mateo Pedroso house (eighteenth century), with its striking continuous balcony dividing the facade. Artillery cannon in the foreground.

Left: Pedroso house, mixtilinear vestibule arch leading to the lower gallery.

Above: Pedroso house, main entrance and part of the facade.

Left: Springing point of an arch, and ceiling of the Pedroso house.

Opposite page, top left: Pedroso house, the wooden inside balcony of the mezzanine.

Opposite page, top right: Pedroso house, the rhythm of arches and columns.

Opposite page, bottom: Pedroso house, upper gallery with a view of the patio.

Left: Pedroso house, central patio.

Casa del Conde de la Reunión de Cuba
(Casa de la Condesa de la Reunión)

This residence was built around 1809 by the notorious slave-trader Santiago de la Cuesta y Manzanal, first Conde de la Reunión de Cuba—a title he acquired in 1824. His wife was María de la Concepción González Larrinaga. Despite its late date, the house reflects the taste of the last third of the eighteenth century. It presents a doorway with a series of molded jambs, a streetside wooden balcony complete with a small roof held up by brackets, and a vestibule arch of mixed straight and curved lines. Its narrow patio has no galleries on the longer sides, but an extraordinary balcony projects out over it, covered by a roof.

Indoors the house is decorated with floral friezes, in which the island's native flowers and beasts are conspicuously absent. This was a common omission until the twentieth century; Graziano Gasparini maintains that the failure of the artist or his employer to acknowledge the nature close to hand is no more than a symptom of provincial thinking, the kind given to craven imitation of the standards of some distant, longed-for metropolis.[67]

This is the house that was fictionally re-created by the Cuban writer Alejo Carpentier in his novel *The Age of Enlightenment*. It currently functions as a cultural center dedicated to the same writer.

House of the Count of La Reunión.

Top left: La Reunión, upper gallery with wooden balcony and friezes.

Above: La Reunión, detail of the sinuous wooden balcony, dating from the early nineteenth century.

Left: La Reunión, view of the gallery from below.

Church and Convent of Nuestra Señora de Belén

It is said that the baroque came to Havana when the church and convent devoted to Our Lady of Bethlehem (Nuestra Señora de Belén) were built, on the corner of Luz and Compostela. The front wall is made up of three superimposed sections, a familiar feature in Havana churches of the eighteenth century, with successively ascending orders in the classical fashion. In the first section, the entrance portal is framed by a large splayed arch, and the third section presents a niche containing sculptures. Inside, the aisles are roofed with barrel vaults, and a cupola rises over the transept, possibly the first of its kind in Havana. The aisles, the vaults, and the cupola were until recently covered with murals, which were destroyed by a fire in 1992. Some murals have been preserved on the facade.

The attached convent has no features of architectural note on the outside, except for the restrained detail of superimposed pilasters at the entrance. The main cloister is organized around galleries of arches over columns, on both levels. The so-called Bethlehem Arch is striking for the way it leaps like a bridge over Acosta Street. It was built in 1772, when the convent was enlarged to include existing buildings on the other side of the road.

The church and convent were dedicated by Bishop Compostela as a refuge for penniless convalescents leaving hospital. The works were in danger of remaining unfinished when a merchant named Juan Francisco Carballo donated the funds needed to complete and enlarge the premises for use by Bethlemite priests arriving from Mexico. Carballo was assassinated in 1718, but this did not interrupt the work, which was nearing completion. The institution's tasks were extended to include assistance to convalescents, daily food distribution, and free education. Carballo's will guaranteed the completion and upkeep of a building that is a true gem of Cuban architecture.

Until 1925 it was the seat of the Colegio de Belén, run by Jesuit priests and one of the most important teaching institutions of the country.

Above: Entrance to the Convent and Church of Belén.

Right: Doorway to the Church of Belén, with a niche containing a nativity scene.

Opposite page: Belén, detail of the niche and its free-standing sculptures.

Church and Monastery of San Francisco de Asís

The church and monastery of San Francisco stands on Oficios Street between Amargura and Churruca and may be dated to the 1730s. Joaquín Weiss describes it as "rudimentary baroque," due to the severity of its lines. The church, shaped like a Latin cross and roofed with a barrel vault, conveys an impression of power through vigorous arches resting on pilasters. The vault is pierced with lunettes to let in the light, and to create a backdrop for the lateral terrace that opens onto the Plaza de San Francisco: the succession of lunettes creates a rythmically undulating pattern. The exceptionally lofty, forty-two-meter tower was only completed at the end of the eighteenth century, and remained the city's highest point for many years; the monumental cloister, lined by three levels of galleries, can still claim to be the largest of its kind in Havana.

The Plaza de San Francisco was the venue for many religious festivals, such as the Day of the Kings, a popular subject with painters and lithographers of the day, and other events of folkloric significance. Under the Republic the monastery was converted into the Administración de Correos, until this was moved in the 1950s to new offices in the Plaza Cívica.

The complex has been turned into the Museo de Arte Sacro and concert hall.

Top left: San Francisco de Asís, arches and ox-eye window in the side aisle.

Middle left: San Francisco de Asís, curves and columns of stone.

Bottom left: San Francisco de Asís, part of the lateral terrace, showing buttresses and lunettes.

Above: The Fountain of Lions, donated by the Count of Villanueva to the Plaza de San Francisco.

Opposite page: Lateral entrance to the monastery of San Francisco, with the Fountain of Lions in the plaza of San Francisco.

Above: San Francisco de Asís, galleries around the patio.

Right: San Francisco de Asís, galleries on three levels.

Above: San Francisco de Asís, view of the cloister galleries from below.

Left: San Francisco de Asís, looking through the central patio.

Left: San Francisco de Asís, the main aisle.

Below: San Francisco de Asís, the altar.

Havana Cathedral

Set between Mercaderes and San Ignacio, Havana Cathedral is the greatest baroque monument in Cuba, at the same time as it constitutes both a symbol and an evocation of the city. Its construction was begun toward 1748 in what was then called the Plaza de la Ciénaga, as a temple for the Jesuit fathers. But when this order was expelled in 1767, the half-finished church was designated to be the Parroquial Mayor (principal parish church), in which form it was concluded by 1777. In 1788 Havana was promoted to the rank of Diocese, and the parish church became a cathedral.

The building presents a front so harmonious as to rival any other monument of its type. It is composed of three sections stacked in pyramidal form: the lower mass is pierced by three portals, enhanced by the complex jambs that were such a hallmark of Havana monuments during the second half of the eighteenth century. The first and second levels are separated by a swirling cornice. Francisco Prat considers that the facade of Havana Cathedral is comparable with that of Murcia in Spain: "it would be hard to find any Borrominesque examples to better it in Hispano-America, and few peninsular specimens are more impressive."[68]

The interior has suffered many changes over the years. The first major alteration was instigated by Bishop Espada, in the early nineteenth century: the old baroque altars were discarded along with the religious statues, which he deemed to be "incorrectly worked." The same fate befell the paintings, including that which depicted the banishment of Bishop Morrell in 1762, and they were replaced by copies of the European masters courtesy of Perovani, Vermay, and their disciples. The new altars, by Pedro Abad Villareal, were in neoclassical style, and the main altar was carved by Antonio Solá. The original wooden roof was replaced by a vault of gesso and stone completed in 1950.

In the view of Nissa Torrents, the cathedral ". . . transmits an easy charm, a well-being within the world, a criollo languor that has no truck with solemnities,"[69] while for Cuban Cardinal Jaime Ortega, Havana offers its face to the world in the rhythmic facade of its cathedral, which is "ever-welcoming and ever-expectant."[70]

Above: Havana Cathedral, bird's eye view over the altar.

Right: Havana Cathedral, upper facade and bell tower.

Plaza de la Catedral

The Plaza de la Catedral lies between Empedrado, San Ignacio, Mercaderes, and the alleyway of El Chorro. Its original name was Plazuela de la Ciénaga, or swamp, because it was an insalubrious patch prone to flooding, being the outlet for the waters of the Royal Channel. Governor Juan de Texeda had a marker installed there in 1592 to register the fact. The square took definitive shape and acquired its greatest social and religious importance around the second half of the eighteenth century.

The Plaza de la Catedral and the buildings that surround it offer a setting of extreme harmony and beauty. According to Graziano Gasparini, it is "a circumscribed urban space that feels intimate and is perfectly to scale with the cathedral complex: one of the prettiest 'drawing rooms' in America."[71]

Top: Havana Cathedral, view of roofs, towers and dome.

Above: Cathedral Square, seen from the house of don Luis de Chacón.

Church of La Merced

The construction of this church, located on Cuba Street between Paula and Merced, was begun in 1755 and continued well into the nineteenth century. Joaquín Weiss observes that there are instructive contrasts to be drawn between this church and the Havana Cathedral. The cathedral relies on breadth, and La Merced tends upward; the concave facade of the greater building is counterposed by the rectilinear front of the lesser, whose columns are marshalled into the center of the composition, framing the church door in order to stress its verticality. In contrast to "the cathedral's elements of rich elaboration and fantasy, we have the austere forms . . . of La Merced."

During the second half of the nineteenth century, the interior walls were lavishly decorated by major Cuban and European painters, such as Miguel Melero and son, Herrera, Chartrand, Petit, Didier, and Zuloaga. The nearby cloister is ringed by extremely high columns, holding up enormous round arches.

The twentieth century heralded a period of great popularity for this church, which became a venue of choice for society weddings, although it appealed to all social classes.[72]

La Merced, the cloister.

La Merced, the main altar.

The Foremost City
in Spanish America

Havana . . . is a perfect paradise. One feels close to civilization once more at the sight of such a well-built town . . . Havana is the foremost city Spain possesses in all her American dominions.

— *Diary of Sir John Maxwell Tylden, 1814–1815*

It was during the nineteenth century that Cuban nationality was at last forged. From early on, poets began consciously working with notions of *lo cubano*, elevating natural features like pineapples and palms to the status of symbols. They drew complex identifications between the natural, the feminine, and the motherland, until characteristics that are integral to the Cuban way of being—nostalgia, gaiety, irony, irreverence, and sensuality, among many others—came together in a definitive articulation. The great themes of those days were incomparably romantic: the spiritual exaltation of landscape, exile, and distance.

One of the first writers to put such sentiments into words, in her letters and books, was Mercedes de Santa Cruz y Montalvo, Countess of Merlín.[73] Living almost her whole life away from Cuba, she expressed a poignant vision of it as an enchanted, lost paradise, and this makes her the precursor, in a sense, of a whole lineage of writers who were to evoke their Caribbean isle from the often irrevocable perspective of exile. She did not return to Havana until 1842, when she found the city transformed by a rash of public works and luxurious private homes, many of them inhabited by members of her family—like the Palacio Pedroso, where she stayed—and the scene of frequent parties in her honor.

The nineteenth century was an epoch of romance. Its history in Cuba is packed with proud patricians who dueled with one another over minute points of honor or conspired for the ideals of equality and freedom, who were capable of emancipating their slaves and giving up huge fortunes to take up arms against the Metropolis, offering their lives for the motherland. That century sounded another deeply romantic chord in Cuba when the island was visited by a succession of learned voyagers whose passion it was

to explore the world, a period pastime that prompted the publication of travel diaries and picture-albums of prints and sketches. The German friend of Goethe, Alexander von Humboldt, came through in the early decades. In his Cuban excursions, accompanied by the artist Bonpland and some select Havana intellectuals, he "discovered" and named the flora and fauna of the island, and gathered much information that he was later to pour into the universalist, humanist vision so characteristic of the Romantics—a vision that was not blind to the grave contradictions of Cuban society.

This was also the time when Cuba defined the fundamental priorities of its economy: it would be the island of sugar, coffee, tobacco, and slavery. Black slaves had been present since the beginning of Spanish colonization, but during the nineteenth century they undoubtedly became the driving force of the economy. The collapse of the sugar industry in Haiti gave Cuba the opportunity to seize a considerable portion of the international market, and confident lobbying swept away the long-standing obstacles to the progress of this industry. Within a short lapse of time, permits were granted for the importation of thousands of Africans as well as machinery for use on the plantations; the statutes of land tenancy were altered to suit the industry's needs, and by 1818, full freedom of trade had been obtained.

It is a telling fact that just as sugar was consolidating its ascendancy, the first criticisms of the city's image were finding their way into *El papel periódico de La Habana* (1792): the wooden balconies were little better than rickety scaffolding, the baroque doorways were in the worst of taste, the vaunted skill of Negro craftsmen was an impediment to the progress of any cultured art of building, and the government palaces expressed sadly garbled notions of grandeur.[74]

View of Havana bay in an oil painting by F. Ceveau.

Clearly, the baroque no longer meshed with the cultural aspirations of the new sugar barons, who among other changes had become less provincial and increasingly looked to the wider world, as a consequence of perfecting sugar production to meet international standards. Not only the merchandise but also its makers now traveled abroad, crisscrossing Europe, the Antilles, and the United States in search of a high-yield species of cane, a new chemical potion, or a special measuring instrument. Thus the plantation owners broke out of their local isolation to forge a network of global relations based upon classic bourgeois interdependence. In 1792 contruction began on the first neoclassical project in the country in Havana: the Casa de Beneficiencia, a charitable institution sponsored by the sugar magnates and the Royal Economic Society of Friends of the Country, and designed by the Italian-born engineer Francisco Vanvitelli.[75]

Sugar threw Cuba open to the world, and the world came to Cuba. A large number of foreigners with an interest in the slave trade or other businesses settled here. They were followed, for brief or long stays, by a bevy of foreign artists and craftsmen-musicians, engravers,[76] painters, sculptors, architects, goldsmiths, ironsmiths, and many others—mostly from England,

Italy, France, and the United States. These artists helped to spread a new aesthetic sensibility that found its most ardent supporter in the figure of Bishop Espada. Arriving in Havana in 1803, the prelate embarked upon an active term of social-minded management, launching various projects such as the new public cemetery (1806) that would be named after him; its gates were designed along neoclassical lines.

Within the walls of Havana itself, the new trend aggressively imposed itself with mass demolitions of old houses in order to erect more fashionable ones in their place. As of the mid-eighteenth century, the entire area within city bounds had been built up, and the number of buildings has since remained more or less stable at around three thousand—even up to the present day, when it has if anything declined, owing to the nineteenth- and twentieth-century habit of using up several lots for a single large building.[77]

There are many distinctive features enabling us to recognize a nineteenth-century mansion or *palacete*. One of the most conspicuous is, of course, the presence of cast or wrought iron. We find it in windows, balconies, gates, staircases, inner corridors, and railings, in the amazingly varied balcony dividers, and in lamps and lamp posts, often with the most faithful classical

Opposite page, left: Wrought-iron lyre-shaped window bars.

Opposite page, right: Wrought-iron balcony divider (guarda vecinos).

Left: Wrought-iron gateway.

Above: Wrought-iron gas-lamp holder.

embellishments: cornucopias, frets, ovals, lyres, arrowheads, or urns. Alongside this we find the classical style of doorways, the addition of dust guards on brackets over the bays, the reframing of wall sections with such devices as attached pilasters, the arrival of raking cornices, and the inevitable parapet with its simple or flamboyant chalices of glazed pottery or some other material; and finally, uncovered balconies supported on great slabs of stone, projecting over the street. The colorful facades were sometimes enlivened with ornamental bands or scenic murals, sometimes painted to convey the illusion of stonework.

The nineteenth-century house shrank from tortuous perspectives, seeking a fluid and harmonious whole. It substituted flat roofs for the old frame structures, covering these on occasion with board-and-plaster ceilings. Large windows filtered light and air through shutters called *a la francesa*; light was broken down as though in a kaleidoscope by the magnificent *mediopuntos.*[78] The gay colors splashed onto walls that were themselves shades of blue, pink, green, and yellow and tinted all the objects on their path.

Inside, the plain, rectangular panelling of the doors eschewed the elaborate incisions of the previous century. Marble floors replaced the old, dark pavements of tile. The main staircase touched unprecedented heights of monumentality, splendor of design, and richness of material. Finally, the court was converted into a central ornamental component, becoming filled with fountains, statues, benches, flowering plants, and shrubs. The house thus appeared transformed, even though little had changed in structural terms. In short, these were mansions fit for elegant, gracious living, complemented by superb furniture.

Side by side with the numerous pieces of furniture and artifacts that were imported from abroad, it was usual to place other pieces made in Cuba. Cuban furniture is primarily differentiated by its use of the island's native timbers: cedar, ebony, mahogany, rosewood, and others. It includes tried and tested objects of local use, such as rocking chairs, *comadritas* (armless rockers), *tinajeros* for water filtering and cooling, and smoking chairs. Though of eighteenth-century French origin, the rocker suited the Cuban temperament to perfection. It is constantly evoked by travelers who were bewitched by the image of Havana beauties rocking back and forth, lazily fanning themselves beside trays of cool drinks and tropical fruit. As for Empire-style furniture made in Cuba, like the *escaparate* wardrobes, it is charmingly provincial and

Top: *Part of a gallery with a* mediopunto *reflected on wall and floor.*

Above: *Rosette of inlaid marble.*

Right: *French shutters and stained-glass window.*

well worth appreciation. Meanwhile beds were increasingly replacing lined cots, couches were coming into vogue, and sewing cabinets appeared. All these items reflected the influence of neoclassicism, largely as a result of greater commerce and exchange with the United States.

Nineteenth-century stately homes and middle-class dwellings contrasted greatly with the living conditions of the poor. The underclass had to make do with jerry-built shacks that were chaotic and crammed into narrow streets that ran with mud, a festering, unhealthy, and unpleasant environment for the many people of varied social status, occupation, and race who lived there. In the lower-class barrios of Havana, such as Jesús María, the precarious structures clung on through cyclones and torrential downpours. From the seventeenth century onward, on the other hand, bourgeois homes were simplified versions of higher-ranking ones: compact, unassuming colonial buildings with frame roofs, *tejaroz* eaves, shuttered French windows, *mediopuntos*, and room dividers. These houses might feature delicate mural decorations inside, and attractive though simple adornments on the facade.

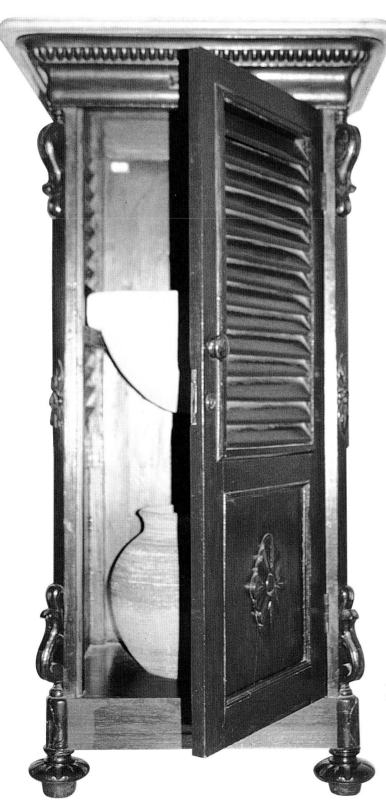

Empire-style rocker.

Nineteenth-century tinajero, *a free-standing contraption for purifying water.*

They were all reinterpretations—in some cases, genuine miniatures—of colonial palaces, a constant trait of Cuban architecture that continued into the Republican era.

European and North American travelers left us books and pictures that afford vivid glimpses of Cuba and the social life of Havana in those days. Brightly colored awnings were strung up over the streets to ward off the sun, causing dazzling contrasts of light and shade. Lumbering carts piled with barrels of molasses contrasted with the graceful, nimble gigs driven by coachmen who looked like true "black princes" in their high leather boots, black redingotes, silver buttons, and top hats. Spanish soldiers flaunted their various uniforms, coiffed with plumes, berets, or peaked caps with red bows; merchants paced gravely in hat and coat, among tax collectors clutching their leather-bound books and gold-pommelled staves, as well as dashing criollo aristocrats prancing by on horses. Fugitive slaves jostled with hollow-eyed gamblers, sailors on shore-leave, prostitutes hunting sailors, and aimless friars. The incessant pealing of bells mingled with the shouts and chants of street vendors. All this riotous movement swirling around the docks impressed visitors forever with "the clangor of bells in one's ears, the taste of guava on one's lips." The thunder of cannon's booming from the fortress of La Cabaña was the signal, morning and evening, for the opening and closing of the city gates. As soon as the cannon sounded, just before dawn, campesino farmers streamed in, carrying their produce to market, and so began another day in Havana.

During the second decade of the nineteenth century, Havana spilled irrevocably beyond the artificial constraints of its walls and the occupation of the outskirts was begun, formalizing what had already occurred in haphazard fashion during the previous century. This time a different conception of space was applied: buildings were set on larger plots of land, in contact

Above: The Gallant Coachman, *oil painting by the Spanish-Cuban artist Víctor Patricio de Landaluze (1828–1889).*

Right: Modest colonial home.

Republican house in El Vedado.

with nature, the opposite of the crowded situation that prevailed inside the walls. Military engineers directed projects that sought to endow the new cityscape with a sense of unity, in clear neoclassical spirit. They encouraged the use of porticos as a means of communication between street and house, and as an element of urban ornamentation. The portico became a prominent feature of the main carriageways in the district we now call "Centro Habana," an area that was already taking shape in the first plan for the amplification of the city in 1817, directed by Havana engineer Antonio María de la Torre.

The urbanization of the zone beyond the old city walls was the occasion for a deepening animosity between criollos and Spaniards, in the context of the feud between Captain-General Miguel Tacón (1834–1838) and the chief of the Exchequer, Claudio Martínez de Pinillos, count of Villanueva.

Tacón, whose disdainful attitude toward the criollos made him the most hated governor of colonial times, surrounded himself with a coterie of Spanish businessmen loyal to the Crown, and embarked upon a far-reaching program of public works whose repercussions on the urban landscape can

still be felt today. This governor improved many facets of the city, paving the roads with the tarmac invented by the Scotsman McAdam, digging sewers and drains, labelling, numbering, and lighting the streets, opening extra gates in the walls, and installing new public markets and fishmarkets. He repaired existing buildings such as the Casa de Gobierno and the San Juan de Dios Hospital, and erected new ones, including a prison and the theater that bears his name; he commissioned decorative monuments such as the fountain of Neptune, tidied up the Plaza de Armas, reordered the Paseo de Extramuros and the Campo de Marte, widened San Luis Gonzaga Street (also known as the Calzada de la Reina), and laid out the Paseo Militar, subsequently renamed for Charles III.

The works completed under the aegis of General Tacón thoroughly established the new architectural canon, and it can be claimed that neoclassical Havana is the Havana of Tacón. The scale of these works entailed the collaboration of architects, engineers, and master-builders, the majority of them Spanish and in some cases from other countries. They represent the dawning of an *auteur* architecture, attuned to the potential of local craftsmanship.

The Teatro Tacón, located at the beginning of the Paseo de Extramuros, is a good instance of the above. Architect Antonio Mayo built it in 1836 to dominate the most important part of the new neighborhood. Its stage machinery was revolutionary, as was the internal telephone system devised by Antonio Meucci for more efficient communication during performances (Meucci's telephone came years before that of Graham Bell, although it was never credited to him). The Countess of Merlín left the following vignette of the theater's scintillating interior:

> This theater is rich and elegant at once; it is painted white and gold; the curtain and decorations provide a glittering spectacle, even though the rules of perspective are imperfectly observed. The patio is furnished with magnificent armchairs, as are the boxes, which are fronted by a slender golden grille through which curious eyes may feast upon the tiny feet of lady spectators. The governor's box is larger and more ornate than that of any king elsewhere. Only the grandest playhouses of the great European capitals can equal that of Havana for beauty of decoration, splendor of illumination, and the elegance of the audience, all yellow gloves and white breeches. In London or Paris, such a theater would be taken for an immense salon of the highest cachet.[79]

The policies of the Count of Villanueva, on the other hand, reflected the interests of reform-minded criollo magnates. His contributions to the city include the Fuente de los Leones (1836) in the Plaza de San Francisco, and another fountain called De la India or "Noble Havana," installed in 1837 at the end of the Paseo de Extramuros; both were the work of the Italian sculptor Giuseppe Gaggini. The Fuente de la India was an allegory of the city, a

Image of the Tacón theater and Paseo de Isabel II, on a cigar-box label printed in the mid-nineteenth century.

The Fountain of the Lions (1836), by the Italian sculptor Giuseppe Gaggini.

The Fuente de La India, or "Noble Havana," also by Gaggini, 1837. It has become one of the city's emblems.

symbol of criollo values, an expression of the intense self-awareness of the sugar aristocracy. The statue of a beautiful indigenous woman stood for the autochthonous expressed in a contemporary idiom, true to the civilizing, internationalist spirit of the famous salons hosted by Domingo del Monte, writer and patron of the arts.

The Count of Villanueva sponsored two further major projects, of vast urban and economic scope. The first was the Ferdinand VII Aqueduct, built between 1831 and 1835 under the direction of Manuel Pastor: the city's expansion had made this a necessity. Secondly, he established a railway that was a triumph for the Cuban patrician class, in that it was championed by the sugar planters and reflected their economic clout. Cuba was ten years ahead of Spain in introducing this revolutionary means of transport, a move that would radically transform the conditions of sugar production. Cuba's railway was the first in the Spanish-speaking territories, the second in the Americas, and the fifth in the world at large. The Villanueva rail terminal was built by an American engineer, Alfred Kruger, and became the first Neo-Gothic construction in Havana.

The rivalry between the two officials brought multiple benefits to the city itself. Their activities were abetted by the considerable economic importance of a region that was maintaining a steady output of close to one and a half million *arrobas* (forty million pounds) of sugar a year, thanks to the labor of more than forty-five thousand slaves.[80] Havana grew to three or four times its former size during this period. After an absence of several years, writer Cirilo Villaverde marveled at the capital's development through history. He described it as a

> . . . maritime city, pliable as wax in the hands of its owners and makers, [that] has always bowed to the form they wished to give it. Each one . . . has stamped her with his imprint. Under the ferule of politician and warrior, her favorite indulgences have been castles, artillery, cannon, and military camps; under the courtier, she has shown off her palaces, cathedrals, boulevards, gardens, fountains, monuments, and ever-finer streets. At such transformations, as speedy as they were magical, her sons . . . never tire of gazing at her in wonder: a fresh and gorgeous city, rising from the depths of the sea . . .

For Villaverde, Havana was also like an irrepressible Indian girl who

> . . . tossed her headdress, stood up and marched forward laden with
> strange feathers, precious gems and silks which she obtained . . . from
> the sugar, coffee and tobacco of her fertile fields. In vain, then, were
> walls erected and ditches sunk. Both these she has breached, and
> saunters southward to Jesús del Monte, whose small church on its ver-
> dant hill seems . . . posted there by the hand of Providence, to stop
> the city from tumbling further into the country. To the southwest,
> past famed estates and cheerful cottages, she has leaped the deep
> Casiguaguas and not halted her advance until coming up against the
> wall of the Quemado. To the west, trampling the mangrove swamps
> of La Punta and San Lázaro, she seems bent on proceeding until she
> kisses the walls of El Príncipe . . .[81]

In 1846, the population had reached 129,994 people, of whom 92,343 resided outside the city walls.[82] It was here and in the outlying neigborhoods that a new type of living space emerged: the *casa quinta*, or house and gardens, in response to changing lifestyles due to higher levels of cultural development and the refinement of manners. A rapprochement with nature was sought, and with this came the desire for a seclusion that would be shared only with one's socioeconomic peers. Another factor was the quest for a healthier environment, shielded from oppressive heat, cholera, and yellow fever. The first example of this type of house was perhaps Bishop Espada's 1819 residence facing the Campo de Marte, and surrounded by delicious gardens: several travelers allude to it as the "gardens of the Bishop." Governor Tacón followed up with a summer retreat for the Capitanes Generales on the brand-new Paseo Militar, known as Los Molinos. This type of construction spread rapidly through the district of El Cerro and, decades later, to El Vedado.

Over a period of approximately fifty years, the Calzada del Cerro emerged as the main thoroughfare of the new neighborhood. Toward 1873, Samuel Hazard admired it in the following terms:

> It is a very handsome street, about three miles long, lined on each side
> with beautiful and comfortable residences of the fashionable and
> wealthy, for whom this with its surroundings is the principal place of res-
> idence, particularly in the summer. Here is an ample field for the study
> of tropic architecture, hardly any two houses being alike, yet all with the
> same general plan, very different indeed from our ideas of comfort and
> yet, probably the best plan that can be adopted for this climate.[83]

Said plan confined itself to a single story (occasionally one may find two, or partial sections built up). The portico ran along the front, and sometimes to the sides. This feature is fundamental in the conception of the *casas quinta*, which were originally brought to nonurbanized areas. Later, when the area's progress had stabilized, these arches succeeded one another continuously, giving rise to the long colonnades that ennoble the Calzada del Cerro.

House of the Alfonso family on Calzada del Cerro, with cast-iron columns and stone parapet.

Opposite page: Gallery and courtyard of the Alfonso house.

The arrangement of these houses was very similar to that of the ranch houses on the sugar or coffee haciendas, except that the town versions preserved the inner court, something that had been virtually eliminated from country homes. However, the relation of the house to the environment by way of the portico betrayed the same aspiration of integration with the landscape, an intention to make the most of the refreshing bounties of light and air. In both cases, the architectonic and ornamental complements were reminiscent of those in stately homes, on occasion reaching extremes of Oriental luxury, as in the fabled estate of the Count of Fernandina.

The houses of El Cerro inspired voyeuristic delight in J. Milton Mackie:

> The mansions are gay and brightly colored, almost all white with fringes of pink, sky blue or apple green. Nothing is more charming than an evening stroll through . . . El Cerro, for the houses—including the patios—are all brilliantly lit by gaslight and keep doors and windows flung wide. The stroller, looking straight in through the passageways, may glimpse an orangery at the back or jars spilling over with equally bright flowers. He may too observe the members of the family gathered in groups in the patio, or seated by rank of age and sex on two formal circles of chairs . . . You can hear the music as you pass, and see the dancing. You also hear the mellifluous whisper of soft Spanish voices, and their musical, tempered laughter, you see the fingers slipping over a keyboard or strumming the strings of a blue-edged guitar. Enchanted by the vision, you exclaim: what a social life![84]

Houses of this kind, like nineteenth-century housing in general, still embody the highest achievement of our country's architecture. By this time the building of houses benefited from a long history, in terms of evolution and of adaptation to the environment. Cuban architecture had become attuned to the possibilities of the workforce, the available construction materials, and the national way of life. A dialogue had been established between an architectural tradition and the neoclassical forms that were applied at a remove from their original models, in a way that bordered on the popular, to create something unique and unrepeatable, which well deserves the name of *lo cubano*.

El Templete

To one side of the Plaza de Armas, on Baratillo Street between Enna and O'Reilly, is the spot said to be that of the foundation of Havana. An obelisk was put up here in 1754 to commemorate the event. It was topped by a bronze statue of the Virgen del Pilar, and a stone relief was carved onto the base depicting a silk-cotton tree shorn of its leaves and branches. This column, erected in the days of Governor Francisco Cagigal de la Vega, marks the place where legend has it that the first Mass and town council meeting were celebrated, under the shade of the spreading ceiba tree.

Many years later, Havana had developed so much that it was deemed high time the modest column was restored and another more suitable monument developed, in keeping with the city's status. This is how the Templete came into being,

a few yards away from the obelisk and in view of the sea. It was designed and executed by Colonel of Engineers Antonio María de la Torre y Cárdenas and unveiled on March 18, 1828.

The monument took the form of a small Graeco-Roman temple. It was astonishingly up-to-date, an exceptional quality in the Latin America of those days. Inside, three canvases by the French painter Jean-Baptiste Vermay were hung; Vermay, a disciple of David, was also the founder in 1818 of the San Alejandro school of painting. The pictures describe the first Mass, the first council meeting, and the inauguration ceremony of the Templete itself, which unfolded with great fanfare in the presence of authorities and personalities at a Mass led by Bishop Espada. The portraits of the Havana notables of the day include that of the bishop, in a promi-

nent position on the left of the huge canvas, and many figures of the criollo nobility.

El Templete, the tree, and the obelisk are enclosed within an iron fence with bronze spikes, between posts of San Miguel stone with urns crowned by bronze pineapple forms, alternating with orbs. A bust of Christopher Columbus was placed in the gardens in front of the column, taken from Bishop Espada's house on the Campo de Marte. Havana was forging a memory of itself for times to come.

Each November 15, on the eve of the anniversary of the city's foundation, the doors of the Templete are opened to allow the people to perform a venerable Havana tradition: they march three times around the silk-cotton tree in the garden, making a wish on each circuit. It is said that these wishes are (almost) always granted.

Front of El Templete, opened in 1828 to commemorate the civic and religious foundation of the city. This monument and its ceiba tree are important symbols of Havana.

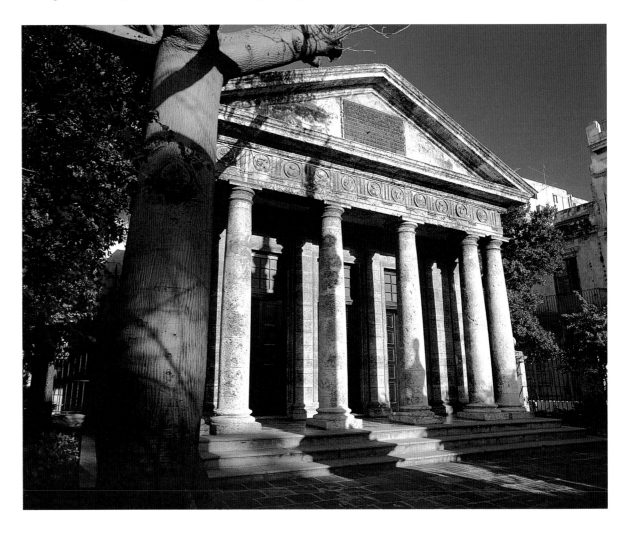

Casa de los Marqueses de la Real Proclamación

The Casa de los Marqueses de la Real Proclamación is one of the more remarkable buildings of the period. In spite of its imposing scale, it maintains a commendable sense of balance and proportion, qualities that are difficult to appreciate at its location, the intersection of two narrow streets, Cuba and Luz.

The facade displays some of the conventional attributes brought by neoclassicism to nineteenth-century architecture, such as pilasters, dust guards over the bays, prominent balconies on massive stone brackets, iron balustrades, and a parapeted roof. The vestibule leads into the gallery surrounding a small, square courtyard. Houses as large as this tended to occupy more and more land, so that the patios were getting smaller—although they remained essential for collecting and storing rainwater in tanks. The monumental staircase underscores the high social rank of the first owners, as well as the architectural merit of their mansion. A beautiful colored light is filtered through the stained glass and beamed onto walls and floors, while the marble paving intensifies the play of reflection and light.

The precise date of construction is not known, but judging by its characteristics the house can be assumed to have been built during the 1810s, probably by Manuel José Recio de Morales, V Marquis de la Real Proclamación, who died in 1839.

In his story *El penitente*, Cirilo Villaverde writes about the daughter of a man called Antón Recio and about her thwarted love affair with an enlisted naval captain, who sets sail from Havana in 1780, under the command of Bernardo de Gálvez, to take Pensacola and Mobile in Florida. Villaverde was an excellent chronicler of Cuban life, but as a novelist he naturally disguised the characters' true names and the actual date of this incident. Yet everyone knew that the book was in fact alluding to this house and the dynasty of the Recio family, who were among the earliest settlers in Havana.

Grand staircase of marble and iron, in the home of the Marquis de la Real Proclamación.

Palacio del Marqués de Almendares (Palacio Zuazo)

The lofty palace of the second marquis of Almendares, in the tiny *plazoleta* of Belén, on the corner of Compostela and Luz, has a splendid, pillared front portico. Both floors are embellished by round arches, the upper ones with the addition of stained glass. In 1798, the then proprietor of the house, Ambrosio María Zuazo (a native of Seville who served as council trustee and Ordinary Mayor of Havana) built on the portico and the upper level.

In 1852, Ignacio de Herrera y O'Farrill, second marquis of Almendares, was the owner of six sugar plantations and more than ten thousand slaves, and his extravagant lifestyle was eventually to ruin him; it was he who now bought the house and contracted the architect Ciriaco Rodríguez to redesign it. This conversion lent the building its present aspect. Historian Francisco Pérez de la Riva writes that the Marquis's reckless spending "could only be equalled by that of the Osuna family in Spain, and Havana folk were wont to say, like the Spanish in allusion to their Duke, 'not even if you were the Marquis of Almendares.'"[85] With lordly indifference, the Marquis presided over the depletion of his great fortune and the procession out of the house of priceless furniture, paintings, sculptures, lamps, porcelain, and the rest, until the end of his days in 1884.

Balcony and reiterated round arches of the Marquis of Almendares house.

Palacio de Aldama

In 1838, Domingo del Monte wrote to his brother-in-law José Luis Alfonso, Marquis of Montelo: "Our father-in-law has purchased land in the best part of the Campo de Marte, and he thinks to build a small house there of elegant and simple construction, and if he does so according to the plans that I have provided him with, it will be the best, the only one in Havana to exhibit even a suspicion, a trace, of respect and love for the beauties of Art."[86] As Del Monte foresaw, the palace built between 1840 and 1844 by Domingo Aldama, a wealthy Spanish merchant and landowner, was the most acclaimed building in nineteenth-century Havana. The original plans were drawn by the Venezuelan engineer Manuel Antonio Carrerá, but as Del Monte pointed out, the finished building responded "not to Carrerá's plan, but a much modified version."[87] There is evidence to indicate that the final design of the Palacio Aldama was the work of Jules Sagebien, a French architect residing in Matanzas.

Main entrance to the Palacio Aldama.

Palacio Aldama, colonnade.

The building occupies nearly an entire block on Reina Street, between Amistad and Águila, and is composed of two large dwellings joined by a single facade. The internal organization adheres to the "stately" pattern, although the kitchen is unconventionally located in the mezzanine. The main attraction of the Palacio de Aldama consists of its ornamentation. In 1875, it was valued at the then considerable sum of 625,000 pesos, containing a varied range of marble floors, sumptuous details in iron and bronze, wonderful use of precious woods for the doors and doorframes, and rich classical moldings on both walls and ceilings; some ceilings are also decorated with murals inspired by those of Pompeii. These interiors were filled with richly carved furniture, Chinese and Japanese bronzes, Persian rugs, Gobelin tapestries, majestic sconces, and great alabaster jars.

The structural point of departure was markedly rectangular. The facade boasts a lintelled Tuscan colonnade, one of the first to appear in Havana; it swiftly became a must throughout the new neighborhoods. The upper level begins flush with the top of this portico and consists of a rhythmic series of Ionic pilasters set to either side of the fifteen bays, producing a truly monumental effect. Each opening is covered by a dust guard and equipped with shutters and *mediopuntos* to reinforce the round arches. The balcony, with its cast-iron balsutrade showing Empire-style candlestick motifs, courses uninterrupted across the front to underline the formal unity of the building, further emphasized by the continuous parapet.

In January 1869, the palace was attacked and plundered by mobs of Spanish volunteers. This was during the tragic days when the defenders of the colonial regime perpetrated extreme acts of violence and pillage against Cuban families, only a few months after the outbreak in the province of Oriente of the first war of independence in October 1868. Today the house is the seat of the Instituto de Historia.

Above: Palacio Aldama, view of the central court, entresol, and upper gallery.

Right: Palacio Aldama, exterior balcony.

Opposite page: Palacio Aldama, the front doorway.

Right: Palacio Aldama, iron gateway to the central patio.

Far right: Palacio Aldama, alabaster urn.

Below: Palacio Aldama, upper gallery.

Top left: Palacio Aldama, banister and neoclassical doorway.

Above: Palacio Aldama, another view of the grand staircase showing marble inlays on landings.

Top right: Palacio Aldama, elaborate banisters of the grand staircase.

Right: Close-up of the neoclassical swans adorning the base of the banister.

Quinta de los Molinos

This bucolic place was the summer residence of the Capitanes Generales, and also acted as transition quarters when they left the service. It was built under the administration of General Tacón. Located on the former site of the tobacco-processing mills of the Real Fábrica de Tabaco, it was to one side of the Paseo Militar (later Paseo Carlos III) and embedded in lush parkland, among sculptures, fountains, and kiosks.

The house features large bays closed by shuttered French windows and rectangular *mediopuntos* of geometrical stained glass. The upper story, set back a few yards from the lower, has a pitched roof covered with tiles. This level is reached via a handsome wooden staircase. The veranda is fronted by a simple iron railing with pillars topped by glazed ceramic urns.

The original building, lacking the top floor, was designed by engineers Félix Lemaur and Manuel Pastor. The upper story was added when the place was refurbished by a Cuban engineer, Mariano Carrillo de Albornoz, during the 1850s. The spacious gardens were closed off by a gate between entrance pillars recovered from the Campo de Marte in 1887, the prelude to a magnificent drive lined by rows of trees and paved with pebblestones.

After the end of Spanish domination on the island, this was the residence of the Generalísimo Máximo Gómez, and under the Republic, it was annexed by Havana University to house the School of Agronomy. It has now become the Casa Museo de Máximo Gómez.

Above: Quinta de los Molinos, internal arches and rectangular stained-glass panels.

Above right: Quinta de los Molinos, the parapet roof with typical urns.

Right: Quinta de Llos Molinos, the garden.

Left: Quinta de los Molinos, the Dolphin Fountain in the garden.

Below: Quinta de los Molinos, the villa surrounded by its garden.

Quinta de los Condes de Santovenia

This outstanding house is along the Calzada del Cerro, in the middle of vast grounds. Around 1846 it was held to be among the five largest and loveliest *casas-quinta* in existence. Construction began in 1832 and was concluded in 1841 on behalf of the second count of Santovenia, Manuel Eusebio Martínez de Campos. In that year, a chronicler for *El diario de La Habana* rapturously described it as follows:

> Its sumptuousness is dazzling, not only for the tropical nature of its architecture, but also for the treasures within: the extensive iron railing that entirely surrounds it, with the count's crowns in embossed bronze and his golden spears; the interminable series of columns with proud capitals, like a Pompeiian mansion; the pretty play of fountains, the glistening lake sliced by some fragile bark, the lovely garden replete with scents, the great English park, all charming tokens of the comfort enjoyed by its wealthy proprietor.[88]

The portico spreads along the whole facade; it is composed of a long series of lintelled columns, linked by iron railings. On the ground floor, the colonnade is the preamble to the entrance; upstairs, the terrace invites the occupants to revel in the view of the gardens with their pergolas, statues, fountains, and fruit trees. The porch baluster is formed by pillars and railings, and that of the upper floor additionally boasts glazed urns. Ventilation and light are obtained through slatted shutters and bright *mediopuntos*, in line with the conventions of this new approach to building.

Much frequented by the celebrities of the nineteenth century, this property was the scene of fabled receptions and balls. The *habaneros* were unforgettably impressed in 1872 when Grand Duke Alexis, third son of Tsar Alexander II and heir to the imperial throne, came to stay at the Santovenia house. He was conducting a grand tour of the United States and parts of Latin America. At the end of the century the owners of this house donated it to the church as an old people's home, and that is the function it still serves.

Above: Quinta of the Counts of Santovenia, portico and colonnades.

Right: Quinta of the Counts of Santovenia, main facade.

Opposite page: Quinta of the Counts of Santovenia, main entrance and lattice gate.

Above: Quinta of the Counts of Santovenia, gazebo in the garden.

Above right: Quinta of the Counts of Santovenia, reception room.

Right: Quinta of the Counts of Santovenia: one of the drawing rooms.

Opposite page: Quinta of the Counts of Santovenia, drawing room with wicker medallion chairs.

Quinta de Doña Luisa Herrera

Domingo Herrera, fourth count of Jibacoa, acquired the house on Calzada del Cerro, between Buenos Aires and Consejero Arango, in 1846; after he married Luisa Herrera y O'Farrill in 1821, it remained identified with her name. In 1884 it passed to the sixth Count of Jibacoa, Francisco Herrera y Montalvo, when he wed María Arango y Mantilla. During the twentieth century the building was partially altered for the last time, to become the headquarters of the Ironmongers' Club. It reverted once more to the Arango family when the club built its own headquarters on Playa de Marianao.

Above: Quinta of Luisa Herrera, iron gateway with cockfight scene.

Right: Quinta of Luisa Herrera, main staircase.

*Quinta of Luisa Herrera, side view
from the grounds.*

Casa del Marqués de Pinar del Río

Located on Calzada del Cerro between Carvajal and Patria, this house was built in the second half of the nineteenth century by Leopoldo González Carvajal: Marquis of Pinar del Río, leading politician, co-proprietor of the Cabañas and Carvajal tobacco company, and owner of large farms in Pinar del Río. It is representative of the houses that were built as permanent residences, linked to their neighbors by continuous porches.

The main entrance is flanked by pilasters. Large projecting shelves crown the elegant window bars, and the doors are shuttered, with stained-glass rectangular *mediopuntos* in floral patterns. To one side, a beautiful, intricate iron grille gives onto the side entrance, guarded by two marble lions. The top of the grille displays the Marquis's crown.

Opposite this house was the famous quinta belonging to the Count of Fernandina, now derelict. The Pinar del Río house has been a nursing home for years, and is run by nuns.

Above left: House of the Marquis of Pinar del Río, internal bay fitted with room dividers.

Above right: House of the Marquis of Pinar del Río, side entrance, showing the intricate iron grille and a marble lion.

Right: House of the Marquis of Pinar del Río, view of the long lintelled portico.

Opposite page: House of the Marquis of Pinar del Río, the side-entrance grille.

Casa de José Melgares

This *casa quinta*, on the intersection of Calzada del Cerro and Santa Teresa, was built around 1860 by architect Antonio Benítez Othon, a graduate of San Fernando in Madrid, for José Melgares y Fernández de Castro and his wife María Teresa Herrera, daughter of the second marquis of Almendares. The house has a columned portico as we might expect, but in this case the columns are especially monumental. The patio is lined with shuttered galleries embellished with rectangular stained-glass windows displaying geometrical patterns. Behind these arcades are the entrances to halls and chambers.

A party was held here in 1872 for the wedding of the Melgares's daughter Teresa, attended by Grand Duke Alexis of Russia. When the Melgares-Herrera family lost the property, they moved to the house of the Marquis of Aguas Claras in the cathedral square. The quinta remained empty until 1890, when it was taken over by the Count of Fernandina, who had deserted his palace on Calzada del Cerro and Carvajal. In 1893 the house burst into life once more on the occasion of a grand reception in honor of Princess Eulalia de Borbón and her husband Antoine d'Orléans, who had arrived in Havana in May of that year. Eulalia recalled the event in her memoirs:

> The party held in my honor by the Counts of Fernandina impressed me vividly by its elegance and lordly distinction, all considerably more refined than the Madrid society of the period. . . . Their house was the center of aristocratic life in Havana, and their balls were the most luxurious of all that society cast in the Parisian mold. . . . I had always heard praise for the beauty, pride, elegance and above all sweetness of Cuban womanhood, but the reality surpassed my expectations by far. I left friends behind me in the capital of Cuba whose memory has been with me all my life, especially the Marquises of Duquesne, Villalta, Casa Montalvo, and Almendares, and the Countesses of Fernandina and Peñalver. . . .[89]

In 1924 this house became a clinic, founded by the Association of Catholic Cuban Women. Today it is a pediatric hospital.

House of José Melgares, patio and its galleries.

Above left: House of José Melgares, mediopunto *fanlight with radiating panes.*

Left: House of José Melgares, window with colored panel.

Above: House of José Melgares.

The City of Columns

One house has light green walls, with pink cornices and moldings; its neighbor is of eggshell blue, picked out in salmon; the next is gray and orange, with touches of white—or lilac and yellow, or pink and blue—all this gleaming and shimmering in the hot, scorching air, until it seems like a vast, radiant, dissolving vision.

—W. M. L. Jay (J. L. M. Woodruff), My Winter in Cuba, *1871*

Toward 1850, engineer Mariano Carrillo de Albornoz produced an urban development plan that laid out the thoroughfares of Belascoaín and La Infanta. The city had spread as far as the edge of these roads, in a continuous flow that was only interrupted by the open land on which the old walls still stood—land that now lay at the heart of a city in expansion. The walls had lost all military raison d'être, and in 1863 their demolition was authorized, paving the way for the definitive profile of nineteenth-century Havana.

The urban and architectural renewal of Havana during the second half of the century posed its own problems. From a formal point of view, the city and its buildings found themselves strictly regulated by means of the most thorough and exhaustive set of statutes yet promulgated: the building ordinances of 1861. It took 476 articles to enshrine the hierarchy and function of roads, the types of buildings, the shape of blocks, the characteristics of lay-out, and the requisites for new suburbs, as well as to list the innumerable dispositions for "urban policing."

The ordinances dictated that arcades should be built in all the main plazas and streets, giving rise to what Alejo Carpentier has called "one of the most singular constants of the *habanero* style: the incredible profusion of columns, in a city that is an emporium of columns, a jungle of columns, an infinite colonnade, the last of the cities with so overwhelming a surplus of columns."[90]

The new distributions of land represented an appreciable source of income. In the case of one district—the area circumscribed to the east by Paseo del Prado, and to the west by Calzada de la Infanta—new buildings were coming up not on land ceded by the municipality, but on lots created by the fragmentation of the privately owned country properties that formerly sprawled around the outside of the walled town. At the same time, the budding urbanizations were increasingly dominated by a social type who seemed to lay his hands on everything: the Spanish businessman. At street level every building added to the endless parade of commercial establishments, which themselves bore witness to the swing of economic power from criollos to Spaniards. If Havana was, up to midcentury, the fief of Cuban patricians, it seemed condemned to spend the second half as the domain of Spanish traders.

The process whereby one group eclipsed the other is too important to be passed over. The Cubans had come up against serious economic problems that they were powerless to overcome. By perpetuating slavery the landowners backed themselves into a corner. The financial burden of huge slave crews, the increase of which was the only way to keep up with the competition in the sugar market, delivered the producers into the hands of the traders. The Countess of Merlín summed up the predicament of Cuban planters with lucid concision:

> However extensive the properties may be, the immense overheads occasioned by the elaboration of the sugar imply costs which rise, for a plantation of three hundred Negroes, to six or seven hundred thousand reals per year and require an early outlay of funds, which obliges the proprietor to borrow against the yield of each harvest. The trader, alone in being able to capitalize his profits, makes sizeable loans at an arbitrary interest, which frequently ascends to two and a half percent monthly. His income in such conditions is more secure than the borrower's, whose harvests are moreover exposed to fluctuations in price and dependent upon the inconstancies of temperature and a thousand

Columns lining a street in Havana.

Top left: The soft light of a Havana evening.

Top right: Chamfered corner, on Prado and Neptuno Streets.

Middle left, and above: Continuous arcades of pillars and columns.

Right: The Balaguer building.

other accidents, and it may occur that the latter finds himself in the impossibility of making due payment when the time for reimbursement arrives. The exorbitant interest doubles the debt, payment becomes difficult and then impossible, and the trader soon finds himself the possessor of a sum equal to the value of the entire property.[91]

This systematic extortion on the part of Spanish merchants deepened the existing fractures between them and the criollo landowners, and on the political plane provoked an armed retort from Cubans who stood up for the right to decide their own destiny. During the second half of the nineteenth century, Cuba was racked by a protracted struggle for independence (1868–1878), which, though it was the catalyst for consolidating national consciousness, and forced or stimulated a certain racial integration, also ruined and in some sense disintegrated the very class that had spearheaded it.[92]

Soon before the war, the new sector in power—the Spanish oligarchy—appropriated the land plots beyond the walls. Displaced criollo patricians surveyed with a jaundiced eye the development of this new district of Las Murallas, whose final plans were approved in 1865.

The urbanization of the land was based around the route of two long avenues running parallel to El Prado Street[93] crossing the zone from north

Top: Cigar-box label, from the La Carolina tobacco factory.

Above: Pilaster reflecting the classical orders.

to south and intersected by streets that were the prolongation of those already existing beyond the old city walls. The constructions presented an impressive formal coherence, derived from the consistent use of a handful of architectural options: the omnipresence of the portico, its notable height, and the decoration of the facades, which provided the classical model with an international veneer as a statement of modernity.

The building ordinances issued in 1861 determined that ground floors should be five and a half meters high, and set a limit on the total elevation; nevertheless, City Hall reserved the right to authorize higher buildings in exceptional cases. The Las Murallas development availed itself of this exception, with the result that its lower floors were assigned a minimum of six meters. The buildings raised to these specifications were referred to as being "on stilts" due to the disproportionate height of the porticos, whose pillars are taller than the lights of the arches will allow, in reckless pursuit of ever greater monumentality.

The same document regulated degrees for balconies, pilasters, and columns, as well as the dimensions of cornices and balusters; they banned the use of eaves and resolved that corners must no longer be sharp, but rounded or chamfered. Whitewash was out: buildings had to be painted in colors. Finally, the ordinances pronounced in favor of respecting "the rules of art, the demands of symmetry, and the conditions for public comfort and ornamentality."[94]

The architectural renewal amounted, then, to modifying the overall scale and the treatment of the facades, which unanimously followed the academic canon of ascending orders: Doric-Tuscan, Ionic, and Corinthian. The pilasters framing the bays served to accentuate the symmetry of the front; as a rule, constructions became sparser insofar as they adhered to international codes that heralded, to some extent, the eclecticism that was to take over during the first decades of the twentieth century. It is fair to say that the edifices of the period that concerns us constitute a bridge between the colonial building tradition and the architectural taste that would develop in the twentieth century.

With respect to the distribution of space, the traditionally flexible organization of the stately mansion was preserved. Its scope for different functions made it adaptable to all kinds of social uses: hotels, recreational associations, factories, coffeehouses, and of course homes. Inside the building a number of options became standard, such as laying tiles on sections of the walls—a practice that was by no means new, but came to be de rigueur during the second half of the nineteenth century, stretching into the first decades of the twentieth. Other features were consequences of the magnification of scale, such as the flat ceilings that replaced pitched structures, or the rectangular window over the door, which helped to fill the greatly elongated bays while contributing to cross-ventilation. Internal bays tended to become garnished by elaborate surrounds of wood, and fitted with room dividers incorporating clear or tinted glass panes that might in turn be adorned with transfers of landscapes, European *scènes galantes,* or the monogram of the owner of the house. Such dividers were indispensable given the size of the bays, while the limited barrier they formed contributed to the ventilation of the rooms. In the estimation of Ramón Meza, the houses were

> . . . bright and sunlit in the rooms of choice. The flat, plaster ceilings are fretted around the edges, and full of reliefs and moldings in the center; the floors are of white marble or intricate mosaics, the walls stuccoed or painted in soft half-tints; the dividers are edged with gilt incisions and covered in gleaming landscapes; the stained glass that completely surrounds the slight frame of shutters lets in the light through its blue or irridescent panels.[95]

Top left: Mosaic with geometric pattern.

Top right: Mosaic with floral pattern.

Bottom left: Decorative mosaic.

Bottom right: The decorative variety of nineteenth-century mosaics.

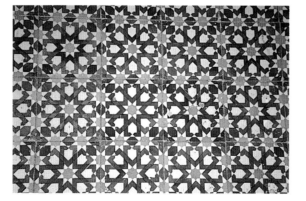

Along the great avenues of downtown Havana—Galiano, Reina, Belascoaín, and Infanta—a new breed of domestic construction appeared: the *casa comunera*, as it was christened in the ordinances of 1861. In terms of the exterior appearance of the facades and the enduring presence of porticos, it resembled the mansions that preceded it; however, the *comunera* house overturned the internal spatial distribution inherited from the stately or storehouse-home. In the first place, the mezzanine disappeared, banned by the regulations. The ground floor ceased to function as a storeroom for the inhabitants, and became occupied by separately run shops, bars, or cafés. Each upper floor normally contained two independent living spaces, rented out to separate households. The staircase was shared by the whole building, and the patio shed its galleries, shrinking into a narrow rectangular yard that extended toward the back. This kind of housing, a precursor of the apartment building, became widespread during the first decades of the twentieth century.

During the second part of the nineteenth century, rocketing sugar production played havoc with the storehouse-home, which explains the gradual obsolescence of the mezzanine and the changes to interior living arrangements. The multiplicity of storerooms were being replaced by gigantic warehouses sited next to the port and the train stations: one such was the Santa Catalina warehouse, built by the North American architect James Bogardus on the bay of Havana, and inaugurated in 1862. The cast-iron structure experimented with by Bogardus on this occasion was among the first in the world.

It is precisely the use of iron, not merely as decoration but also as the structural backbone of walls and roofs, that made the most significant impact upon the architecture of the period. Examples are plentiful among the monumental buildings of the new allotment of Las Murallas. The iron and glass covering of the inner gallery of the Pasaje Hotel caused a veritable sensation: it spanned the building from street to street, with monumental porticos at either entrance. A year later, in 1877, the Payret Theater opened its doors. This was the creation of Fidel Luna, a Catalan builder hired by his compatriot, entrepreneur Joaquín Payret: it sported an extraordinary iron armature cast by a Belgian foundry, Valentin Bataille et Cie. That same year, the three small squares outside the Puerta de Monserrate were flattened to make way for today's Parque Central, equipped with fine cast-iron railings and lamp-posts from New York City. Shortly afterward, around 1881, Miguel Jané contracted builder Juan Pagé to build the Jané Circus-Theater on Zulueta Street, between Dragones and Monte. Inside the circular arena, spectators could gaze entranced at the formidable iron girders of the roof, which tapered to a cone in the middle.

A few yards from the Jané Circus-Theater, down Dragones Street, the Basque entrepreneur Ricardo Irioja had a theater built and named after himself in 1884; it was later rechristened Teatro Martí. The Irioja theater was the work of a Cuban engineer, Alberto de Castro Bermúdez, a graduate of the Professional School of Havana and of Rensselaer Polytechnic in the United States. The building was raised upon iron columns in linteled fashion. During the same period, a similar solution was chosen for the Colón market courtyard and for the interior halls of the great tobacco factories located at the heart of the new urban extensions.

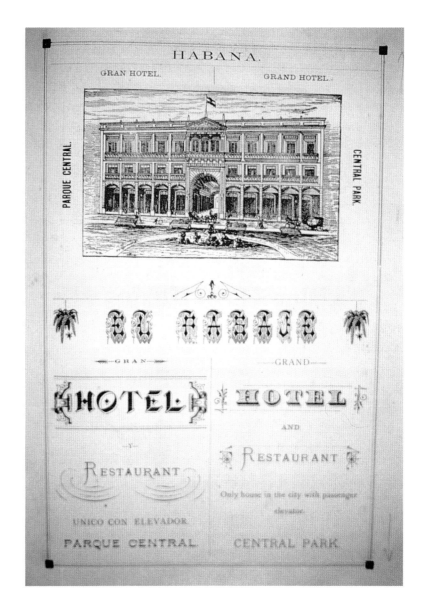

Advertisement for the Hotel Pasaje in Prado Street, published in a Havana catalogue in 1884.

The Hotel Pasaje today.

These and other pioneering buildings presented novelties galore. The Pasaje Hotel imported the first hydraulic elevator in Cuba. On Dragones and Prado, the Aragonese Gregorio Palacios built a complex in 1879 that had storerooms and shops on the ground floor, apartments on the first, and a hotel at the top; the imposing facade was clad in Portland cement. And in the Roma Hotel (1881), bathrooms with built-in showers were installed.

As far as interior decoration was concerned, this period was one of mismatched furniture and the confluence of several styles at once. Very popular were the "medallion" chairs, so-called because of the oval shape of their backs. The light, fine wickerwork of back and seat was ideal in the tropical heat. Such chairs offered a Cuban interpretation of the style labelled as "Second Empire" in France, as "Victorian" in England, and in Spain as *isabelino*. All the variants might be qualified as a sort of rococo, marrying the supple curves of the latter with the severity of neoclassicism. Other items of furniture, with a specific local form and function, became common in Havana homes at around this time: *canastilleros*, *jugueteros*, *coperos*, and so on. The simplest, most popular versions of the lathed wicker seat (known in Cuba as *muebles de perilla*) were in use throughout the nineteenth century and up to the First World War. Neo-Gothic and Neo-Romantic furniture also charmed the Havana of those days, along with that Spanish combination of Renaissance and baroque that would prove such a favorite in Cuban homes during the first half of the twentieth century.

Causing no violent break with preceding architectural traditions, modernity made its niche in Havana in academic guise, implanted by trained professionals. This was one of the principal factors of change. The Escuela General Preparatoria was founded in 1855 to provide formal training in the building arts, as a first effort to move beyond the random transmission of knowledge through workshops and the traditional master-apprentice relationship; its graduates were able to complete their studies in Spain. In 1861, the square called Alarife Municipal was rebaptized as Arquitecto Municipal, in honor of the alumni "of the School of Architecture, whose studies in Madrid are funded by the Island's Municipalities . . ."[96]

During the second half of the nineteenth century, the capital acquired the unified, compact, and monumental appearance that characterizes it today, a function of the dense succession of buildings and the dearth of open or green spaces: these are reduced, properly speaking, to the Paseo del Prado, the Parque Central, the Plazoleta de Albear, the Campo Militar, and the Paseo de Carlos III. The urban scheme does, however, vary from district to district, thanks to the private initiatives encouraged throughout the period. A clear instance of this is the area known as Vedado, in which the concentrated Hispanic model was rejected in favor of the Anglo-Saxon suburb, or garden city.

In contrast to El Cerro, which became haphazardly built up along the meanderings of its famous Calzada, Vedado was the creation of a preconceived urban plan. In 1859, José Domingo Trigo and Juan Espino

House of Juan Bautista Docio in Línea Street.

approached City Hall for permission to begin developing the district of La Chorrera. The following year, José Jacinto Frías applied in his own name and that of his brothers[97] to parcel out their property of Vedado. When sales turned out to be sluggish, the Frías brothers launched a general-interest magazine entitled *El porvenir del Carmelo*, which they used to advertise the new development of 105 blocks and 1,186 plots. Land was also set aside for churches and markets, a park, a school, a hospital, and a barracks.

In 1877 another petition relating to Prolongación del Vedado was approved, with its properties extending as far as Calle 19 and the beach district. This time it was submitted with the relevant plans and calculations; those relating to Vedado and Carmelo were drawn up by Luis Yboleón Bosque, and those for the Balzaín hacienda, by José de Ocampo. Both these engineers were relatives of the Frías brothers. The grid of Vedado was thereby oriented northeast/southwest and composed of streets intersecting at right angles. Those destined for tramway routes were to be twenty-five meters wide, and the rest were to measure sixteen. Each block equalled one hectare, with sides one hundred meters long; the blocks would be divided into twelve plots, four of them corner properties. These plots would have five meters for a garden at the front, and four for the portico. The corner lots would benefit from the same conditions twice, in the direction of both streets. The Vedado houses were created on a roughly uniform basis: they tend to be porticoed villas surrounded by green spaces.

By the end of the Ten Years' War, the Vedado had attracted some twenty summer houses and the Havana Baseball Club. As of the 1880s, however, its prestige mounted despite the many disputes over property. Young people were drawn to it because of the fresh air and the glittering shoreline; here they could bathe, play society games, and dance,[98] as well as attend concerts and plays at the elegant Salón Trotcha on Calzada 4, a venue opened by Buenaventura Trotcha in 1883.[99]

The new suburb possessed its own collective transport system, in the form of horsedrawn *guaguas* that linked it to the city. Eventually Calle 9 started to be called Línea in honor of the tramline that followed it, stopping every hour on the way between Havana and Carmelo. During the bathing season it passed more frequently, and ran as far as San Lázaro and Prado. By the end of the century Vedado enjoyed fresh water, piped in from the Albear canal, and electric lighting. It was to be the last of Havana's territorial expansions under the colony; the Republic would use this already considerable infrastructure as a starting point for the development of the great Havana of the twentieth century.

At the close of the nineteenth century, the Cuban people waged their war of independence (1895–1898) under the leadership of José Martí. In 1898 the United States declared war on Spain, whose humiliating defeat forced it to hand over its remaining colonial outposts to the victors. On January 1, 1899, at twelve noon, Spanish sovereignty came to an end in Cuba and the first American intervention began. On May 20, 1902, the Republic of Cuba was born.

Allegory of the Cuban Republic on a late-nineteenth-century cigar-box label.

Casa Conill

The house of Catalan businessman Juan Conill is located on Teniente street, between Cristo and Villegas, opposite the Cristo plaza and church. It exemplifies the persistence of the stately home model, as well as the changes to which this model was subjected. It was probably built around 1869, the date inscribed on the iron gate; however, Guido Conill, a descendant of the first owner, claims that it was built much earlier, on the grounds that he remembers a print of it in the house, marked with the date 1852.

The design preserves the time-honored disposition of lower floor, mezzanine, and upper floor. But there is a patent impulse to play down the importance of the middle level, expressed in the row of gigantic pilasters on the facade to unify lower and mezzanine sections. The continuous balcony supplies the line of connection between the two floors. The house lacks a portico, but is aggrandized by exterior classical motifs. A satisfying relationship is achieved between the stilted arches of the bays and the rectangular lines of the pilasters, surmounted by Corinthian capitals.

Above: Conill house, part of the front balcony, with iron divider at the end.

Right: Conill house, view from Cristo plaza.

Top left: Conill house, detail of an internal arch.

Top middle: Conill house, wrought-iron gate.

Above: Conill house, patio and galleries.

Left: Conill house, first-floor hall.

Palacio de Balboa

The Palacio de Balboa cuts an exceptional and isolated figure in the development of Las Murallas. Built by the Madrid architect Pedro Tomé under the direction of his Catalan colleague, Jaime Sabadell, it was the first mansion to appear on Egido Street; the owner was a Spanish functionary named Pedro Balboa. The palace is decades ahead of its time in prefiguring the kind of suburban dwelling that would typify Vedado. Tomé brought to Havana the Anglo-Saxon model of villa and garden that was already popular in Isabelline Madrid. Breaking with the habit of cluttered spacing, he also introduced a novel plan of internal distribution: downstairs were the reception rooms, the dining room, the kitchen and annexes; upstairs, the bedrooms. The external decoration of sober neo-baroque moldings clearly situates the mansion within the revivalist tendency.

Two gala balls were held here in honor of Grand Duke Alexis of Russia when he was on his Latin American tour. The ball was a wild success and had to be repeated, since the Grand Duke, who was also an active officer with the naval squadron that was escorting him, happened to be on guard duty for the first occasion.

The building was later converted into offices to administrate Havana Province.

Above: Balboa Palace, the sculpted top of the facade.

Right: Balboa Palace, the arms of Cuba, added when the building became the seat of the provincial government.

Opposite page: Balboa Palace, interior courtyard galleries.

Above: Balboa Palace, facade detail.

Opposite page: Balboa Palace, interior courtyard.

Palacio de la Marquesa de Villalba (Casa Moré)

In 1831 Cecilio Ayllón, of Salamanca, then governor of Matanzas, became the VII Marquis of Villalba after the previous holder of the title, Francisco de Paula de Villanueva, died, leaving no heir. Ayllón was also the owner of two plantations in the vicinity of Matanzas, the most productive sugar-producing zone in the country. Between 1874 and 1878, his widow used her centrally placed plots in the Las Murallas area—on Egido, between Monte and Dragones—to build one of the largest palaces of the colonial era.

It was designed by a Cuban architect graduated in Madrid, Eugenio Rayneri Sorrentino, and like the Palacio de Aldama, consists of two great houses unified by a single, consistent facade. The building remained faithful to the ground plan of criollo mansions, but on an ostentatiously enlarged scale. At ground level a towering portico on "stilt" pillars fronts the building on three sides; the corner arches are pointed, while the remainder are round. The main staircase is grandiose, and the neo-baroque curlicues on ceilings, doorframes, and railings make this an eclectic building before its time, an impression endorsed by the Second Empire look of the principal door, which is made of cast iron.

This house was inhabited by José Eugenio Moré, Count of Casa Moré (a title he received in 1879) until his death. Moré was a leading Spanish planter and politician who settled in Cuba, marrying María Mercedes Ajuria in 1842.

Villalba Palace, heavy, ornate bronze door.

Top left: Villalba Palace, second-floor gallery.

Middle left: Villalba Palace, another view of the second-floor gallery.

Left: Villalba Palace, detail of ceiling and arches.

Above: Villalba Palace, close-up of a door protected by a finely worked grille.

Hotel Inglaterra

The Inglaterra was founded in the second half of the nineteenth century, in an existing building on Prado and San Rafael—the site of the famous coffeehouse belonging to the Spaniard Juan Escauriza, who had been trading since 1843. Around 1891 the building was altered by architect Francisco Fernández Villalmil, who gave it three floors and a portico. Another floor was added during the twentieth century, and the interiors were modernized.

This hotel, very well placed at the center of the Las Murallas quarter, was reputed to be the best in town. A new café called El Louvre was opened downstairs, which gave its name to what became a favorite meeting-place for criollo youth—"La Acera del Louvre" (the sidewalk of the Louvre). The "sidewalk boys" were targets for the violent excesses committed by Spanish volunteers in 1869, such as the riots at the Villanueva Theater and the sacking of the Aldama house; many of these young men went on to enlist with the insurgent Cuban troops.

The hotel was equipped with all the facilities that North American investors were prone to install in this kind of venture. Especially, as Cuban writer Raimundo Cabrera observed,

> . . . since the ease and low cost of communications with the United States has encouraged so many Yankees to winter over here and teach us how to set up and manage such establishments. There are already some hotels that occupy splendid premises, and where the electric wiring, the reading room, the writing room, the elevator and other amenities have been imported from America . . .[100]

Right: Advertisement for the Hotel Inglaterra, from a Havana directory printed in 1884.

Far right: Hotel Inglaterra, the facade seen from Central Park.

Above: Hotel Inglaterra, Sevillean Dancer, *bronze figure by the prolific Catalan sculptor Mariano Benlliure.*

Above right: Hotel Inglaterra, lobby.

Right: Hotel Inglaterra, lobby and restaurant are decorated with a Mauresque touch.

Hotel Inglaterra: the overlap of styles in a period of transition.

The Cigar Factories of Pedro Murías and Calixto López

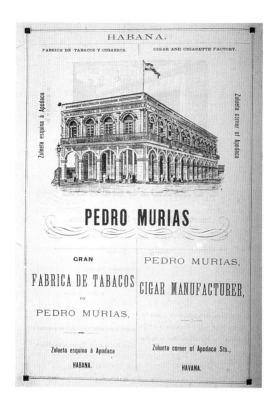

The tobacco factory belonging to the Spaniard Pedro Murías was built around 1880. It occupies roughly half a block, similar in size to the neighboring residences, which it also emulates in terms of general structure and the decoration of outer and inner walls. Calixto López's factory, one of the most important producers of Havana cigars, was built some six years later; in this instance the owner's home was built into the plant on a mezzanine. Inside, narrow cast-iron columns were deployed for a more advantageous use of space.

The factories of cigars, cigarettes, and loose tobacco were owned by both Spanish and Cuban entrepreneurs, and provide good examples of the functional versatility of the new breed of buildings, as well as of the economic supremacy of the new oligarchy.

Spanish journalist Tesifonte Gallego expressed his admiration for the mighty industrial monuments along Zulueta Street in these words: "Near the Arsenal . . . two proud palaces rise up. Both of them are tobacco factories. One, amidst galleries of monumental arches, belongs to Pedro Murías; the other, property of Bances y López, is lone, colossal, such as a prince might envy."[101]

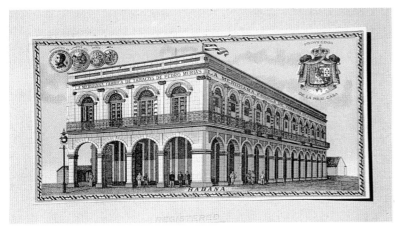

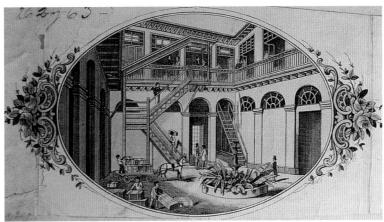

Opposite page, top: Advertisement for the Pedro Murías tobacco factory, from the 1884 directory of Havana.

Opposite page, bottom: The Pedro Murías factory looks no less imposing today.

Top: The Calixto López factory, on a cigar-box label.

Above left: The Pedro Murías factory represented on a nineteenth-century cigar-box label, with the Spanish coat of arms denoting its appointment to the royal household.

Above right: Label showing the inside of a tobacco factory, where several innovative architectural solutions can be appreciated.

Church of Santo Ángel Custodio (Iglesia del Ángel)

The Church of Santo Ángel was renovated in the Neo-Gothic style in 1866. It had been founded during the seventeenth century on a small rise formerly known as Peña Pobre, then as Loma del Ángel, on Compostela street between Cuarteles and Chacón. The renovation was concluded in 1871, and the Ángel promptly became fashionable in high society, so much so that it was upheld as the "blue-blooded" church. The facade, dominating the little square of the same name, bristles with lancet arches, pinnacles, and spires in the Gothic manner. Within, the three vessels were supplemented by an ambulatory, a hitherto unknown space in the building traditions of Cuba. All the same, its best perspective is from the rear, toward the recent development of the Murallas district.

José Martí was baptized here in 1853, and several other historical figures lived in the vicinity, including Bishop Juan José Díaz de Espada, head of the diocese of Havana for thirty years (1802–1832), and the memorable writer Vidal Morales. The temple and its environment were brought to life by Cirilo Villaverde in his regionalist novel *Cecilia Valdés o la loma del ángel*, and this is why there is a bronze bust of the author in the square. Víctor Patricio de Landaluze included the church in a painting with an irresistibly *habanero* feel, titled *El místico del ángel*.

Above: Santo Ángel Custodio, general view of the spires.

Top: The neo-Gothic pinnacles of Santo Ángel Custodio. In the foreground, a salient surviving from the old city wall.

Irioja Theater (Teatro Martí)

This theater was originally named after its Basque builder and proprietor, Ricardo Irioja. It epitomized the diversity of functions proper to the new construction wave. Located on Dragones Street, between Prado and Zulueta, it was inaugurated on June 8, 1884, with one of the public dances to which Havana folk have been addicted for centuries. The Irioja was considered the most "criollo" of all the new playhouses and the best for staging homegrown *teatro bufo*, or slapstick farce. Many comedies by journalist and playwright Ignacio Sarachaga made their debuts here, and poet José Fornaris labelled it "the coliseum of a hundred doors."

The building was made in accordance with a project by Alberto de Castro, and proved remarkably innovative in its internal structure. It was surrounded by a pleasant garden full of waterfalls, sprinklers, ponds, and little tables, where the audience repaired during the interval and after the show. In 1893 the traveler J. C. Prince noted in his book *Cuba Illustrated* that these gardens reminded him of "the Champs Élysées, or the concert-cafés of Paris." Internal unity is ensured by a score of slim iron columns, repeated to support the tiers.

Irioja went bankrupt in 1899 and the building was bought by Rafael Pastoriza, who renamed it Eden Concert. Before long it changed hands again, and the new owner, Generoso González, gave it the name of Teatro Martí in memory of Cuba's national hero. From 1900 to 1901 it seated the convention that drew up the first constitution of independent Cuba, a document that remained in force until 1940 (except for the appendix known as the Platt Amendment, giving the United States license to intervene on the island as guarantors of peace and public order. This unacceptable curtailment of Cuba's sovereignty was repealed by bilateral agreement in 1934).

The Teatro Martí was bought by José Cano in 1905, and managed later on by his daughter Juanita. It was a center for zarzuelas, both Spanish and Cuban (among those who sang there were Plácido Domingo's parents) and the popular Spanish revue *Cabalgata*, as well as the Pubillones circus. Most famous of all was the vernacular theater company run by the well-loved Cuban actors Garrido and Piñero, who epitomized the comic types of the Negro and the *gallego*, or Spaniard.

Left: The Irijoa Theater, or "Coliseum of the Hundred Doors." Turn-of-the-century photograph from the time it was relaunched as the Teatro Martí.

Above: Teatro Martí, detail of facade.

358 Reina Street

The Calzada de la Reina, connecting the Paseo del Prado and the Paseo Militar, was one of the great thoroughfares of the period. It is also the address of one of the most outstanding architectural structures of the turn of the century. Number 358, between Lealtad and Escobar Streets, was built at the end of the nineteenth century with two stories and no mezzanine. Inside we still find the classic patio surrounded by colonnaded galleries, but the columns are of iron, and the arches blocked by stained-glass windows. The decoration of the facade testifies to the shift toward eclecticism. On the upper floor, a terrace fronted by three arches juts out over the street, a feature that was to become commonplace during the following decades. The balcony retains its iron baluster, and the house is topped with an elaborate stone parapet rail, of modern aspect.

358 Reina: the balcony.

Casa de la Familia González Curquejo

Between 1880 and 1885, building commenced in the new plots of the Vedado area. On the corner of Línea Street and Avenue B, Dr. Antonio González Curquejo built one of the first residences in the district, and one of the few that have survived from this period. The house emulates, on a smaller scale, the pattern that dominated the El Cerro development: two stories, surrounded by porticos. It is set back from the road, and the gardens are defined by railings, which are separated by posts topped with urns. Yet this barrier is low enough to allow the house to be seen, and thus a direct relationship emerges between the building and its environment. This pattern proved highly influential during the early part of the twentieth century, the period when most of the Vedado zone was constructed.

The González Curquejo house in El Vedado, view of the facade.

Casa de Francisco López García

This house was completed around 1888 on Línea Street, between D and E. It took the form of a porticoed bungalow in the midst of a garden. The entrance is reached through a tall iron grille as fanciful as lacework, framed by pillars, each of which is crowned by an urn. The house became the property of the Alfonso family, whose alterations left it as it is today. Unusually for its time, the building lacks an inside court (still present in the Palacio de Balboa), and this absence came to constitute the major difference between colonial and Republican houses. Here, the interior arrangement of drawing room, dining room, bedrooms, kitchen, pantry, and so on is radically different from that of colonial homes: the twentieth-century house is here presaged.

Above right: López García house, stone ornament on a wall post in the shape of an acorn.

Above: López García house, a glimpse of the porch.

Right: López García house, exterior view of entrance and garden.

Casa de Cosme Blanco Herrera

Virtually opposite the previous example, at Línea 505 between D and E, industrialist Cosme Blanco Herrera built another nineteenth-century house that contained prescient innovations. As was standard for Vedado, it consists of a villa in a garden—yet it almost completely turns its back on the criollo tradition, looking instead to the southern cities of the United States, particularly New Orleans, with its flowery, Frenchified grilles. The house has a portico supporting a terrace that is strictly tailored to the dimensions of the lower structure, so that the glassed-in spaces on either side of the central, open terrace are set back, following the design of the lower level. The composition and decoration of this building follow an eclectic sort of classicism. Like the López García residence, it outlines new approaches that prefigure the century about to begin.

Cosme Blanco Herrera house, view of the facade.

Colón Cemetery

A competition to design a new cemetery in the Vedado area was won by the Spanish architect Calixto de Loira, with his concept of the graveyard as a Roman city. Work was begun in 1871. The plan of the cemetery is based on five crosses, with Francisco S. Marcotegui's octagonal chapel at the center of the composition. The chapel was hung with paintings by Miguel Melero. The main door is by architect Eugenio Rayneri Sorrentino, in a Romanesque-Byzantine idiom. Over it stands a sculpture of "Faith, Hope, and Charity" carved by José Villalta Saavedra.

The Colón cemetery is the resting place of prominent historical figures. It is notable for its monuments of funerary art in more than one style and its many sculptural ensembles; for the confection of these works from the most expensive materials, and for their consummate execution.

Among its most striking sights are the pantheon of the eight students of medicine who were shot in 1871; that of the firemen who succumbed fighting the blaze at the Isasi Ironworks, a collaboration between architect Julio M. Zapata and sculptor Agustín Querol; the mausoleum of Antonio Guiteras and that reserved for the National Police, both with sculptures by Teodoro Ramos Blanco; the tomb of Nicolás Rivero, crafted by Moisés de Huerta; the pantheon of the Falla Bonet family, with a sculpture by the Catalan Mariano Benlliure Gil; and the tomb of Oscar B. Cintas, which has a beautiful relief of a Madonna and child.

The chapel of Catalina de Lasa has a magnificent Lalique glass dome and doors of black and gray marble, incised with angels and roses. Her disconsolate husband, Juan Pedro y Baró, planted two royal palms in front to commemorate the phrase with which Catalina was wont to express her homesickness, like Heredia, La Avellaneda, and Merlín before her: "Ah, how I miss the palm trees of my homeland!"

Certain more humble markers have also become famous, less for the public worth of the individual buried there than for the originality of his or her epitaph. One marks the grave of an inveterate gambler. It takes the form of a game of dominos, hewn in marble, and reproducing the last game played by the deceased—the one that caused her fatal heart attack.

The Colón Cemetery is one of the most engrossing in the world, on a par with Père Lachaise in Paris, the cemetery of Geneva, or La Recoleta in Buenos Aires.

Above: View of the Colón Cemetery through an arch.

Right: The central chapel of the Colón Cemetery.

Right: Detail of the Firemen's Monument, dedicated to those who succumbed in the course of duty in 1890. The Sister of Charity is accompanied by a goose, associated with the perils of human existence.

Far right: Firemen's Monument, the bat as a symbol of destruction.

Right: The tomb of a keen domino player, reproducing the move that killed her.

Far right: Tomb of Cuban world chess champion José Raúl Capablanca, adorned with a gigantic king.

Tomb of Cuban musician Eduardo Sánchez de Fuentes, who composed the famous habanera *number "Tú."*

Far left: The spirit of the Architects' Mausoleum is expressed by an Egyptian pyramid.

Left: Statuary on the tomb of Mercedes Alentado de Beato.

Far left: The door to the Catalina Lasa chapel, made of marble and Lalique glass etched with roses and angels.

Left: Ex-votos dedicated to La Milagrosa, in the mausoleum of doña Amelia de Adot.

Pavilion of the Albear Aqueduct

The pavilion or station by the water reservoirs of the great aqueduct stands on Fomento Street between Chaple and Recreo, in the El Cerro district. It is a sober and gracious building in neo-classical style, composed of nine stilted arches over tall pillars and Tuscan pilasters. The flat roof is bordered by a parapet of pillars and simple cast-iron railings.

The building was designed by Francisco José de Albear y Lara, director of Cuba's Office of Public Works, and his chief assistant, Joaquín Ruiz, and constructed from 1890 to 1893. This was the occasion for Albear and his team to conduct the first topographical survey using contour lines that had ever been undertaken in Havana. The aqueduct itself was started in 1891, under the name Isabel II, but by the time it was opened in 1893 it had been renamed for its late creator. It is also known as Acueducto de Vento, after the place where the springs that fed it were located. The works were contracted out to the firm of Runkle Smith and Co., from New York, which had collaborated since 1889 on the Palatino reservoirs and their network of pipes. Gardens were planted around the pavilion in 1927.

Above left: Covering of the pipe of the famous Albear Canal, in El Cerro.

Above: A turbine, part of the pumping system of the acqueduct in Vento.

Right: The water reservoir pavilion at the terminus of the acqueduct.

The Garden City

El Vedado, a quarter worthy of great Buenos Aires . . . was a promise haloed in dreams during my day; now it is a reality, faithful to the dream if not more so . . . it has all the bearing of a great capital, and its climate is a cut above that of any suburban district in the world.

—*Eva Canel*, Lo que vi en Cuba (a través de la isla), *1916*

The advent of the twentieth century did not bring with it any substantial changes to Havana's urban profile; it would be truer to say that the first years of the Republic amounted to a continuation of the nineteenth century. The capital now enjoyed electric lighting and the telephone, making it one of the most progressive cities in America, yet on the other hand it lacked paving on all but the most important streets of the old center. Early photographs and postcards show cows and goats wandering along such major roads as O'Reilly and Obispo. The clanging bells of draft animals, the rumble of pushcart wheels, and the cries of the drivers as they hawked their wares and shouted pedestrians out of the way created a noisy tumult, punctuated by the calls of street vendors.

The old Teatro Tacón threw doors and windows open to relieve the heat, so that the strains of musical performances drifted out to mingle with the din of the streets. After the show, families would congregate at the nearby Louvre coffeehouse in the Hotel Inglaterra. Next to the theater was a shop that sold gramophone records of operas, American one- and two-steps, monologues and dialogues by well-known actors, boleros, and *danzónes* played by Cuban brass and *pailitas* (kettledrum) bands. The youthful Republic lived at the pace of a provincial Spanish town, with little female participation on a public level and many picturesque characters. Its men still jealously observed the codes of honor of Count Athos of San Malato or the marquis of Cabriñana, and engaged in sensational duels that were the stuff of Havana gossip.

After 1902, the American political and economic influence that had been steadily mounting through the last decades of the nineteenth century asserted itself more powerfully. Cuba had entered the twentieth century still bleeding from the lacerations of war. The country was literally devastated,

and most criollos, whether exiled or insurgent, found themselves ruined; the economy remained in Spanish hands and North America exerted a decisive pull in terms of commerce. Cuba was fast turning into a country that depended on imports and substantial foreign investment in key sectors of the economy, and this situation would become lamentably entrenched.

However, the huge sums invested by North Americans contributed to the recuperation of domestic capital during the first decades of the century, and World War I enabled Cuba to become the dominant sugar producer of the globe. This generous fount of capital, popularly celebrated as the "*danza de los millones,*" underpinned the construction boom that flourished between 1910 and 1929, leading to the reorganization of the district of Las Murallas and the creation of new suburbs.

Up until the 1920s Havana's population grew at a rapid rate, as did that of the rest of the country, fuelled by the influx of legal or clandestine immigrants who were eager to share in the economic bonanza. The new arrivals included Europeans (chiefly Spanish), Chinese, Mexicans from the Yucatan peninsula, and people from elsewhere in the Caribbean. The city's population doubled from a quarter to half a million in those twenty years. Leaving its old world behind, Havana was seeking to find a niche in the twentieth century. Artistic and literary vanguards, both European and Cuban, were reviewed in *Social*—a bold magazine edited by cartoonist and publicist Conrado J. Massaguer between 1916 and 1933. In 1927 *Revista de avance* came out, under the direction of Jorge Mañach, Francisco Ichazo, and Juan Marinello, among others. This was a forum that sought to strengthen the links with international currents, while simultaneously cultivating Cuba's cultural roots.

Avenida de los Presidentes

Top left: House of Pérez de la Riva, on Avenida del Puerto. Once a ministerial building, it is now the Museum of Music.

Top right: Palacio Cueto. Its art nouveau aesthetic contrasts with other buildings on the Plaza Vieja.

Above left: Stylized floral patterns and female heads adorn the capitals of columns in Cubano-Catalan art nouveau.

Above right: Another example of the sensual, organic capital reliefs favored by the Catalan masters working in Havana.

Left: Railings with Republican star.

For the first time in its history, Havana began to be urbanistically divided along social lines. The upper class settled along the coastal fringe, moving westward from Vedado to Marianao beach, and seeding the development of the Miramar, Altos de Miramar, Biltmore, and Country Club districts. The middle and lower bourgeoisie were concentrated in the new barrios springing up to the southwest, such as La Víbora and Lawton; the poorer classes occupied marginal areas between these planned expansions. Functionally speaking, the city center was now transfered to Los Murallas, and this was where the new institutional buildings were grouped for the administration of public government, activities, and recreation.

In architecture, two strands of Cuban eclecticism were visible in those years, loosely associated with different social ranks. The first was popular in character and all but eludes classification: a specialty of the Catalan builders working in Havana, it flowered in gloriously decorated buildings that might justly be called neo-baroque. Among other recurrent motifs, this genre was enamored of the lone star emblem—which appears on the flag as a symbol of the united soul of the nation—and employed it to stud facades, ceilings, railings, and windows.[102]

Related to the above, and generated by the same group of architect-builders, was the art nouveau or "floral" trend, whose forms, somewhat schematized, were applied as decoration: female heads with flowing tresses bound up in ribbons merged in and out of sinuous tendrils on the walls of some of the smartest as well as the more modest dwellings. Cárdenas Street, in today's downtown Havana, offers a good sampling of these proto-"modernist" details, strewn on balconies, railings, arches, ceilings, mural paintings, tiles, mosaics, doors, and screens.

The urban design could be a compact amalgam or could be broken up by green spaces. In the first instance, detached homes with two or more levels and porticos onto the main street stood in tight rows, housing a family on each floor. Their old designation of *comunera* houses had been replaced by the more contemporary *casas de apartamentos*. The disposition of space was nevertheless inherited from colonial houses, although the patio gradually disappeared or became a narrow lateral passageway connecting the front part of the house with the rear. During the twentieth century, the patio altogether lost its crucial former purpose of collecting rainwater in tanks, since the Albear aqueduct had made it obsolete. Some changes could be observed in the distribution of the rooms, as for example the dining room, which was moved farther back to be nearer the kitchen: the disappearance of house slaves had palpably affected the modes of domestic life. Such buildings had also lost their multiple functions of the past, becoming exclusively residential.

In middle-class districts the houses were usually of one story, with the same internal distribution as previously. Others were small porticoed villas, fronted by a little yard, like a miniature reproduction of the grand version that spread through Vedado, the origins of which were rooted in the late nineteenth century. The court was eliminated and the internal order ramified out from a central hall that crossed the house from the front to the rear.

The second strand of Cuban eclectism was the academic genre, adopted in many mansions of the wealthy class, although its ultimate turf was Vedado—the suburb that had established itself by 1910 as the only chic place to live. It was a learned architecture, of a kind that had not been seen before in Cuba,

Top: Mansion in El Vedado.

Above: Porticoed villa on Línea Street in El Vedado. Site of Saint George's College.

Left: The five-pointed star used as a decorative element on a false keystone under a balcony.

and was mostly propagated by Cuban graduates of the School of Architecture, founded in 1900 as part of Havana University. Some of these professionals had also studied abroad or been influenced by foreign architects. Among these was Thomas E. Newton, who transmitted his penchant for academism to many Cuban followers. Eugenio Rayneri Piedra, César Guerra, José Rafecas, José Ramón Toñarely, Rafael de Cárdenas, Francisco Centurión, Raúl Otero, and Leonardo Morales were among those at the forefront of the movement to break away from the colonial building tradition.

The new architecture dipped into a wide range of styles. In the short span of three decades, Cuba came into contact with the millenarian building experience of western Europe, in a way that was deliberate as never before. In his book *La Habana actual*, Pedro Martínez Inclán articulated a widely shared desire to endow the capital with works of art that would put it on a par with European cities. The architects of the first Republican generation disposed of new materials with which to attain this goal: concrete and steel. Now the architectural limitations that had handicapped colonial structures, obliging them to abide by certain dimensions and relationships of load, could be transcended. The architecture of this period, while firmly adhering to the principles of symmetry, achieved much greater freedom of composition. Leonardo Morales, one of the main practitioners of Cuban eclecticism, offered a succinct analysis of the evolution of taste:

> At the beginning of this period . . . of the Second Republic [after the second American intervention, launched with José Miguel Gómez's government in 1909], the author and Messrs. Albarrán and Bibal . . . followed the direction indicated by Newton. These buildings were well proportioned, but of a quasi-Greek rigidity. Later we progressed to the Italian Renaissance . . . After that there were some variants on Louis XVI, and I dare say that from 1914 to 1924 our architecture was a blend of this latter style and Italian Renaissance, in a fusion that was characteristic of our country and produced many distinguished works. . . . The Spanish Plateresque was introduced circa 1924, and became outrageously modish for a while. Then the Florentine came into vogue, and the Californian Mission, and finally . . . Cuban colonial and art deco. The recent period has, therefore, spawned a plethora of styles in the absence of precise time-frames, for at the same time as one style came into fashion others that until lately had claimed that honor were still under construction.[105]

Venetian-style home of Estanislao del Valle.

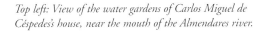

Top left: View of the water gardens of Carlos Miguel de Céspedes's house, near the mouth of the Almendares river.

Above: Stained-glass window in the house of Joaquín Gumá, Count of Lagunilla, on 5th Avenue and 22nd Street, Miramar.

Left: The same water gardens on the edge of El Vedado.

Such versatility reached its most alarming pitch during the 1920s, with the evocation of every source imaginable: Mudejar, Romanesque, Gothic. This last fad was responsible for a veritable spate of castles. The moneyed classes favored the two-story detached home surrounded by lawns, and some experimented with exotic "Japanese" gardens, such as that surrounding the Carlos Miguel de Céspedes house at the end of Almendares Street.

The preferred orientation for these luxurious homes was at the so-called friar's corner, to the northeast of the block for maximum shade and the most refreshing winds, the side that the drawing room and master bedrooms gave onto. The service areas, kitchen, pantry, and garages were condemned to the "infernal corner" grilled by the sun. The ground floor was reserved for social spaces and those of domestic service, while upstairs were the bedrooms and bathrooms, a common amenity by this date.

These houses stressed the importance of the entrance porch and the parlor, which was the starting point for a large sweeping staircase illuminated by leaded glass windows showing historical scenes, coats of arms, religious imagery, or floral and geometric patterns. Certain themes were recurrent, such as that of the great sailing ships that used to make the perilous crossing to

Top: Havana Yacht Club, on the second roundabout in 5th Avenue.

Center: The Casino Español club and spa.

Bottom: Havana Yacht Club, rear view.

and from Europe, or the shields of Cuba as a manifesto of national pride. The oldest dynasties, however, confined themselves to a monogram or other merely decorative motifs, as in the case of the count of Lagunillas.

This architecture also paid careful attention to interior decoration, which tended to proceed from New York. This was initially due to the efforts of H. F. Huber, who frequently visited Havana and finally opened a branch of his store there. The first house to be decorated by Huber was that of banker Hermann Upmann, in Vedado. Huber's success was quickly capitalized upon by other foreign firms that set up shop in the city to supply an avid clientele ranging from the government to rich private citizens. Tiffany's of New York, for example, found a market for its impressively varied stained-glass windows and lampshades, not only in the great mansions but also in less prosperous homes throughout the country.

It was not long before Jansen of Paris followed suit, with the difference that its Havana subsidiary employed Cuban carpenters and cabinetmakers, as well as artists including Rogelio Atá and his son; this firm remained in Cuba for many years. The Theodore Bailey house on the elegant Paseo del Prado came later and specialized in artistic furniture and interior fixtures. Bailey was one of the decorators who collaborated most closely with Massaguer's groundbreaking magazine *Social*.

The campaign launched by that journal and the decorators' efforts encouraged builders of luxury residences and commercial premises to hire professionals to handle the interior details. The Spanish Renaissance was popular in the Cuba of those years, especially where architectonic ornamentation and furniture were concerned. A good example of this trend is offered by the dining room in the Oscar B. Cintas house in Vedado, which was furnished with fine pieces in Spanish oak and displayed an enviable collection of paintings by Joaquín Sorolla, Gerardo Murillo, and Madrazo on the walls.[104]

According to Bailey, the scientific study of interiors is a twentieth-century phenomenon. Previously it had been the rule for architects to provide building plans with interiors left blank, for clients to fill as they pleased when the house was ready. From the late 1920s to the early 1930s, two Cuban women worked on the interior decoration section of *Social*: Bertha Arocena, a journalist and writer, and Clara Porcet, who subsequently went into furniture design and moved to Mexico to open a studio. She was particularly interested in the science of bathrooms.

The North American influence was reflected not only in interior design, but also in the participation of powerful companies like the Purdy & Henderson Co. or the T. L. Huston Contracting Co., who built memorable buildings catering to every kind of social, public, or administrative need. Local firms such as Arellano y Mendoza, and Morales y Cía., also completed major projects. Havana was becoming modernized, and the content of its architectural patrimony was diversifying. There were banks, hotels, hospitals, recreational societies, clubs, teaching institutions, commercial complexes, services, and government buildings, all situated in zones determined by function.

Most estate developments, on the other hand, acquired an exclusively residential character, with the exception of Vedado, which welcomed hotels,[105] clubs such as the Vedado Tennis Club, theaters such as the Auditorium, and hospitals: the Calixto García Hospital, in particular, became an enclave of

The Railway Terminal.

Facade of the Ursuline Convent in Old Havana.

learning, notably after Havana University was relocated there. Public institutions and government offices were generally confined to the downtown Murallas district, leaving the old colonial center relatively intact. But the historic area did not escape the edification of a number of public and private buildings, such as multistoried apartment houses, which violated the atmospheric integrity of Old Havana both in height and volume.

The deterioration of colonial buildings set in when their owners deserted them for smart, modern developments elsewhere, and poorer people moved in. Such residential properties now became known as *solares*, while other old buildings were turned into offices, workshops, and warehouses. Since the nineteenth century, in fact, *solar* or tenement housing had been expressly contructed; these rental rooms were also called *cuarterías* or *ciudadelas*. The rooms were aligned on either side of a central passageway, which led to a communal set of sanitary and washing facilities at the back. Each room was equipped with a tiny cooking area to one side of the door. The *solares* were occupied by people on very low incomes, whose vitality found outlets in raucous collective fiestas where everyone joined in to play *son* music, thump out *rumbas de cajón*—using crates as percussion instruments—and rehearse routines for the parades and pageants of Carnival.

The public buildings erected at this time brought a new element to the profile of the capital in the form of skyscrapers inspired by the masterpieces of the Chicago School. These towers, of moderate height, were nevertheless sharply at odds with the low-rise skyline of the city. They consisted of a shaft

and a top cornice, ornamented in academic style and displaying a profusion of windows that opened on small balconies. The Hotel Presidente was built in Vedado on Calle G and Calzada; apartment buildings went up, including that by Horacio Navarrete on Paseo and Calle 25, and another two on Avenida de los Presidentes.

The civic center was further built up with prominent Republican constructions in eclectic style, to form a monumental architectural ensemble of undeniable value. The configuration of this new environment was spearheaded by the revamping of Paseo del Prado in 1902, using asphalt for the first time. A monument to the poet Juan Clemente Zenea was placed at one end of the Paseo in 1920. The Parque de la Punta zone was improved, gaining a gazebo designed by Charles Brun (1921) and a memorial to the students of medicine who faced the firing squad on that spot in 1871.

The first section of the Malecón seawalk was also begun at this time. Nearby, the demolition of the Cortina de Valdés had cleared the edges of the canal where it met the sea, and opened the city to the ocean. This ground was used to construct the provincial government building, which later became the Presidential Palace, as well as other outstanding houses lining the central thoroughfares of Prado, Zulueta, and Monserrate-Egido. There were also some public projects of clear architectural note, such as the Commercial Employees' Center, the American Tobacco Company building, the Sevilla Hotel, the Gran Hotel, and the Isla de Cuba hotel; the shopping complex known as Manzana de Gómez, the new Ursuline building, the Galician

Center and the Asturian Center, the Spanish Club, the Secondary Education Institute, the police station on Dragones and Zulueta, the Red Cross building, the railway terminal, and the National Capitol, among many more. Havana's urban development during the course of the first decades of the Republic was reviewed in a 1932 text by architect Pedro Martínez Inclán:

> Thus at the beginning of the twentieth century, Havana was urbanized as far as the Calzada de la Infanta. . . . The development of Havana conformed to two elemental rules for the growth of cities. It spread to the mountains (to La Víbora) and followed the shoreline (Vedado, Marianao, etc.). The Acosta suburb, in La Víbora, was one of the first to emerge. The whole of La Víbora, which now covers a surface three times greater than that of the Havana that extended to La Infanta, far from obeying the fundamental rules of urban planning, was developed by evading, through any pretext to hand, our already antiquated ordinances. . . . The lands designated for common use were reduced to a minimum. The wide avenues that had been projected were seldom realized. Each lot was developed in isolation, without reference to the rest. The primary network of roads required by any well-organized city was never contemplated. Let us not even speak of zoning. Parks and gardens were squeezed into one hundred square meters and given a few flowerbeds and some spindly trees.[106]

It was not until the presidency of Gerardo Machado (1925–1933) that comprehensive urban planning projects were set in motion. But though Machado was determined to broadcast a progressive image, he was handicapped as of 1929 by the profound economic and political crisis. Earlier, however, he partially rationalized the urban complex and commissioned the imposing National Capitol. Havana was set to be a "tropical Paris" or the "Nice of the Americas."

View over the Paseo del Prado, seen from the Hotel Inglaterra.

Avenida de los Presidentes in El Vedado.

The urban reorganization of Havana called for the services of the celebrated French town planner Jean-Claude Nicolas Forestier, who enjoyed great prestige in both Europe and Latin America. In line with the aesthetic tenets of the École des Beaux-Arts, Forestier amplified the ideas already explored in projects by Raúl Otero (1905), Enrique J. Montoulieu (1923), and Pedro Martínez Inclán (1925), which implied a system of diagonal trunk roads and *rond-points* or rotaries. The plan took in the coastline—the sea would be decisively integrated into the city, with a distinctive touch— and envisaged the creation of parks and gardens complemented by the highest quality of urban facilities. Forestier was also prepared to move the whole civic center to the higher ground of Catalanes, the site of present-day Revolution Square. The design of the roomy Paseo de Almendares and the Gran Parque Nacional sought to insert verdant breathing-spaces into the dense weave of the city.

This plan, although incompletely carried out, represented the first comprehensive urban planning of Havana and changed the face of the city forever. The Paseo del Prado was redesigned as it now stands, the Campo de Marte was reborn as the Plaza de la Fraternidad, and Avenida del Puerto (1927–1937) was created to join up with the shoreline at Malecón. The latter extended from plaza to plaza, each dominated by commemorative monuments, making it into one of the busiest social magnets of the city to the present day. At the point of confluence of the two roads, Avenida de las Misiones was opened (1928–1929), stretching from the concourse of La Punta to the north portico of the Presidential Palace. In El Vedado, Calle G became Avenida de los Presidentes, and Avenida de los Alcaldes replaced Paseo Street; both were graced with parks and monuments along their entire length. The principal urban spaces thus became interconnected, with the bonus of significant monumental works. Modern Havana had been sketched out.

Dionisio Velasco Residence

On the corner of Cárcel and Avenida de las Misiones, at the entrance to Havana bay, Dionisio Velasco built one of the first great mansions of the Republican era. It is also judged to be the crowning achievement of the Catalan masters. This work by Francisco Ramírez Ovando has a splendid facade that has understandably drawn the admiration of observers, and has points in common with Philadelphia's City Hall and the Executive Office next to the White House.

Inside, however, the rooms are small, and communicate by means of winding passageways, in spite of the presence of a central court. The carpentry is remarkable, as are the plaster moldings on the ceiling. When Nena Velasco and her husband Álvaro González Gordon lived here, the house was famed for its collection of historic Cuban etchings and lithographs, part of which was exhibited at the Palacio de Bellas Artes in 1956.

From the tower and much of the house, it is a pleasure to watch the comings and goings on the canal as it meets the bay, bringing to mind a comment by Alejo Carpentier: "Of all the ports I know, Havana is . . . the only one that offers so precise a sensation that the boat, on docking, has penetrated right into the city."

Today, this house is the Spanish Embassy.

House of Dionisio Velasco, Avenida de las Misiones.

Casa de Dámaso Gutiérrez

The house built for Dámaso Gutiérrez on Loma del Mazo in the La Víbora district (1910) is held by many to be the most important work by architect Mario Rotlant. It celebrates the forms of art nouveau in cast concrete outside and plaster inside, all the elements having been crafted in Rotlant's own workshop.

The house is set on a rise, at the summit of one of the hills that billow around the outskirts of Havana. It is a two-story structure with a tower on one corner, a feature that was much exploited by architects of the first decades of the century. It has front and side porticoes, themselves preceded by a terrace at the top of a double flight of steps. The complementary decorative details, such as balconies, arches, railings, and mosaics, give free rein to Rotlant's love of art nouveau. The columns are topped off with splendid capitals in the shape of a female head—another recurring feature in the popular architecture of the period.

House of Dámaso Gutiérrez.

Masía l'Ampurdà

The chalet named Masía l'Ampurdà, on Revolución Street at the level of Josefina and Gertrudis in La Víbora, was erected in 1919. Here fantasy runs riot through a profuse display of art nouveau. Resembling a miniature castle, the house is surrounded by a garden that is terraced into various levels, dominated by the tower. The walls are coated with rustic whitewash, lending the place an artisanal air, and the decoration is based on pink and green mosaics that highlight walls, stairs, and columns, as well as serving as flooring. The columns have sunflowers in relief on the capitals. Down in the garden, the voluptuous lines of art nouveau animate the curves of the mosaic benches as they do in Gaudí's Parque Güell in Barcelona. This bizarre concoction is without a doubt a gem of decorative architecture.

Top right: Facade of Masía l'Ampurdà.

Right: Masía l'Ampurdà, side entrance; note the sundial on the tower.

Opposite page: Masía l'Ampurdà, detail of the porch.

Above: Masía l'Ampurdà, ironwork with inset glass.

Top right: Masía l'Ampurdà, a mosaic-covered bench in the garden.

Right: Masía l'Ampurdà, bench arm.

Masia l'Ampurdà, garage entrance with wrought-iron door.

Palacio de la Condesa de Revilla de Camargo

This residence was built at the corner of Seventeenth and E Streets by a wealthy planter, José Gómez Mena, for his sister María Luisa, the countess of Revilla de Camargo, who was known to her intimates as María Cagiga. With nods to Versailles and the Petit Trianon, this French classical-revival building was completed in 1926 under the supervision of architect Adrián Maciá, to a plan drawn up by his French colleagues P. Viard and M. Destuges; it stands out for the stunning luxury of its concept. The facade was chiselled out of hard *capellanía* stone and displays two corner sculpture groups of cherubs, reminiscent of the work of Augustin Pajou, who carved decorations for the facades of Palais Royal and Palais Bourbon. The white Carrara marble floors are inlaid at the most effective points, and the entrance hall, of double height, leads to an awesome staircase; the dining room walls are clad with panels of the finest marble.

The countess collected valuable French furniture signed by cabinetmakers of renown; one piece was a secretary that had allegedly belonged to Marie Antoinette. She also possessed some excellent paintings by French artists such as the landscape painter Hubert Robert, and various portraits of herself by the Spanish artists who were fashionable in the days of her youth. The interior decoration was entrusted to Carlos Ortiz, the Cuban representative of the Maison Jansen of Paris. Ortiz returned during the 1950s to redesign the loggia, which contained murals by Mario Carreño depicting the birth of Venus. This space, with its French art deco furniture imitating braided rope, achieved a delightful environment that was tropical and fresh.

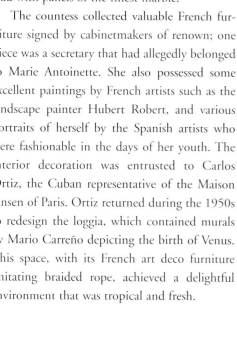

Main gate to the palace of the Countess of Revilla de Camargo.

María Cagiga was famous for her glamorous receptions in honor of European nobles and royals: she entertained the kings of Belgium, the dukes of Windsor, and the counts of Barcelona. Her home is evoked in another novel by Alejo Carpentier, *La consagración de la primavera*, whose main character is conceivably a cross between the author and the countess's great-nephew, Pancho Vives y Gómez Mena.

The mother of Pancho Vives, also named María Luisa, was a great benefactress of the arts in Cuba; her portrait was painted many times, most successfully by Carlos Enríquez and Mario Carreño, who also happened to be married to her when Alfred Barr, director of the Museum of Modern Art in New York, visited Havana in the summer of 1942 to acquire works of art for that institution. According to sculptor Alfredo Lozano, María Luisa gave a most colorful and picturesque dinner for Barr at her aunt's place, to which she invited not only the high society of Havana but also its leading artists, which was an unconventional step to take in those days. Forty years later Edgar Kauffmann Jr., who accompanied Barr on his trip, still recalls María Luisa's outfit that night. She was in a long clinging dress, with her head and part of her face covered by laurel wreaths: "It was live surrealism come to life!"

Today the palace has become the Museo de Artes Decorativas.

Left: Revilla de Camargo palace, sculpted corner group on the parapet.

Below: Revilla de Camargo palace, oblique view of the front facade.

Above: Revilla de Camargo palace, handbasin with dolphins, in the dining room.

Right: Revilla de Camargo palace, hall and grand staircase.

Bottom right: Revilla de Camargo palace, inlaid marble brightens the floor.

Portrait of María Luisa Gómez Mena, María Cagiga's niece, by the Cuban painter Carlos Enríquez (1901–1957).

Above: Revilla de Camargo palace, main drawing room.

Right: Revilla de Camargo palace, view of dining room.

Revilla de Camargo palace:
glassed-in loggia.

Above: Garden of the Revilla de Camargo palace, two of the marble sculptures representing the seasons.

Left: Revilla de Camargo palace, Dolphin Fountain.

Casa de Alfonso Gómez Mena

Originally constructed by Pedro Marín, the home of landowner Alfonso Gómez Mena y Vila and his wife (who was also his cousin), María Vivanco y Vila, stands on Calzada and Avenida de los Presidentes in Vedado. It was built between 1910 and 1912 in the style of a French palace of the Second Empire to a design by Francisco Centurión; the contractors were Morales y Cía. It is a superbly luxurious creation in every respect, deserving of special mention for such details as the beautiful wrought-iron grilles by Ricardo Soler Sendra. The great central hall is as high as the house and with its cupola above and imperial staircase to the rear forms the compositional nucleus of the whole building. Might this decor be alluding to the colonial courtyards that did so much to emphasize the social and architectural superiority of a house, or is it rather

a beaux-arts solution derived from the Second Empire and the Third Republic in France?

The stained-glass windows over the stairwell display a prominent Cuban coat of arms commissioned by original owner Pedro Marín, a native of Camagüey who actively supported the War of Independence. It was preserved by the Gómez Menas, no doubt as a testimony to their Cuban loyalties. All the same, the mood of the palace owes much to a Spain that the family had only recently left behind, although it is also true that the Spanish style was everywhere in vogue during those years. The grand dining room had a Moorish ceiling and a very fine seventeenth-century *bargueño* desk, a small silver bull by Mariano Benlliure on the hall table, and in the drawing room a bronze figure of an altar boy by the same artist. In the small secluded living room

on the second floor, there was a collection of marble busts of the couple's seven children, also by Benlliure. The master bedroom was furnished with art deco pieces made from Cuban mahogany by Maison Jansen.

Like other *palacetes* of the time, this manor had front and side gardens of moderate size and a larger one to the rear, which showcased another spectacular Benlliure: a life-sized bronze sculpture on a bullfighting theme called *El coleo*. It represented a heart-stopping incident at the ring, where men try to distract a bull away from a gored matador by tugging on its tail. After the death of Alfonso Gómez Mena, his family sent the monumental sculpture to the Amistad sugar mill.

At the beginning of the 1950s, the Cuban government bought the house and turned it into the offices of the Ministry for Foreign Affairs.

Opposite page, top: Gómez Mena house, wrought-iron main gate by Ricardo Soler.

Opposite page, bottom: House of Alfonso Gómez Mena.

Top: Gómez Mena house, ornate walls and windows of the principal drawing room.

Above: Gómez Mena house, great marble staircase and stained-glass window featuring the Republican shield.

Above right: Gómez Mena house, shield of the Cuban Republic, surrounded by those of the six provinces, in stained glass designed by Cuban artist Pedro Marín.

La Dolce Dimora

Close to Havana University, on the corner of Ronda and San Miguel streets, we find this copy of a sixteenth-century Florentine villa; the home of politician and writer Orestes Ferrara is one of the most refined and well appointed of the era. It was built in 1927 by the prestigious firm of Govantes & Cabarrocas, whose mettle was demonstrated on more than one occasion in Havana. On the lower floor is a rectangular, double-height living room in the purest Renaissance manner, with a balcony stretching along its principal length. A beautiful stained-glass panel lets in the light on the street side, and opposite this the room gives onto a little court. Part of the top floor is occupied by a columned loggia, evocative of the same period. The mansion has three stories, with terraces that afford views of different angles of the city. It is built of

Jaimanitas stone and enhanced by the presence of such noble materials as Italian marble, European glass, wrought iron, and precious hardwoods.

Orestes Ferrara, a Neapolitan by birth, came to Cuba as a young man enthused by the nationalist struggle for independence from Spain. He joined the Army of Liberation, reaching the rank of colonel. Under the Republic he pursued a career in the field of politics and the higher civil service, holding the posts of president of the House of Representatives, Cuban ambassador to Washington, and secretary of foreign relations under the government of Gerardo Machado (1925–1933). Ferrara had little opportunity to enjoy his house; he was forced to flee the country on August 12, 1933, when Machado's administration collapsed and his secretary of

state was in danger of being lynched. Mobs broke into the house, but without causing irreparable damage. Ferrara returned to his home when the situation appeared more stable. Years later, having survived a couple of terrorist attacks, he moved back to Italy for good, and died there in 1972.

The property was taken over in 1961, destined to house the Julio Lobo Napoleonic Collection, as the museum it is today—which entailed removing almost the entire contents of my father's house to that address. While he and Ferrara lived in Cuba, they were on indifferent terms; but once in exile, the matter of the house brought them together to ignite a genuine friendship. In old age—Ferrara in Rome, my father in Madrid—they exchanged a copious correspondence on the subject of Cuba's future.

Above: Side view of La Dolce Dimora.

Right: Part of the facade of La Dolce Dimora, now the Napoleonic Museum.

Casa de Juan de Pedro y Baró y Catalina de Lasa

The home of the sugar planter Juan de Pedro y Baró was built around 1928 by Govantes and Cabarrocas, while the gardens were laid out by Jean-Claude Nicolas Forestier. It took shape under the stamp and seal of the mistress of the house, my great-aunt, the ravishing Catalina de Lasa, and was hailed as a strikingly new design, original in concept and faultless in execution. It stands at the corner of Seventeenth and Paseo Streets and occupies half a block. The exterior, painted a vivid pink, is in the Italian Renaissance mode; it was actually based on a famous Florentine palazzo. The ceramic cornice is a copy of the Palazzo Strozzi's, and the upstairs windows resemble those of the Chancellery Palace in Rome. It was the first high-ranking residence in Cuba to adopt an art deco aesthetic inside the house.

The mansion has wrought-iron railings and wall lamps made by the French firm Baguez in the shape of art deco roses. The Lalique glass is patterned with roses like much else in the house, doubtless as an allusion to the variety of bloom that became known in Cuba as the "Catalina Lasa" rose. The materials are beautiful and rare throughout, with red marble from Languedoc and the sumptuous Italian marbles of Port-Oro and Giallo di Siena. A graciously austere library marries the geometry of art deco with a panelling of antique mahogany. The tall mirrored doors of the drawing room used to reflect the furniture designed especially for the house by Luis Estévez, Catalina's son by her first marriage.

Family and friends often used to gather on the sun porch, a captivating room with trellises around the walls and refreshing fountains. Another favorite spot for entertaining or relaxing *en famille* was under the portico among the *areca* palms, in wicker chairs. In the past there was a small greenhouse separated from the dining room by a marble step, and Catalina's bedroom was decorated in a lovely shade of "ashes of roses." Her simple but unusual sycamore bed was upholstered in blue chamois leather, like the other pieces in the room. The guest suite was one of the first commissions given to designer Clara Porcet.

In the Havana of the early twentieth century, Catalina's divorce and remarriage to Juan de Pedro y Baró caused such a scandal that they were driven to emigrate to Paris. Her beauty and charm opened all doors to them in Europe, including those of the notoriously hermetic court of imperial Russia. Many years passed before the couple returned to their homeland to build this house, which Catalina barely had time to enjoy before she passed away in December 1930.

Top: House of Juan de Pedro y Baró and Catalina de Lasa, guarded by the couple's hallmark twin palms.

Right: Portrait of Catalina de Lasa.

The Palm Room in the house of Juan de Pedro y Baró and Catalina de Lasa. Archive photograph from the National Library of Cuba.

Opposite page: Baró and Lasa house, front doorway with sitting lions.

Top left: Baró and Lasa house, complex ironwork in the round arch above a door, tracing the initials PB.

Top right: Baró and Lasa house, fanlight of Lalique glass.

Above: Baró and Lasa house, rectangular panel of Lalique glass.

Above: Baró and Lasa house, dining room with art deco furniture.

Left: Baró and Lasa house, art deco appliqué in Lalique glass.

Casa de Pablo González de Mendoza

The González de Mendoza residence is located on Paseo and Fifteenth, in the midst of large grounds dotted with romantic marble sculptures. The gardens ensure the privacy of the house by means of the transitional elements of terraces and steps, which draw the eye along as every perspective converges on the house. Built during the second decade of the century, this building reflects the purest classical period of Leonardo Morales; it is built in the "Vedado Style," the hallmarks of which are balance and sobriety. The Pompeiian bath sunk inside the house itself was the first covered swimming pool in Cuba. Its roof forms an immense skylight supported by painted wooden beams; for parties, the pool was boarded over and the space converted into an unusual dance floor.

House of Pablo González de Mendoza, view of the facade through the wrought-iron gate, tracing the initial of its owner.

Left: González de Mendoza house, statue of a classical goddess.

Below: González de Mendoza house, the first indoor swimming pool to be built in Cuba, doubling as a dance floor when required.

Casa de Eduardo Montalvo

My maternal grandparents Eduardo Montalvo and María Esperanza de Lasa (Catalina's sister) lived on top of a hill on the west bank of the Almendares River, in a house that illustrates the commitment of architect Leonardo Morales to achieving a personal mode of expression. Set on ample grounds, this great house evokes a plantation home insofar as it exploits the frontal arches as a link with nature, and has a rooftop terrace bordered with a parapet and covered with tiles.

The pillars of the portico hark back to colonial times, being particularly reminiscent of the Buena Vista plantation house in Trinidad—shown on top of a similar rise in an engraving by French artist Édouard Laplante, which is reproduced in *Los ingenios*, by Justo Germán Cantero (Havana, 1855–1857). The monumental entrance portico is laden with decorative detail, and yet the house appears light and dainty, with all the refinement of the Morales style.

Above: The Buena Vista plantation house, in an engraving by Édouard Laplante (1818).

Right: The house of Eduardo Montalvo.

Casa de Marcos Pollack y Carmen Casuso

The palatial residence designed by Leonardo Morales in the Country Club district for Marcos Pollack and his wife, Carmen Casuso, is the replica of a Renaissance villa: the use of fused columns and oculi recalls the work of Palladio. The central court is lined with a gallery on both stories. Two of the four sides of each arcade are pierced to overlook the patio, and each column is made of a different kind of marble. Galleries like this were first devised by Flaminio Ponzi for the courtyard of the Palazzo Borghese, and later taken up in a host of baroque villas. The bands and fillets outlining the arches, like the subdivisions of the wall sections, draw attention to the murals—a device that is characteristic of baroque and mannerist villas, as is the sienna color that was used. The mosaics of this patio are uncommon in that they depict tropical fruits: Cuban friezes and murals of earlier centuries tended to represent European varieties.

Pollack himself painted the doors to the grand drawing room, as well as some details on the Discovery of America mural that covers the walls of the same room. He slipped in the faces of several family members, for this tobacco exporter was also a talented artist. The house was completed in 1929, in time for his daughter Elena's wedding to Guillermo Aguilera.

Opposite page, top: Pollack house,
interior of the loggia.

Opposite page, bottom: Pollack house,
loggia in evening light.

Above: Pollack house, fountain, loggia,
and garden steps.

Top: Pollack house, detail of the shield carved into the pendentive of the arches.

Above: Pollack house, the well in the central patio.

Right: Pollack house, view of the galleries, with their columns of different marble and mural paintings.

Left: Pollack house, painted wood rafters and frieze.

Below: Pollack house, painted round arch above a first-floor gallery door, showing Cuban fruits.

Quinta Palatino

At the end of Calzada de Palatino in El Cerro, on the former site of a pretty weekend estate called Las Delicias, a castle-like residence appeared in 1903. Its owner was Rosalía Abreu, sister of Marta Abreu, the heiress who donated so generously to the independence struggle. In the Romantic sense, this building was the first "folly" ever to be seen in Cuba. The project was realized by Charles Brun, whose curriculum already included acclaimed works like a now-vanished gazebo, the Glorieta de la Punta, and the house of Pedro Abreu on Paseo del Prado (afterward the American Club of Havana), both in reinforced concrete from Purdy & Henderson.

The castle is accessed through a porte cochere, with a detailed mosaic ceiling that depicts a classical charioteer urging on his horses. It has two striking turrets of unequal height, both with leaded stained-glass windows and crenellated battlements. Downstairs a sheltered, ivy-clad terrace runs the length of the dining room, drawing room, and study and round the small circular chamber; the roof is of glass. The ground floor is divided into several palatial reception rooms, the dining room, a billiard room with Moorish echoes, pantry, kitchen, and other service rooms. On the first floor were the family quarters, and above, the servants' and housekeeper's rooms. These levels are linked by a bronze staircase of highly intricate design.

The walls of the vestibule and other downstairs rooms are decorated with large frescoes by Armando Menocal, depicting battles from Cuban wars such as the battle of the Loma de San Juan, in which Teddy Roosevelt's Rough Riders were deployed during the Spanish-American War. In 1908 a gigantic statue was placed in the round entrance hall; made of bronze, marble, and semiprecious stones, it represented Bellona, goddess of war, and was created by Jean-Louis Gérome. The interiors were complemented with expensive furniture and fittings, from Jacob chairs to Tiffany lamps. The original Buvet tapestries were exceptionally valuable, since they dated back to the French Revolution. In 1948 the French Government expropriated the home of Pierre Abreu for reasons of state, and its contents were shipped out to Havana,

Opposite page: The Quinta Palatino, from the bottom of its lush, landscaped gardens.

Above: Another angle of the Quinta Palatino.

where Abreu redecorated the castle with his priceless furniture and objets d'art. Of special note was a dining room set that had belonged to Edmond Rostand, author of *Cyrano de Bergerac*; the table and chairs were the work of the great French cabinetmaker Jacob.

The mansion is surrounded by formal gardens, landscaped by Forestier in the style of French academic classicism with neat parterres, artificial lakes, fountains, ponds, aviaries, and sculptures. The park was planted with a wide variety of trees and animated by mallard ducks and peacocks. However, it was the plentiful and varied monkeys that most caught the eye, causing the place to be nicknamed "Quinta de los Monos"— and prompting the disquiet of dancer Isadora Duncan when she dropped in at the castle:

> Another house where I visited was inhabited by a member of one of the oldest families who had a fancy for monkeys and gorillas. The garden of the old house was filled with cages in which this old lady kept her pets. Her house was a point of interest to all visitors, whom she entertained lavishly, receiving her guests with a monkey on her shoulder and holding a gorilla by the hand. . . . I asked if they were not dangerous and she replied nonchalantly that apart from getting out of their cages and killing a gardener every now and then, they were quite safe. This information made me rather anxious and I was glad when the time came to depart.[107]

The Abreus were prolific in beneficial works and cultural patronage in both Havana and Santa Clara, as well as making handsome contributions to the independentist cause. Two schools were founded in the neighborhood of their house: the Santa Rosalía for elementary students, and the Palatino for workers, specializing in electricianship. In Paris the Abreus left a permanent legacy at the Cité Universitaire, in the form of the Maison de Cuba, which would "forever be open to our students," as Pierre Abreu affirmed during the inaugural ceremony in February 1933. Sure enough, it has lodged Cuban students in France ever since.

Not all is yet known about the paramount contribution made by this family to Cuban society: their connections in Europe to a range of important personalities have yet to be researched. We do know of the intimate correspondence between Rosalía's daughter Lilita and two of the giants of Francophone literature, Jean Giraudoux and Saint-John Perse; both men were deeply in love with the Cuban beauty and through their letters bring us a little nearer to the inner world of Lilita Abreu, *la belle étrangère*.

Top: Quinta Palatino, view of the palm grove, and curved stained-glass windows of a drawing room.

Above: Quinta Palatino, Mauresque arches and plasterwork.

Quinta Palatino: cupola, banisters, and stained-glass windows.

227

Above: Quinta Palatino, statue of Bellona, by J-L. Gérôme.

Right: Quinta Palatino, chapel in the grounds.

Centro de Dependientes

The Social Palace of the Commercial Employees of Havana, on Prado and Trocadero, was unique among Spanish associations in that it did not define its membership on the basis of their region of origin, like the Asturian Center and others, but on the basis of their trade. The building was raised in Venetian Gothic style by Arturo Amigó between 1903 and 1907, and is reckoned by some to be the finest monument in all the city. The ceilings and grand staircase were among the first works to be carried out in steel-reinforced concrete produced on the island. The four stories contained ample space for the various available facilities, including classrooms, gym, library, game rooms, fencing and music rooms, a cafeteria, and a vast salon where balls, parties, and cultural events were held.

For a modest fee, comparable to that charged by the regional centers, members had access to all the services provided by the society, including a health clinic of the same name. Any member of the commercial trades, regardless of the nature of his or her job, could take advantage of the splendid premises and the society's cultural and educational programs.

In 1937 this building hosted the first exhibition of modern art, showing paintings and sculptures that made a momentous impact upon Cuban culture.

*Above: Centro de Dependientes, note the
Venetian references.*

*Opposite page: The Centro de
Dependientes for commercial employees,
general view from Paseo del Prado.*

Centro Gallego

This leisure-society building for the Galician community is on Paseo del Prado, between the streets of San Rafael and San José, on the site of the Teatro Tacón. The old playhouse was incorporated into the center under the new name of Teatro Nacional (later García Lorca). The first stone of this impressive palace was placed on December 8, 1914. Two architects collaborated on the project: Paul Belau from Belgium and the Cuban Rodolfo Maruri; the contractors were Purdy & Henderson. For all its bravura, the facade achieves good relations of proportion and fluidity of line, qualities that in conjunction with the corner turrets and the sculptural groups at the summit, by the Italian Giuseppe Moratti, cause an especially pleasing impact on the eye.

The interiors are elegantly decorated and make imaginative use of marble, iron, stained glass, and precious hardwoods in all the great rooms. There is a stunning grand staircase, guarded by outsize white marble angels.

Legend has it that on perceiving the majesty of this palace, the Asturian community decided to burn down their own social center and build a new one that would put the Galicians in their place. Whether this is true or false, the Centro Asturiano never did overshadow the edifice designed by Belau and Maruri.

Top: The Centro Gallego, in a 1930s photograph.

Right: Centro Gallego, ebullient upper facade.

Left: Centro Gallego: the bronze Angel of Fame, coiffed with a laurel wreath, symbolizes the building that now contains the Gran Teatro de La Habana.

Below: The roof of the Centro Gallego, its towers crowned by angels.

Centro Gallego: sculptural ensemble that surmounts one side of the building, framing the arms of the city.

Opposite page: Centro Gallego, balconies and sculptures.

Above: Centro Gallego, the top of the stairs and the upper gallery.

Left: Centro Gallego, the base of the monumental staircase.

Opposite page: Centro Gallego, first staircase landing, with part of the upper gallery.

Centro Asturiano

The Asturian community's social center stands on the block formed by Zulueta, San José, Monserrate, and Plazuela de Monserrate. It was built from 1923 to 1928 in *capellanía* stone by Purdy & Henderson, following the prizewinning design of Spanish architect Manuel del Busto and supervized by builder José Gómez Salas and draftsman Luis Betancourt. The exteriors, dominated by sober towers, were inspired by the Herrerian and Plateresque forms so typical of the period. Many in Havana rate the restraint of the Asturian Center above the gaiety and bubbling fantasy of its Galician predecessor.

Major sums were invested in this project, and it abounds in luxury materials: marble, lead mullions, ironwork, mosaics, granite, and precious woods. The finish is of faultless quality. At its entrance the space is dominated by a soaring staircase lit by a large skylight bearing scenes from the journey of Columbus to the Americas; this theme was important to the center, for many of the first *indianos*, or Spanish émigrés, were natives of Asturias. The ceiling paintings were done by Mariano Miguel.

Tower of the Centro Asturiano, viewed from the Centro Gallego.

Left: Centro Asturiano, tower view from Central Park.

Below: Centro Asturiano, view from the Hotel Inglaterra.

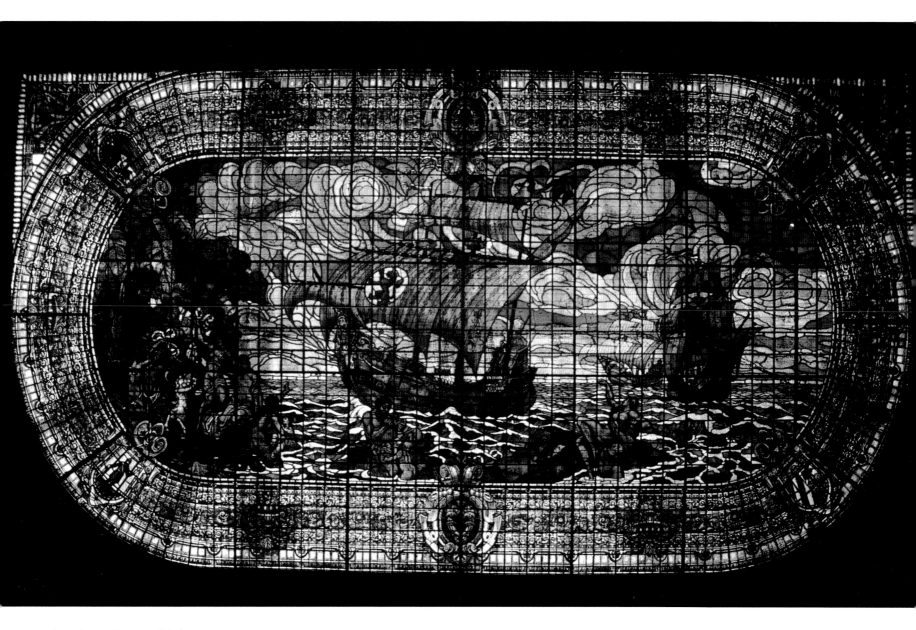

*Above: Centro Asturiano, skylight
decorated with the three caravelles of
Columbus's historic expedition.*

*Opposite page: Centro Asturiano, detail
of the cafeteria, with Sevillean tiles.*

Quinta Covadonga

The health clinic managed by the Centro Asturiano was located on Calzada del Cerro, occupying lands formerly owned by the count of Jibacoa. In 1896, the Asturian industrialist Manuel del Valle conceded this *casa quinta*, which he had recently acquired, to his regional association for the purpose of establishing a sanitarium by the name of Quinta Covadonga. The offices were placed in the original house, and a quantity of new pavilions mushroomed around it to house the various services and medical departments, without sacrificing the lush gardens with their fountains and groves. These outbuildings of one or two stories were designed so that every room had access to the ample indoor and outdoor colonnaded galleries by way of two large wooden doors, each surmounted by an adjustable stained-glass window to let in light and air.

All the sanitariums and health clinics run by the Spanish regional centers were similar in terms of setting and structure. Almost all, moreover, were built during the same period: the Benéfica and the Hijas de Galicia, both belonging to the Centro Gallego; the Castellana, the Canaria, the Balear, and that of the Dependientes, or commercial employees. Although as the years went by the architecture of hospitals took a different direction, these sanatoriums went on adding fresh pavilions built with the latest techniques, keeping pace as best they could with the progress of science. This form of hospital was transplanted back to Spain by the *indiano* Ramón Pelayo, marquis of Valdecillas, when in 1929 he endowed his native village of Ardeyo in Santander Province with the Casa de Salud Valdecillas. His health center conformed to the same architectonic pattern as that of the Cuban regional association sanitariums, which was not perhaps the most advisable option for the chilly climate of northern Spain. The cumulative approach of multiple low-rise pavilions had already been superseded in the rest of the world, and hospitals were henceforth being conceived as tall individual constructions. By going against the grain of most medical institutions and reproducing the format that had been current a decade before, was the marquis of Valdecillas paying a tribute to his adoptive Cuban homeland?

The marquis had amassed the bulk of his considerable fortune in sugarcane, as the proprietor of the Rosario mill in Aguacate, in the province of Havana. This property was later to be acquired by my father.

The Quinta Covadonga, on Calzada del Cerro. Detail of the administration building facade.

Casino Español

The Casino Español, or Spanish Club, is yet another conspicuous venture by the former colonial community in Havana. The three-story building in Spanish Renaissance style, with turrets at the top corners of the facade, was built in 1914 by architect Luis Dediot on the fashionable Paseo del Prado, between Ánimas and Virtudes. Like all the addresses along this boulevard, it emphasizes the front arcade, providing ample space for members to sit and chat and catch the breeze from their creaking rockers. Inside, a gorgeous marble flight takes us up to the great salons with their rich furnishings and murals. There was a magnificent library like those of the regional centers, with furniture and shelving made of Cuban hardwood.

This club, as its name indicates, did not select its membership on the basis of their native province in Spain; instead, the members all came from a wealthier class than that catered to by most other regional centers. Nor did it offer medical and educational services to the members, as did other clubs. It was a strictly recreational and social club with all the leisure facilities of a clubhouse in Marianao Beach, where centers such as the Club Náutico, the Círculo Militar y Naval, the Hijas de Galicia, and the top-notch Havana Yacht Club were to be found, as well as the public beach of La Concha.

In *La vuelta al mundo de un novelista*, Vicente Blasco Ibáñez writes that the ballroom of the Casino Español demonstrates that there are salons of such grandeur in America that they might as well be throne rooms.

The Casino Español on Paseo del Prado. Detail of the Grand Salon on the second floor.

Gardens of the Tropical Brewery

The Tropical and Polar breweries, the products of which were much appreciated in Cuba, built plants in the Puentes Grandes area, where Havana first settled after it was moved to the north coast in 1519. The rival companies both surrounded their factories with extensive landscaped gardens lapped by the waters of the Almendares river, on the banks of which they set up quirky pavilions and kiosks for holding parties, lunches, fairs, and other social events.

The park of La Tropical contains an open-sided pavilion with cement columns made to resemble tree trunks, based on the figurative caprices of Antonio Gaudí's Parque Güell in Barcelona. This kiosk is covered by a series of cupolas, the center of which is marked by a large, five-pointed art nouveau star, silhouetted in rippling lines that suggest starfish. The gardener's cottage has a pitched roof and balconies with slender turned rails. There is also a chapel and a couple of outdoor diners, the Salón Ensueño and the Mamoncillo, this last called after the venerable tree that shades many a table beneath it. But the most intriguing construction here is undoubtedly the Castillo, intended as the administrator's residence. More than a castle, it is a miniature *alcázar* palace in the Moorish tradition, clad in bright mosaics, and it stands as a monument to the skill of Cuba's master plasterers. This was the period during which they most excelled in an art that is, today, on the brink of extinction. The floor plan and the monumental staircase follow the conventions of the day, but the pools and sprinklers reinforce the Moorish references.

Top: Gardens of La Tropical brewery. Note the Gaudiesque aesthetic of a covered recreation area.

Right: The Alcázar, or administrator's house in the gardens of La Tropical, with its Arabic decor.

Hotel Plaza

This hotel opened in 1906 on the corner of Zulueta and Neptuno, and was designed by Ricardo Galbis Abella around part of an existing late-nineteenth-century structure. It is one of the supremely representative buildings of early Republican Havana, and is deployed around a central court overlooked by the galleries of each floor. The corridor arches are blocked with shuttered French windows and *mediopuntos* tinted white, ocher, and red, while the facade is heightened with a discreet patterning in classical style. The building was renovated in 1919 and given a roof garden that also housed a ballroom and a restaurant; it was felt that with the Plaza's roof garden, a corner of New York or Paris had alighted in Havana at last. Only recently was the courtyard covered over with a floral skylight that recalls the transparencies of nineteenth-century Cuban glass.

Hotel Plaza: the main entrance, on a chamfered corner facing the Fountain of Neptune.

Opposite page, top left: Hotel Plaza, updating the classic combination of shutters and stained glass.

Opposite page, top right: Hotel Plaza, the raised central court.

Opposite page, bottom left: Hotel Plaza, skylights from below.

Opposite page, bottom right: Hotel Plaza, a skylight.

Left: Hotel Plaza, central court with the domes of four skylights that illuminate the hall below.

Hotel Nacional

On the site of the old Santa Clara battery, demolished in 1929, the first luxury hotel of Republican Havana rose up. It was designed in Mediterranean Revival style by the New York firm of McKim, Mead & White—one of the most successful offices of its time, which had already completed such lasting achievements as Pennsylvania Station and the New York Racquet Club.

The hotel is in an ideal setting, with sea views. Its main entrance, off O Street, is reached at the end of a driveway lined with royal palms, the national tree of Cuba. The building presents broad terraces overlooking the sea on several sides and encloses a central patio with the traditional galleries. The inside is a profusion of precious woods, bronzes, tiles, and inlay. In its early days, luxury suites were available for heads of state, and the first floor was given to the Apartamento de la República, or presidential suite.

In September 1933, the Nacional was the scene of a bloody confrontation between factions of the armed forces. Taking advantage of the fact that United States Ambassador Benjamin Summer Welles was staying at the hotel, a band of former officers—who had been deposed weeks earlier (September 4) during the uprising manipulated by the future dictator Fulgencio Batista—dug themselves in and engaged in a violent skirmish with government soldiers. At length, and not before the hotel had been dented by a couple of shells, the rebel officers surrendered. There were many casualties.

*Above: Hotel Nacional, the mirador,
with dolphins and concrete wavelets.*

*Left: Rear view of the Hotel Nacional,
seen from the Malecón seawalk.*

Hotel Nacional, lobby.

Hotel Nacional, main dining room.

Presidential Palace

Belgian architect Paul Belau, in partnership with the Cuban Rodolfo Maruri, constructed this palace between 1913 and 1920. It was originally planned as the seat of the provincial government. The building, which occupies a block in the old Murallas development bordered by Zulueta, Colón, Monserrate, and Refugio Streets, can be seen from afar crowning the perspective at the top of Avenida de las Misiones. A monumental white marble staircase leads up to the main floor, and the interior decoration is by Tiffany.

The central section boasts six large stained-glass panels two stories high, each rising up above a door with a neoclassical pediment. The three principal doors open onto the North Terrace, the place from which it became customary for presidents to address the people. Inside, the six windows cast their light into the grand Mirror Room, and here the ceiling is painted with historical scenes by Cuban artist Armando Menocal. One of these is known as the *Apotheosis of José Martí* and shows the liberator at the moment of his death in battle. For forty years this room was the scene of big state receptions and the investiture ceremonies of successive new governments. Next to it was the president's office and further on, the Council of Ministers

meeting room and other smaller rooms reserved for audiences.

The third floor was set aside for the private presidential quarters, and the top, which was added later for services and occupies only the central portion of the surface, is encircled by a wide terrace with a high balustraded parapet.

The Presidential Palace was sacked by the mob when Gerardo Machado's government fell on August 12, 1933, and all his furniture and private belongings were flung into the street and destroyed by angry crowds. Its day of greatest historical moment, however, came on March 13, 1957, when members of the University Students' Directorate burst in through the back door with the intention of killing Fulgencio Batista, the army sargent who had gained power through a coup in 1952 and been confirmed as president in 1954 by a tainted electoral process. The assailants were unable to get to the third floor, and most of them died in the attempt.

Soon after the events of 1959, the house ceased to function as the headquarters of the executive. Today it contains the Museum of the Revolution.

Opposite page: Presidential Palace. To the left, the towers of the Iglesia del Ángel.

Right: Presidential Palace, the dome and, partially obscured, the shield of the Republic.

National Capitol

The National Capitol was built between 1925 and 1929 on a double block marked out by Prado, Neptuno, Industrias, and Dragones Streets, on the former site of the Villanueva sta-tion. Its massive size and dignity make it com-parable to the fortifications built during colo-nial times. Many of the best Cuban architects joined forces on this project, which can be con-sidered the fruit of a brilliant collective effort. The fundamentals of the design were provided by Félix Cabarrocas and Evelio Govantes in 1926, and partially modified by Raúl Otero and

J. N. Forestier. Lastly, José María Bens Arrarte gave definitive shape to the steps at the entrance and dome, also adding the curved volumes at either end.

The front of the monument is enhanced with a colonnade. A broad flight of steps, flanked by two heroic bronze figures in neoclassical style—the work of Italian artist Angelo Zanelli—takes us through the three sculpted bronze doors of the main entrance into the middle of the majestic Salón de los Pasos Perdidos (Hall of the Lost Steps), which is two stories high, with marble floors and walls.

In the circular center of the long Salón, set into the floor, lies a twenty-three-carat diamond that marks Kilometer Zero of the Central Highway; there was a scandal when this gem disappeared for several weeks during the second administration of Ramón Grau San Martín (1944–1948). A few meters beyond, directly beneath the dome, looms a towering bronze statue: *La República*. Also by Zanelli, it represents a woman in a Greek tunic holding a spear and a shield bearing the arms of Cuba. On her head is a Phrygian cap adorned with the five-pointed star. *La República* is the second largest indoor statue in the world; first place goes to the golden Buddha of Bangkok.

The right wing of the building used to house the Chamber of Representatives in a stepped semicircle like an amphitheater. The deputies' seats were of finest Cuban hardwood, and there was a dais for the president of this body and galleries for the press and the public. The hemicycle that corresponded to the Senate, in the opposite wing, is designed on the same pattern, although there were fewer seats, in view of the smaller number of senators per province.

The Capitol radiated a magnificence that had hitherto been unknown in this country. It was a triumph of harmonious balance between architecture and interior space, and between applied decoration and furnishings.

Above: National Capitol, the left wing of the building, with one of the monumental statues.

Left: National Capitol, view from Prado Street.

Havana University

In 1905 the first buildings were coming up on the new site chosen for Havana University, which prior to moving to Vedado had been squeezed into the old Santo Domingo monastery premises in Old Havana. The campus dominates the city from a bluff hemmed by L Street, Twenty-seventh Street, Avenida de la Universidad, and Ronda Street, where the Pirotecnia Militar used to stand in the previous century.

The new complex was based on separate buildings for each department linked by green or paved spaces, emulating the layout of North American universities and in particular that of Columbia University in New York City. The first pavilions were grouped around the Plaza Cárdenas to constitute an ensemble of marked architectural homogeneity. Features of note include the colonnade of the science faculty, by Pedro Martínez Inclán, the academism of the Law School, the rationalism of Joaquín Weiss's library, and the classicism of the Rectory, with its double porch of Corinthian columns. Presiding over the long flight of steps and surrounded by another four faculties stands the statue of the Alma Mater, a symbol of the university spirit sculpted by Mario Korbel.

During the first half of the twentieth century, Havana University was both a house of learning and a hotbed of political activity. After 1930, the University Students' Federation took a decisive lead in public life with all the force of a political party. A high degree of self-government enabled Havana University to conspire freely against the government of Machado during its last years, and it was the students who impelled Ramón Grau San Martín, holder of the chair of physiology, from the School of Medicine to the presidency for the first time, in 1933. Under this government, moderately social-democratic measures were passed. Throughout the 1940s, the campus was torn by the disputes of rival gangs at a time when political violence was spreading. Fulgencio Batista's coup in 1952 turned the university into a stronghold of opposition: demonstrations were organized in defiance of bloody police repression and the assault on the Presidential Palace was planned. Subsequently, classes were suspended, and the campus closed until 1959. Since then it has been divested of its autonomy as a center of learning.

Havana University: the great flight of steps leading up to the rectory.

Left: Havana University, colonnade of the Felipe Poey Natural Sciences Building.

Below: Havana University, rectory and statue of the Alma Mater.

Tradition and Modernity

Most encouraging is that the rehabilitation of criollo values can be seen to go hand in hand . . . with a shift of collective culture toward the wider horizons of the world. . . .

—Alejo Carpentier, "La Habana . . . vista por un turista cubano," 1939

Within the context of eclecticism, the revival of elements of colonial architecture was paradoxically a blow against tradition, as we shall see. The appearance of *Arquitectura* magazine in 1917 was the first signal for a reassessment of colonial aesthetics. Numerous articles were published on the subject by architects such as Luis Bay Sevilla and José María Bens Arrate, as well as historians of stature, such as Francisco Pérez de la Riva and Emilio Roig de Leuchsenring. In 1936, Joaquín Weiss brought out the first book on Cuban colonial architecture, while Emilio Roig and others launched a fervent press campaign in support of the conservation of historic monuments.[108]

In those days, however, the "national" in architecture was equated with the baroque. Such was the thesis advanced by Republican historians, and by those architects who in like spirit were pasting baroque elements onto new buildings as an instrument of renewal. Early attempts to quote the idiom of Cuban baroque entailed reviving the jambs around doors and window bays and setting ox-eye windows, mixtilinear cornices, and parapets and roofed balconies into buildings that were otherwise of eclectic inspiration. This opened the door to more far-fetched details culled from the broader Latin American or Spanish traditions—including even Californian colonial—in versions that might fit within the Cuban context.

Then Eugenio Batista appeared on the scene. Batista approached the colonial heritage not from the angle of individual features, but from that of its pared-down essentials. He took the constants that are repeated in Cuban buildings, such as courts, galleries, and shutters, and emptied them of stylistic connotation, so that they simply expressed their perfect adequacy to the tropical environment. In this way a whole new potential was discovered, one that would be explored in many works by the avant-garde architects of Cuba.

Meanwhile, in this transitional phase, the fashion for internationalist options held sway throughout the 1930s and much of the subsequent decade. This certainly left Cuban architects in a better position to handle new building techniques and materials. The style that Leonardo Morales called *arte nuevo*, which received the international tag of "art deco" in the 1920s, was one of the most popular tendencies of the moment.

Many interesting buildings were predicated on this style. To mention but a few: the López Chávez house by Esteban Rodríguez Castell; the López Serrano building by the firm of Mira and Rosich; the Children's Hospital and the Maternity Hospital by Govantes and Cabarrocas: the Fausto theater by Saturnino Pajarón; the América theater by Fernando Martínez Campos and Pascual de Rojas; the Duplex cinema by Luis Bonich; and what is surely the jewel in the crown: the Bacardi Building by Esteban Rodríguez Castells, José Menéndez Menéndez, and Rafael Fernández Ruenes.

The second dominant aesthetic of this transitional period was that adopted by monumental buildings of state. Though ostensibly rationalist, they betray the primacy of symbol over function in their persistent fondness for gigantic colonnades, stress on verticality, and baldly symmetrical composition. Prominent examples include Moenck and Quintana's School of Medicine, the School of Veterinary Science by Manuel Tapia Ruano, the School of Odontology by Esteban Rodríguez Castells, the headquarters of the Economic Society of Friends of the Country, by Govantes and Cabarrocas, and the Marianao Workers' Maternity Hospital by Emilio de Soto.

It was not until the 1940s that the modern movement carried the day in architectural practice, shorn at last of classical reminiscences, whether formal or spatial. Several factors contributed to the dissemination of the movement.

Naturaleza Muerta, *Amelia Pelaez.*

Top left: Main entrance to the López Chávez house (41st Avenue and 44th Street), in art deco style.

Top right: Front door and porch of the López Chávez house, by Esteban Rodríguez Castells.

Bottom left: Facade of the Economic Society of Friends of the Country, on Carlos III Avenue, built by the firm of Govantes y Cabarrocas.

Bottom right: The house of Martín Fox, with a mosaic mural designed by painter José Mijares.

Above: Lobby of the Havana Hilton, with its modern domed skylight.

Left: The house of Richard Neutra.

Top: Stained-glass window by Cuban modernist painter René Portocarrero (1912–1985), in the Restaurante Las Ruinas.

Above: Urban meets rural folklore, in an oil painting by Mariano Rodríguez (1912–1990).

In 1939 José Luis Sert stopped off in Havana on his way to the United States. A refugee from the Spanish Civil War and vice-president of CIAM (International Congresses of Modern Architecture), Sert inspired a group of youthful architects to found ATEC two years later (Technical Union of Contemporary Studies). In 1945 Richard Neutra began teaching at the School of Architecture. Two years later, his students along with a posse of antitraditionalist professors symbolically set fire to the treatise of Andrea Vignola in the school quadrangle. In 1948 the Mexican architect Carlos Obregón Santalicia presented his work in Cuba, and Walter Gropius himself gave a course of lectures at the Colegio de Arquitectos the following year.

At first, almost all the attempts at modern architecture in Cuba passively reflected the formal innovations of the movement, heedless of the actual conditions of this country. Some buildings flaunted enormous swaths of plate glass that invited the sunlight straight in, then had to be fitted out with blinds and air conditioning to mitigate its effects. The main advantage of the building activity of the 1940s was that it familiarized Cuban architects with the technological revolution underlying the new symbolical and expressive discourses of the modern movement; the expert handling of reinforced concrete soon changed the face of Havana beyond recognition.

Many buildings used the "orthogonal" method based on the post-and-beam system. Among these we may mention the Workers' Maternity Hospital in Marianao, already noted above and dictated below; the Radio Centro building (1948) by Junco, Gastón, and Domínguez; the residential towers referred to as the Retiro Odontológico (1953) and Retiro Médico (1956), both by Antonio Quintana, Rubio, and Pérez Beato; the Court of Accounts (1954) by Aquiles Capablanca; the house of the younger Noval by Mario Romañach; and the FOCSA building (1956) of Ernesto Gómez Sampera.

In some of those buildings (as in others like the house of Noval senior, also signed by Romañach in partnership with Silverio Bosch), much emphasis was given to unsupported projecting features. The first experiments in this new cantilevering confined themselves to such salient elements as balconies, terraces, and eaves. Later, whole sections of a building would be brought forward, in a joyous show of "Look—no hands." Another discovery was the concrete shell, pioneered in Cuba by Max Borges Jr. in one of the most noted buildings of the 1950s: the Tropicana cabaret. This innovative building was encased with a spiral or conchiform arrangement of large, vaulted bands made of concrete, set against glass through which may be glimpsed the wooded gardens outdoors, part of the former Truffin estate. Other interesting examples are the dome of the Ciudad Deportiva, by Nicolás Arroyo and Gabriela Menéndez, and the dome over the lobby of the Havana Hilton, by Welton Beckett.[109]

A glance at the wide spectrum of buildings listed above is enough to give us some idea of the very different types of programs that were carried out during those years. All this activity was facilitated by an excellent communications network, in which the tunnels under the Almendares River and the bay played a crucial role. The most spectacular growth, however, occurred in the housing domain, both urban and suburban, individual and collective. The housing boom was one result of the investment of capital accumulated after World War II, and was encouraged by a new and favorable juridical background: the Apartment Property Law and the Rental

Oil painting by Carlos Enríquez (1901–1957).

Accommodation Law were passed in 1952, and the first official, guaranteed mortgage system became operational the following year. Real estate investments multiplied exponentially as a result.

With regard to individual housing and apartment buildings alike, two distinct architectural trends emerged: one, which we may call "modern," embraced new criteria of spatial distribution and functional use, but remained ultimately anodyne and expressionless. The other was more properly "avant-garde," and sought to generate space on the basis of function. It achieved genuine heights of architectural merit by incorporating certain values of our national culture to synthesize a uniquely Cuban architecture, in a way that had been intuited by Leonardo Morales, theorized by Joaquín Weiss, and put into practice by Eugenio Batista.

The evolution of housing under the aegis of the modern movement was directly linked to three factors: first, the economic growth of the country, entailing substantial investment in all forms of real estate; second, the population explosion in Havana, which overtook the million mark around 1955; and third, the demands of a confident middle class that was reshaping the city according to new criteria of well-being and comfort.

Detached homes adopted a square ground plan with a porch at the front and well-defined spaces, some of which were novelties in the household, such as libraries, music rooms, ironing rooms, or guest rooms. The wealthier families had a swimming pool. Scale was brought down to human levels and a more efficient relationship was established between the purpose of a room and its furnishings. The real estate speculation that tended to promote the greatest possible number of units at the lowest possible cost meant that in popular housing the basic components of the model were drastically simplified by comparison with the creations of private initiative.

Apartment buildings were undoubtedly the biggest theme of this period, springing irrepressibly up throughout the 1950s—for example, the tower blocks for the middle-class market in Vedado. Such apartments regularly followed a basic sequence of lounge/dining room/kitchen, and were seriously marred by lack of privacy. Among the exceptions were the building on Seventh Avenue and Sixtieth Street in Miramar by Mario Romañach, and the Retiro Médico by Antonio Quintana. The first was redeemed by the recourse to colonial elements, the sensitive handling of light, and the use of crafted materials such as brick and wood, enabling Romañach to create a more fluid, less impersonal environment. In the second, Quintana broke away from the standard blueprint with a very intelligent distribution of interior space.

The avant-garde building wave was headed by a large group of architects who had graduated after 1942, the date when the restrictions imposed on the profession by the civil engineering lobby were finally lifted. Their clientele was the petite bourgeoisie of the middle and often intellectual classes, with moderate budgets and cultivated minds, well prepared to assimilate the latest in architectural experimentation.

The new approach was adept at drawing out the relations between spaces and their settings. In most cases the plots concerned were large enough to permit ground plans of unconventional design, from irregular polygons to hexagons to circles, with any combination of straight or rounded angles. Sometimes the irregularities of the terrain could be exploited to create interesting sparks between surface and volume. The preference for a continuous sequence of spaces did not blur their separate functions, and much attention was paid to the transitions between indoors and out. The concepts of patio, gallery, and balcony came back in modern dress, and

The stairs leading to the René Portocarrero window in the Restaurante Las Ruinas.

tropical nature was enthusiastically merged with the man-made. Artisanal features such as stone or brick and rustic textures also returned, alongside complementary ones of proven suitability to the climate, such as latticed jalousies, slatted shutters, stained glass, overhanging roofs, and so forth. The placing of each house, the nuancing of its light, and the choice of colors were all the outcome of careful study, in both urbanistic and climatic terms.

Some of the older families still kept the furniture of their ancestors, and brought it with them when they moved to a modern house: in this case they rarely mixed it with contemporary furniture. Others got rid of their colonial heirlooms and filled their new abodes with things that sat better, in their view, with the aesthetic of the building.

There was a clear sympathy between this architecture and the fine arts. Many houses of the period displayed works by leading figures of modern Cuban painting and sculpture, and public buildings followed suit. There were murals by René Portocarrero in the National Theater, and eight frescoes by Rolando López Dirube in the sporting complex of Ciudad Deportiva; Amelia Peláez decorated walls in the new Court of Accounts building; sculptures by Alfredo Lozano and Eugenio Rodríguez stood in the Palace of Fine Arts; and the ESSO building commissioned murals by a large group of painters, of whom the best known are Wifredo Lam, Amelia

Peláez, Mariano Rodríguez, René Portocarrero, Carlos Enríquez, Cundo Bermúdez, Carmelo González, and Enrique Moret. Wifredo Lam also did the murals in the Medical Insurance Building.

The achievements of Mario Romañach, Nicolás Quintana, Frank Martínez, Manuel Gutiérrez, Emilio del Junco, Miguel Gastón, and Joaquín Cristófol, among others, marked an important stage in the development of a first-rate architecture in Cuba.

It may very well be Emilio del Junco[110] who best succeeds in distilling the essences of Cuban constructive traditions. He freely sifted the stained glass, shutters, gates, jalousies, mosaics, marble, and ironwork of old into a mixture bound by new materials and techniques, in an arresting, creative way that was never simply mimetic. He drew deep from the colonial well to find a new point of departure: a contemporary Cuban architecture that had at last found its true path. Toward the end of the 1950s, I began to look for the ideal architect who might achieve the symbiosis of modernity and tradition that I wanted for the house of my dreams: Emilio del Junco was the man who most closely corresponded to such a vision.

Mario Romañach was another of the finest exponents of this search for a modern Cuban house that would be a synthesis and reinterpretation of the best Cuban traditions in light of new techniques, new materials, and new ways of life. Romañach believed that architecture is the medium that translates the needs and resources of a society; he felt that buildings, landscapes, and cities should express the ideals of the social body. For him, the meaning of a building derived from the synthesis of form, technique, and function, strongly and thoughtfully influenced by its physical and social setting—by the direct, specific relation of that building with its site and with human lives and longings. This synthesis, already apparent in his works in Havana in 1947 and 1948, was to become gradually deepened and enriched by his attentiveness both to the architectural history and climatic conditions of Cuba, which dictate the control of light and the perpetual quest for shade and air.

But the process of architectural evolution was abruptly suspended and redirected, due to the events that brought down the Batista administration (1952–1958). Under the revolution, the construction binge of the 1950s was capped with a brief period of exploration and audacity before giving way to the stagnation that continues up to the present. With few exceptions, the appearance of the city remained frozen in time. But during the early flush of the 1960s, the stars of the previous decade found an echo in the debates about the future direction of the profession, and their ideas were taken up by younger people, the most memorable of whom is Ricardo Porro.

Porro was commissioned along with two Italians, Vittorio Garatti and Roberto Gottardi, to realize the project for the new Havana School of the Arts, which was built between 1960 and 1965 on the golf course of that most exclusive institution, the Country Club, now renamed the Cubanacán. The Drama School was Gottardi's, Music and Ballet was allocated to Garatti, and Ricardo Porro was given the task of designing facilities for Modern Dance and Visual Arts.

In his ideas for this complex, Porro offered a quite unprecedented expression of *lo cubano* in architecture. The interpretation of the national soul undertaken by twentieth-century architects comprises three epochs. The first relied on reproducing certain aspects of baroque and colonial monuments, mimetically transferred in the spirit of eclecticism. The second implied a distillation within the canons of the modern movement of those formal, plastic, and environmental values that are the crux of traditional Cuban architecture. And the third stage is the work of Ricardo Porro, who dared go one step further, toward the architectonic representation of a Cuban quintessence.

In order to understand Porro's work fully, it is necessary to start from two premises: his theory of architectural process, and his vision of *lo cubano*. Porro posits a dialectical relationship between image and function, "image" being conceived as a poetic component. And he apprehends the quality of "Cubanness" through oneiric and sensual life, the fruit of Cuba's cultural hybridity and the nature of its countryside. As he put it:

> Cuba is sensual, everything targets the senses, and no wonder. It's an island bathed by the breeze, a soft, intimate landscape you could almost stroke with your hand. . . . The fertile land is sensual, and the way the girls walk. . . . Spanish harshness is dissolved into sensuality. The tragic sensibility . . . softens and is gone.[111]

In Porro's analysis, the "more nuanced sensuality of the European crossed with the forthright sexuality of the African ultimately gave birth to that dreamlike and voluptuous baroque that every now and then reaches a point of paroxysm." Thus the decorous Cuban baroque of the early years surged up to explosive heights during the twentieth century, an apotheosis palpable in the writings of José Lezama Lima or Severo Sarduy. Porro associates the sensuality of the baroque with the sensuality of Cuba, and insists on eroticism as a manifestation of life. His are essences, inscribed into an architectural language of intense formal expressionism, and so from his roots in *lo cubano* he touches the universal.

After 1959, architecture in Cuba concentrated on addressing social problems and issues of economic development. Prefabricated structures took over, devoid by their nature of any concern with quality or aesthetics. Nevertheless, the search for national identity through the medium of architecture, attached to the time-honored constants pinpointed by Eugenio Batista, survived in one or two isolated ventures. The use of craftsmanlike materials and techniques in defiance of industrialization, and the encroachment of tropical flora into architecture by means of open or covered spaces where vegetation runs riot, also persisted during the early years of the revolution.

The house of Emilio del Junco: Side view of the patio, in which we can appreciate traditional elements of Cuban architecture revisited with a modern slant.

Havana University Library

The library of Havana University by Joaquín Weiss illustrates the tendencies that prevailed during the transition to modernity. It is placed to one side of the Plaza Cadenas, in a proud building that betrays Weiss's devotion to classicism. Because of his contributions to the knowledge of Cuban colonial architecture and due to his influence upon Republican architecture, Weiss is regarded as the father of architectural studies in Cuba. He was also an able teacher who exerted a far-reaching effect upon the young architects who were destined to confront the renewal of the field under the postulates of the modern movement. His views on how best to incorporate the new ideas within the context of the cultural and physical conditions on the island lent a solid theoretical basis to the building activity of the 1950s.

Art deco facade of Havana University Library, designed by Joaquín Weiss.

Marianao Workers' Maternity Hospital

This obstetrics facility is one of the most successful art deco buildings in Cuba. Of a similar stamp to many others then appearing in Havana, especially those intended for medical and clinical purposes, Emilio de Soto's Workers' Maternity Hospital softens the outline, thanks to the curved design of the plan, which gives the impression that the building welcomes the women who arrive there with open arms. The entrance portico is accompanied by a sculpture symbolizing motherhood, the work of Teodoro Ramos Blanco. Inside is a remarkable mural by Esteban Valderrama, also an allegory of maternity. The edifice was completed in 1940, and was awarded a Gold Medal by the National College of Architects in 1942.

Above: Mural painting by Esteban Valderrama in the Workers' Maternity Hospital.

Right: The Workers' Maternity Hospital. Detail of the front, highlighting the statue by Teodoro Ramos Blanco.

Tropicana Cabaret

The famous nightclub is located in the midst of a romantic, exuberant garden that used to be part of the Villa Mina, the country retreat of Mina Pérez Chaumont de Truffin, on Seventy-second Street and Forty-fifth Avenue, in Marianao. The house was quite naturally made a part of the cabaret environment.

Tropicana earned the National College of Architects' Gold Prize for its creator, Max Borges, in 1953. Its roof is a series of shell vaults that preside over spatial sequences of the utmost fluidity and transparency, with a subtle bonding between the interior and the open air. Borges found a place for the lovely Fuente de las Ninfas within the gardens; it had been sculpted by Italian artist Aldo Gamba in 1929 and was originally housed in the National Casino. When this was demolished, the fountain rapidly became the icon of the Tropicana.

A host of famous artists and bands have performed here, both Cuban and international. Its glittering shows use the woods in a thrilling way, as singers, musicians, and dancers perform on high platforms among the treetops, while stars glimmer and the luminous night sky is filtered softly through the leaves.

The Fountain of the Nymphs, by Italian sculptor Aldo Gamba, in the gardens of the Tropicana Cabaret, one of the symbols of this nightspot.

Above: Glass vaulting in the Tropicana Cabaret.

Left: Another view of the Fountain of the Nymphs, by Italian sculptor Aldo Gamba, in the gardens of the Tropicana.

Bacardi Building

The Bacardi Building dates from 1930 and was built by Esteban Rodríguez Castells, Rafael Fernández Ruenes, and José Menéndez. It stands on Monserrate between Empedrado and San Juan de Dios, providing an element of visual transition between Old Havana and its fin-de-siècle and early Republican perimeter. At seven floors it is not an unduly tall building, by the standards of its time and place—just enough to lift it above the surrounding rooftops without transgressing the urban scale.

This is the most successful example of corporate image in Havana, having been adopted since its inauguration as the architectural logo of the Bacardi Rum company. It deserves no less, being one of the most endearing art deco buildings in the city. The structure is symmetrical, its three volumes including a central tower. The seven levels are divided into three sections: a base of two, a shaft of four, and an attic below the tower. Maxfield Parrish contributed a splendid exterior decoration of low reliefs in warm, striking colors that contrast with the polished black granite of the base. The square tower is surmounted by a pyramidal roof where flies the emblematic Bacardi bat, an ancient Hispanic symbol of vigilance, watching over a building that is one of the most significant monuments of its time and place.

Above: The Bacardi building, on Monserrate street.

Right: The Bacardi tower and its bat, the emblem of this successful Cuban firm.

López Serrano Building

The López Serrano, built in 1932 by the office of Ricardo Mira and Miguel Rosich on Thirteenth and L, was among the first skyscrapers in El Vedado. Its vertical piers are stressed in the art deco manner of North American examples. According to Narciso G. Menocal, professor in the art department at the University of Wisconsin, its design closely follows that of the apartment block at One Fifth Avenue in New York City. This project was by Harvey Wiley Corbett, main partner at the firm of Helme, Corbett & Harrison. The López Serrano rises ten floors, with another four in the step-back; it has a steel structure and brick walls. The ground plan is H-shaped for the sake of maximum illumination and ventilation in the apartments, of which there are eight on each standard floor.

This was also one of the first apartment buildings to incorporate small interior courts to ventilate the service areas that had no access to the facade. The floors are of terrazzo and so is the elegant lobby, with its showy ornamental nickel-plated panel. The interior decoration maintains stylistic coherence with the architecture throughout: even the flower containers at the entrance are art deco.

Right: López Serrano building, part of the hall, with its nickel-plated panel showing the cohesion of style and decoration.

Opposite page: View of the López Serrano building, in El Vedado.

Casa de Eutimio Falla Bonet

Eutimio Falla Bonet's house, on First Avenue and Twenty-eighth Street, was built in 1930 by the Batista brothers, Eugenio and Ernesto. It was exciting for its modernity and the free association of elements taken from traditional Cuban architecture. This is not an ostentatious building; its smooth walls, unencumbered by decoration, quietly enhance the window grilles, projected forward like those of colonial houses. The entrance is via a gallery stretching along one side of a patio, which is overlooked by the bedrooms. The lounge and service areas are to the rear, and the swimming pool faces the sea. The roof is sloping and tiled, and the bar is painted with murals by Eugenio Batista that evoke the very criollo images of fighting cocks, lizards, and bunches of bananas.

Eutimio Falla was well cut out to build an innovative house linked to the colonial tradition: it was he who was responsible for the restoration of the Remedios church in the province of Las Villas, and that of Bejucal, on the outskirts of Havana. Remedios is one of the oldest churches in Cuba, and to restore it called for complex solutions that were unheard of in Cuba. A generous man, Falla also sponsored numerous philanthropic works, such as the Oncological Hospital, the Children's Shelter, and the Technical Industrial School, all in Santa Clara.

Below: Mural behind the bar in the house of Eutimio Falla Bonet, painted by architects Eugenio and Ernesto Batista.

Bottom: Eutimio Falla Bonet house.

Casa de José Noval Cueto

Designed by Mario Romañach and Silverio Bosch on behalf of José Noval Cueto and his wife, María Teresa Rodríguez, the house on 17A 17424, Country Club, reveals all of Romañach's flair for the modern idiom. It manages to be airy and imaginative within the limits of a highly defined volume. *House and Home* magazine showcased it in their August 1952 issue, with this comment: "When Walter Gropius returned from Cuba recently, the house he talked about with the most excitement was the extraordinary structure shown on these pages."

The building is raised up on piles to maximize the circulation of fresh air. The various levels and elevated gangways are not merely the ingredients of a complex aesthetic composition; they also ensure that the Cuban breezes will play through the house, refreshing it during the sultry months of summer without the need for air conditioning. Reservoirs placed under the raised structure supply water to the cooling system. The west flank of the house, which bears the brunt of the sunlight, is mostly left blank white—a treatment that pleasingly contrasts with the dominant glass of the rest and keeps the sun at bay when it is most necessary. The east-west orientation of the house has a similar logic, for the breezes tend to blow from the east, and thus the building acts as a ventilated corridor that defeats the sun's attempts to heat through its walls.

Above: Exterior view of the house of José Noval Cueto.

Top: Stairs leading to the first floor of José Noval Cueto's house.

Casa de Luis Humberto Vidaña and Evangelina Aristigueta

For the dwelling of Luis Humberto Vidaña and Evangelina Aristigueta, at 2308 146th Street in the Country Club district, Romañach took account of the unevenness of the ground, the movement of the sun, and the direction of the prevailing winds—all these being matters of profound concern to this architect. He came up with a binuclear structure that afforded the scale of a residential building while allowing air to circulate through all of its rooms. The project was developed on three levels, each contiguous to its corresponding outdoor space, and there is a series of courts that are modern in detail while alluding to broader, colonial-era design principles.

The house has been described as being framed by its roof, as the sliding doors make it look ethereal, as though dispensing with the walls, even though the structure is cast in reinforced concrete. At night this impression is intensified by the lighting: the roof appears to float and the big pool causes a magical dappling of light inside the house. The interplay of large and small pools reminds us of that created by the North American architect Richard Neutra in collaboration with the Cuban firm Alvarez y Gutiérrez for a house in the same neighborhood belonging to Alfred de Schultess. But in this case, the profound tropical-weather sensitivity of Romañach produced a masterpiece of ventilation, something that Neutra had failed to do.

The inside walls were lined with bare, light-beige bricks, which matched superbly with the cedar woodwork. Other fine Cuban woods such as *sabicu* were chosen for the stairs and other focal points, and the effect was completed by the ruddy, earthy shades of antique floor tiles from the Canary Islands. In 1955 the house won the Gold Medal awarded by the National College of Architects of Cuba, the same prize that was granted to the Noval Medio house in 1949. Romañach is the only architect ever to have earned this accolade twice.

The Vidañas wisely instructed their architect to furnish the interior with the best in contemporary international design, as well as ordering a varied complement of Romañach's own range of tables, chairs, cabinets, and even silverware. The lounge was equipped with Barcelona chairs and stools by Mies van der Rohe, and the dining room chairs were by the Danish designer Hans Wagner; another Dane, Finn Juhl, furnished the library. The swimming pool terrace was all Van Kepple Green.

Top: House of Humberto Vidaña.

Right: Humberto Vidaña house, garden.

Casa de Ana Carolina Font and Rufino Álvarez

In the house of Ana Carolina Font, where the roofs seem poised for flight, Romañach used stained glass and Cuban mahogany, and devised a smooth illumination and cross-ventilation system. The Font and Álvarez home in Biltmore (at 1312 214th Street) is remarkable for the way its galleries conduct the transition from space to space, while the windows are designed to filter and tint the light, primarily with indigo glass. Air circulation is controlled by Venetian blinds and free-standing panels, and there are lattices and bars that helped to produce varying degrees of privacy and light and shade, always inviting the breezes. The floors are of white Carrara marble and Catalan tiles, and the carpentry used *sabicu* or mahogany. All the metalwork is of bronze and includes many features designed for the house by Romañach himself.

Above: Álvarez-Font house.

Top: Álvarez-Font house, ground floor.

Left: Álvarez-Font house, detail of concrete lattice calculated to filter light and air.

Below: Álvarez-Font house, stained-glass skylight and wooden rafters.

Opposite page: Álvarez-Font house, side patio.

Casa de Eloísa Lezama Lima and Orlando Álvarez

This house, at 855 Forty-fifth Street, between Twenty-sixth and Santa Ana in the Nuevo Vedado development, was built by Frank Martínez. The architect gave me the following pithy manifesto regarding his work in Cuba:

> The principles that govern any manifestation are archetypal, and during any creative period those principles are applied in accordance with their own particular expression. I don't believe that an architect should copy the architecture of another era, so much as apply the archetypes that gave rise to it. That was how I conceived the house of Orlando Álvarez and Eloísa Lezama Lima. Its spatial concept is contemporary and responds to our time: its spaces flow and mingle into one another; they are transparent. The ground plan with its patios is an offshoot of the climate and of the kind of life that will be led here. In its expression we took account of the sun, the light, the winds, the rain and the local materials used for the construction. Any legitimately creative architecture must respond to these timeless principles. The architecture of the colonial era was transplanted from Spain to Cuba and soon began to change under the influence of the tropical environment, until the time came when this architecture turned into legitimate Cuban colonial architecture. Orlando and Eloísa's house is a manifestation of legitimate Cuban contemporary architecture.[112]

Inner courtyard at the home of Orlando Álvarez and Eloísa Lezama Lima, in Nuevo Vedado.

Casa Ingelmo

In 1951, architect Manuel Gutiérrez built this residence in Bellavista between Conill and Santa Ana, in the Alturas del Vedado neighborhood. The owner was Paulino Ingelmo. Gutiérrez assessed this work for me as follows:

> . . . decidedly tropical, facing toward the winds that blow in through the wall-to-floor, wall-to-wall Venetian blinds, which are themselves further protected by sizeable eaves; while from east to west the walls are full, shutting out the sun. This type of house, inspired by those in El Cerro, is for me the most typically Cuban: the ones in Old Havana were traced on the Mediterranean model, with those interior patios barricaded against the dangers and evil smells of the street. The Cerro type, by contrast, has a portico to the front, right on the street, and large back yards. . . .[113]

Facade of the Ingelmo house, in Nuevo Vedado.

Baracoa Chapel

The chapel of Nuestra Señora de la Caridad del Cobre, patroness of Havana, is on Baracoa Beach in Havana Province, within the parish of Bauta. It was designed by Eugenio Batista in 1954, winning that year's Gold Medal from the National College of Architects. The enthusiasm of Monsignor Ángel Gaztelu, parish priest of Bauta at the time, persuaded Batista and the artists René Portocarrero, Mariano Rodríguez, and Alfredo Lozano to contribute their services free in building and decorating the chapel. This was a time when Cuban architecture, fired by continental nationalistic movements promoting the integration of artistic disciplines (most famously in Mexico and Brazil) was seeking a medium for its own expression.

Batista was one of the leading spokesmen of the movement to transform international modern architecture into a manifestly Cuban idiom. A strong Catholic, he proposed to reproduce the unification of the arts—architecture, stone-masonry, glass-making, painting, and sculpture— that had been the hallmark of the Gothic, but without forgetting that the prime function of a church is to be a setting for the liturgy. In this way the *iglesita de Baracoa*, as it was always known, became one of the first Cuban churches to integrate modern architecture and the arts; it can thus, in all modesty, be compared to the chapel of Saint Paul de Vence decorated by Matisse from 1948 to 1952, or the Sacré Cœur in Audincourt with windows by Jean Bazaine and Fernand Léger.

Monsignor Gaztelu relates that he chose a site on the shores of a lagoon for the chapel, and suggested to Batista that he put a glass wall into the back of the chancel like a window onto the lagoon, making the statue of the Caridad del Cobre on the altar look as though the Virgin had risen from the waters. "Very poetic," replied Batista drily, "but no one would be able to see you saying Mass."

The chapel contains a window of the Virgin by Portocarrero, elaborated in tiny glass mosaics that were manufactured in the Vatican. The same painter was responsible for the canvases that tell the Stations of the Cross, and the great crucifix on the altar is the work of Lozano. The chapel has been declared a national monument.

Inside the nave of Baracoa Chapel, with the mosaic of Havana's patroness La Caridad del Cobre, designed by Portocarrero, and a Christ carved by Alfredo Lozano.

Schools of Modern Dance and Visual Arts

As described above, these two schools were part of the Havana School of the Arts complex, built between 1960 and 1965 on the lawns of the former Havana Country Club golf course. They were youthful works by the Cuban architect Ricardo Porro, now internationally renowned and resident in France. Porro described his impulse for the School of Dance in a revealing essay:

> This building, like the Visual Arts school, is structured as a city. In it I wanted to express two very potent feelings I had about the first, romantic stage of the Revolution: exhilaration, the collective outpouring of emotion, but also anguish,

leading to a state of painful inner tension, of agony in the etymological sense of the word (struggle or combat). The entrance and the practice rooms are images of ecstasy. The fragmented vaults above seem to be inflated by some expansive force. But when we reach the arcades leading to and around the plaza, the angles of the columns point in different directions, shattering the order and provoking disorientation and anxiety. The theme, the "mediated content" here, is the evocation of a given historical moment.[114]

School of Visual Arts, cupola and gallery.

The School of Visual Arts, intended to house the disciplines of painting, engraving, and sculpture, was placed next to the schools of Modern Dance and Music. Porro wrote as follows about its inception:

> The construction material is terra cotta, something you can find anywhere. It was selected for its warmth, but even more because it has the color of *mestizo*, mixed-race skin, the skin of the Cuban people. . . . Here I wanted to celebrate the black roots of our tradition, something that has never before been acknowledged in Cuban architecture. Music, dancing, everything in Cuba has an intense erotic charge. It comes from Africa, and implies not only sexuality, but also fertility and creation. The succession of curves, the sensual forms and earthy materials of the building invoke the human, feminine presence: the entrance is a funnel, the passageway narrow, and the great open plaza has arcades behind which the workshops are articulated. These are conceived as theater-arenas, where the object of study is steeped in the overhead light of glass vaults like female breasts. The greenery is luxuriant, full of long-leaved plants that sensually envelop the building like hair. The square has a fountain with a statue that recalls a papaya (in popular parlance, a term for the female sex). I also wanted the school to be a city unto itself, with places to work, to dream, to walk, to meet (memories of Venice?). Everything is organized into urban spaces that culminate in the plaza. The School of Visual Arts is the city that becomes Eros.[115]

Our romatic Havana does not end with this rapid glance cast down the centuries at its history, culture, and architecture. It continues on beyond—to where other cities and villages unfold in the nooks of its valleys, plains, gentle hills, serene beaches, slow and tranquil streams—in its extensive periphery.

Left: School of Visual Arts, cupolas.

Below: School of Visual Arts, the Plaza with the "papaya" fountain at the end.

Opposite page, top: School of Visual Arts, cupola and flame tree.

Opposite page, middle: School of Visual Arts, cupola and entrance to the funnels.

Opposite page, bottom: School of Visual Arts, a path between the galleries.

Beyond Havana

Let us pass through the unknown villages
touched by the slight shadows of jasmine
the fragrance of the night like a memory.

—*Eliseo Diego,* Por los extraños pueblos, *1958*

Our errant *villa* of San Cristóbal de La Habana finally settled down on the north coast, to the east of the bay, four hundred and seventy-nine years ago. It gave life to younger settlements all around, which in time came to constitute *la periferia*. The growth of Havana seeded new urban neighborhoods such as El Cerro, El Vedado, Marianao, and La Víbora, but the "periphery" of Havana refers to its outlying areas, where the villages and towns have their own distinct countenance vis à vis metropolitan Havana. Such centers still maintain their physical and territorial independence, and were never absorbed into Greater Havana itself.

The history of this process can be said to have begun on October 8, 1607, when Philip III of Spain signed a Royal Order that sanctioned two governments for Cuba: one was to remain in Havana, the other was established diametrically opposite in Santiago de Cuba, on the south coast of the island's eastern tip. For it would not do, ordained the king, for the governor to be absent (as indeed he usually was) from so preeminent a city and port as Santiago. The municipal jurisdiction of Havana was to cover a vast area: to the west it took in the ports of Mariel, Cabañas, and Bahía Honda, and to the east it reached as far as the bay of Matanzas—prior to the foundation of the city of the same name—and stretched up to fifty leagues "of longitude inland and seaward on each side." The Royal Order stipulated that a new governor and captain general of the island of Cuba and of Santiago would now be appointed "just as before they were appointed who had possessed said Title for all the Island."[116] But the Santiago administration remained subordinate to that of Havana, while the boroughs of Trinidad and Sancti Spiritus, and the town of San Juan de los Remedios, were not subject to the governments either of Havana or of

Santiago, but were ruled by their own councils. Ever since then they have been denoted as *Las Villas*.

The king's decree was part of a bid to bolster the island against the pirate and *corsaire* attacks that plagued Cuban coasts—in hopes that this would check the contraband trade being conducted by Spain's enemies on Cuban soil, with great financial prejudice to the Crown. The royal document that placed such extensive lands under Havana's control propelled the city into the next chapter of its story, and soon these territories began to be dotted with small, rustic dwellings, some of which eventually formed the basis for new settlements.

During the seventeenth century, many villages materialized on the outskirts of Havana, in what has been called the "rural heart of the region."[117] The restlessness of the early settlers, constantly on the move in search of better lands to farm, gave rise to the foundation of hamlets and municipalities. The process of territorial occupation was linked to the predominant economic pursuits of the day: cattle and tobacco, on haciendas and *vegas* respectively. The first, being of an extensive nature, encouraged demographic dispersion; the second concentrated the campesino population into productive enclaves. In addition there were some agricultural estates, located in areas of economic value. Nearer to Havana, the need to supply the city with food led to many smallholdings cropping up along the main communication routes between Havana and its outlying areas.

These obscure villages emerged spontaneously, without advance planning, and acquired juridical status thanks to the efforts of the Catholic Church represented by Bishop Diego Evelino de Compostela, who founded many curacies and built as many churches. Compostela arrived in Cuba on November 17, 1687, and wasted no time beginning his labors of reform that

Paisaje, *oil painting by Romero Arciaga.*

Below: The palace of Bejucal. A print in Picturesque Walk through the Island of Cuba, *lithographed by Fernando de la Costa (1842).*

Bottom left: The facade and bell tower of the church of Santa María del Rosario, the "cathedral of the fields."

Bottom middle: The majestic Sauto theater in Matanzas.

PALACIO DEL BEJUCAL

by their nature took years to be accomplished but by their importance long survived him. Among these works were numerous elementary schools; the Seminary of San Carlos y San Ambrosio, for ecclesiastical education; the first girls' college in Havana; the convents of Santa Catalina and Santa Teresa; the convalescents' hospital in the monastery of Belén, and the churches of El Cristo and El Ángel. In the rural zone he founded the parishes of Santiago de las Vegas, San Miguel del Padrón, Jesús del Monte, San Antonio del Río Blanco, Guamacaro, Macuriges, Guamutas, La Hanábana, Guanajay, Santa Cruz, Consolación, San Julián de los Güines, Batabanó, Guane, Pinar del Río, and the sanctuary of Regla, in the small town of that name to the other side of Havana Bay.

The foundation of Guanabacoa was an exception to the rule, as this was an indigenous village that had existed a few miles outside Havana since at least the sixteenth century. It passed unnoticed until 1555, when Jacques de Sores attacked Havana, and its entire population, including the governor and his family, took refuge in Guanabacoa (whose aboriginal name means "place of waters"). After that the village became home to a number of Spanish colonists, and the indigenous population was gradually wiped out. During the eighteenth century this town grew and developed into a center of considerable importance.

At the beginning of the eighteenth century, some villages were still taking root spontaneously while others were created by the interests of wealthy Havana landowners and dubbed *villas de señorío*. The latter was the case for Bejucal, Santa María del Rosario, Jaruco, and San Antonio de los Baños.

San Felipe y Santiago del Bejucal was founded by Captain Juan Núñez de Castilla. By a Royal Letters Patent on April 29, 1713, the king approved the foundation of this municipality "on a level and salutary spot, on the southern slope of the immediate sierra also called Bejucal, and at the foot

Below: The village of San Antonio de los Baños.

Bottom: Neoclassical fire station in Matanzas.

of other lower hills."[118] The founder was required to build the parish church and donate four times forty-two hectares (four *caballerías*) of his lands to be distributed among thirty new settlers and their families. Each beneficiary would receive a plot of land to build a house, and land to plough; Núñez de Castilla was rewarded with the title of marquis of San Felipe y Santiago del Bejucal. In the opinion of Hugh Thomas, however, he "owed his title to his efforts in support of Crown policies against the tobacco farmers during the years 1710–1720."[119] The metropolis took repressive action against the unruly tobacco growers of San Miguel del Padrón, Jesús del Monte, and Guanabacoa, which culminated in the hanging of twelve men in 1723. This incident may be considered as one of the first uprisings against the colonial power.

Santa María del Rosario was founded by José Bayona y Chacón, count of Casa Bayona, on the land of his former sugar plantation of Quiebra Hacha, between 1728 and 1732. The site was similar to that of Bejucal, in a sun-drenched zone surrounded by green hills, off the high road from Havana to Matanzas. The village can be spotted from afar by the high tower of its parish church, built between 1760 and 1766, and rejoicing in the nickname of "cathedral of the fields" due to its exceptional quality. The church has a very lovely baroque altar whose sole rival in Cuba is the altar of the Remedios temple.[120] The Spanish Crown rewarded Chacón with the title of Lord Justice of the Borough. This place was renowned for its healing waters and spa: one of the count's slaves had knowledge of the medicinal properties of the springs and recommended them to his master, who suffered from rheumatism. His ailment relieved, the grateful count had himself painted by Nicolás de la Escalera surrounded by his family, servants, and the helpful slave on one of the scallops of the dome in Santa María. This work depicts "for the first time, representatives of all social classes of both sexes."[121]

Opposite page, top: The Valle palace, in Mauresque style, against the broad bay of Cienfuegos.

Below: Entrance to an estate in Calabazar.

Opposite page, bottom: Elegant neoclassical gateway to the Acea cemetery, in Cienfuegos.

Bottom center: Church in Madruga.

Bottom right: The Malacoff market in Cárdenas.

Top: La Aurora, front arcade of the plantation house.

Above: Casa quinta in the La Aurora coffee plantation.

Matanzas was founded around 1693 on the bay of that name, east of Havana on the same coast; it was destined for a glittering future, since during the nineteenth century the province asserted itself as the biggest sugar-producing region in the country. Its wealth became reflected in its architecture, and Matanzas is probably the most neoclassical city of all. Spread along the foot of a bluff that rings its immense and open bay, it reminds one of a giant amphitheater. With its orderly web of streets, harmonious classical houses, and dignified public buildings, this is a well-planned city of many attractions.

Aware of the importance of communications between Matanzas and Havana, Gabriel de Santa Cruz y Aranda obtained permission from Charles III to found a settlement on his property, San Juan de Junco, that could become "the key to communications between the capital, the center, and the eastern territories of the Island."[122] Each settler would be given lands to farm and a homestead with a ready-made house consisting of living room, bedroom, and kitchen. On June 12, 1769, Captain General Antonio María de Bucarely informed the king that some sixty householders had flocked to the new town; Don Gabriel was gratified as a result with the title of Count of San Juan y Jaruco. Many settlers opened inns providing bed and board for gentlemen on their way to and from their estates along the old road from Havana to Matanzas, accompanied by their retinues.

In the mid-eighteenth century there were some underexploited cabins on the ranch of the marquises of Cárdenas de Monte Hermoso, by the Ariguanabo River: they were for the journeyman lumberjacks who supplied Havana shipyards with lumber. Here, in 1794, the marquis financed the establishment of the borough of San Antonio Abad, later to be called De los Baños—a project his mother had been working toward since 1784. San Antonio de los Baños was, wrote Jacobo de la Pezuela, "a town nestled in a smiling landscape, of regular design with broad streets . . . albeit devoid of the luxuries of architecture . . . and of the order of construction that the climate requires."[123]

During the second half of that century, many further settlements mushroomed in the vicinity of Havana: Quivicán, Güira de Melena, Melena del Sur, Guatao, Jibacoa, San Antonio del Río Blanco, Los Palacios, San Juan y Martínez, San José de las Lajas, Alquízar, Bahía Honda, and Bauta, also known as Hoyo Colorado. Pioneers settled the localities of San Diego de los Baños, Pipián, Tapaste, Caraballo, Aguacate, and San Francisco de Paula, places that were later to sprout into substantial towns. The urban structure of these settlements was very diverse. Those that arose in improvised fashion usually developed according to whim, while those that were founded as a result of private initiative almost invariably adopted a grid framework, in obedience to the foundation plan and to the ordinances.

At the end of the eighteenth century, when sugar began to become very lucrative, the government found itself obliged to intervene in this anarchic eruption of new towns. It was no longer a question of spurring the development of a particular place by attracting settlers, or facilitating the emergence of new centers that catered to private interests. It now appeared imperative to proceed with a particular logic, the aim of which was to create a strategic system for whites to counteract what many of them considered to be an alrming increase in the black population. As well as controlling a large acreage of still-unexploited land that might be used to boost sugar production, this new urban policy also sought to occupy the zones around the ports in order to ease the process of sugar exportation. In the words of Francisco de Arango y Parreño in 1792:

> The careless neglect in which we have lived until now, and the untrammeled expansion of curacies, has left the white population sorely disadvantaged. . . . The hamlets that, properly sited, could apply a firm brake to the seditious notions of the country slaves, are rare, and the few that exist are in altogether the wrong place.[124]

This is the context in which we should approach the activity of Joaquín de Santa Cruz—count of Jaruco y Mopox, son of don Gabriel, the founder of Jaruco, and father of the Countess of Merlín. Mopox was chief of the Royal Commission of Guantánamo, convened to investigate the foundation of a city on that spot and to "reconnoitre the Island of Cuba with the object of embarking upon the exploitation of new lands that might contribute to the prosperity of the Island and create a system of defenses of its territory."[125] This commission represented the greatest effort so far to obtain accurate knowledge about Cuba. It set out from Spain in November 1796 and returned on April 22, 1802. Regions were studied and maps drawn, among others of Guantánamo, Jagua (where the city of Cienfuegos was later founded), Isla de Pinos, Matanzas, and Mariel. Mopox founded a town in 1802 in his demolished haciendas of Bagaes and Palos; he named it Nueva Paz, in honor of Manuel Godoy, "Príncipe de la Paz" (prince of peace) and strongman of the Spanish government. Mopox, whom Humboldt regarded as the best naturalist in Cuba, also studied the possibility of digging a canal from Güines to Havana, in order to link the capital with the southern coast.

The city of Cárdenas (1828), near Matanzas, is a textbook example of the foundation of city-ports at the entrance to large sugar-producing regions. By 1860 it encompassed 147 plantations. The settlement grew into a busy town with enchanting houses and patios, and colorful *mediopuntos*. Cárdenas has a wealth of fine civil and religious buildings, but perhaps the most spectacular, because of its very early iron roof frame, is the Malakoff market. This name was borrowed from that of a fiercely disputed hill in Crimea, when the Crimean War was causing a great buzz in Cuba and was avidly followed in serialized papers and especially in the satirical press. Not only was the market named after Malakoff, but the battle also inspired song lyrics and caricatures, and the crinoline, that wire contraption worn by ladies under their voluminous skirts, was from then on called a *malacof*.

Besides these projects, consistent with strategies of national promotion and inspired by the thinking of the Enlightenment, many other towns sprang up during the nineteenth century. The favorite summer hideaways of the *habaneros*, where they also withdrew in times of epidemic, gave rise to resorts like Madruga, famous for its salutary waters; Calabazar, surrounded by attractive countryside, or Baracoa, by the sea near Bauta. Everyone who was able to bought or rented a house in one of these picturesque, peaceful settings, whether in El Cerro or Puentes Grandes, in Marianao or San Antonio de los Baños, in Güines or in Madruga. There was dancing, performances, and gambling, and people drank the waters between refreshments of fruit, sweetmeats, and cold drinks; all pleasures were intensified in that bucolic, aromatic countryside bathed by burbling rivulets and springs, and in the

Top: Abandoned remains of the Angerona coffee and sugar plantation, in Artemisa.

Middle: Angerona house, where the statue of the goddess of that name still stands.

Bottom: Angerona, view of the arcades.

congenial company of neighbors who were equally bent on having a good time. During the fairs coincident with religious festivals they threw themselves with the same gusto into dancing, gambling on games of chance, and savoring the varied and succulent dishes of criollo cuisine. Many voyagers have told in their diaries of the brilliance of the Cuban sky—its luminous sheen, so different from the muted tones of European skies. At night, wrote William Hurlbut, the tropical world comes awake, quivering with life and light.

Around these villages sugar and coffee plantations were started, many still in existence. In his novel *Cecilia Valdés o la loma del ángel*, Cirilo Villaverde evokes a coffee estate, in the rich zone of Alquízar, that he calls "the famous garden of Cuba":

> Its comely, restful dwellings did not front the wide lanes and roads that ran between the different lots. Rather they sought the seclusion and shade of inner recesses; it seemed that here the gold-orbed orange

tree grew more profuse, as did the native, exotic lime, the mango of the Indies, the broad-leafed breadfruit and the many-varied plum, the bushy tamarind with its pungent pods, the heart-shaped custard apple, sweet as nectar, and lastly the gallant palm, which stands apart from the great family of plants for its straight, cylindrical trunk, smooth and thick as the shaft of a Doric column, and the winsome crest of fronds with which it is perennially crowned.

From the road there certainly could be discerned the entrance gates, portals or—more correctly—triumphal arches, under whose shadow, as under the Caudine Arches, it was necessary to pass before proceeding up a broad driveway lined with orange and palm trees toward the distant seigneurial residence ahead, tucked there among luxuriant groves. Even when one was well inside, the cluster of buildings was seldom in plain view, and not reached as the crow flies, for the drive often forked in opposite directions to describe

Top left: Plantation house on the derelict Taoro property, in Cangrejeras.

Left: Taoro, ruins of the farm workers' quarters.

Above: The Alejandría acqueduct in Güines, as it is today.

two semicircles, one for arrival and one for departure; the one bordered by coffee bushes or a riot of brambles, the other by a garden in bloom that swung suddenly into view to amaze the visitor. Either path could be followed to reach, first, the owner's dwelling and its immediate annexes; next, the millhouse, normally separate, in the middle of something approximating a plaza called *batey*, where coffee beans were spread out to dry, encircled by barns, stables, dovecotes, chicken runs, and the village formed by the straw cabins of the slaves.[126]

Anselmo Suárez y Romero took a more jaundiced view of cane plantations, based on one in Güines:

> I don't know, my friend, sugar plantations . . . are distasteful to me. See one, and you have seen them all. Nothing but huge canefields of sickly green . . . chopped into uneven squares by narrow boundaries, around which press none of the fruitful trees we find near coffee—not *mamey*, not *mamoncillo*, not avocado, and never a whiff of lime or orange blossom; perchance some solitary palm, tossing its dispirited locks at the mercy of the wind . . . And shall we have more joy with the buildings? I fear not. The drainery for the molasses here, the boilers there, the mill over yonder, the overseer's office farther on. The domestic quarters are demarcated somewhat from the rest, but form despite this a sort of quadrangle with it, and the space thus marked out is called a *batey*. The *bohíos* are huddled a short distance behind the utility buildings, and can in their destitution and misery be perceived as the suburbs or slums of the small town that is the whole. The refinery, boilery, and mill are not only large, they are dull, dull to look at from without: long walls and conical roofs, or pitched roofs, as they say; however, the first installation is more squat than the second, and the third less so. The chimney pots and stacks, spewing smoke from the oven and steam from the pans and evaporators, also help to distinguish the boilery from its neighbors.[127]

In 1859, Richard Henry Dana echoed Suárez Romero and other Cuban writers in an elegiac book, *To Cuba and Back*, which mourned the deterioration of the rural atmosphere of Havana's periphery. The rustling trees and the coffee bushes they once shaded had been axed, to make room for monotonous expanses of sugarcane. Gone were the ancient, flowering trees with their fragrant buds and the richly decadent smell of ripe tropical fruits; no more were the birds and their joyous songs, or the flashing butterflies, and the freshness that disarmed Cuba's inclement sunshine was a thing of the past. So too was the carefree life of the coffee plantation—a far more congenial milieu, even for the slaves, than the cane industry. What is more, noted Dana, the fact that the sugar barons did not live on the estates but spent their time in cities such as Matanzas, Cárdenas, and Havana, meant that the slaves were abandoned to the mercies of the overseers, who were generally even more abusive.[128] In his *Political Essay on the Island of Cuba*, Humboldt relates that household slaves were kept in line by the threat of being sent to the coffee fields, while coffee slaves in turn were threatened with going to a sugar plantation.

On the old highway from Santiago de las Vegas to San Antonio de los Baños, lies the town of El Wajay. This is where the Receiver-in-Chief of

Top: Nineteenth-century house in Guanabacoa.

Bottom: Side patio of the Guanabacoa Museum.

Accounts of the Island of Cuba, José Gelabert, founded the island's first coffee plantation (according to his descendants) in December 1748, on his hacienda, La Aurora. He reportedly brought the cultivable seeds from Haiti, with the intention of harvesting the berries to brew a form of aquavit from their husk. This was the genesis of the pioneering La Aurora coffee estate, certainly the oldest in the immediate periphery of Havana. Around 1819 it was the property of Manuel Rafael Recio de Morales, fourth marquis of La Real Proclamación, scion of a venerable criollo line that stretched back to don Antón Recio,[129] a prominent citizen of sixteenth-century Havana. Recio de Morales refurbished the old village church, which had been built of masonry and tiles in 1674, and gave it the neoclassical pediment admired today. The plantation house likewise presents a pleasing neoclassical facade, a large portico resting on ten columns, and a hipped roof covered with clay tiles. The family, being actively committed to the independence movement and counting several *mambíses* among its members of both sexes, allowed the house to be used as an operational center during the war. Like some other historical estates in the province of Havana, this property fortunately preserves its gnarled old fruit trees, including *mamey, zapotes,* and avocados.

Today, most of the once great sugar or coffee haciendas are reduced to ruins. Here and there can be glimpsed a solitary chimney or the occasional tower, like that of the Fénix estate in Bainoa—whose original purpose has been lost, although it must have belonged to a sugar mill, of which there were so many in this region during the eighteenth century—and perhaps the shell of a crumbling barn, or a derelict country seat. Antonio Bachiller y Morales describes the simple facade of the kind of plantation house that could be found in any nineteenth-century village: plain, tall, unadorned, with a tiled roof, windows protected by turned wooden bars, and a door

Top right: El Rosario, palms lining the drive, seen from the administration building.

Right: El Rosario sugar plantation, in Bejucal. Note the ogival stained-glass windows within the round arches.

fronted by a porch on slender wooden columns "with an oratory attached in the case of richer families, today almost all closed; but notwithstanding the shortage of artfulness, you will everywhere see that tropical sky, those majestic palms, those stooping coconut trees and the smiling countryside of Cuba."[130] The remains of the Angerona coffee (later sugar) estate are near Artemisa, and those of the Taoro sugar plantation, on the outskirts of Havana; the municipality of Güines contains the ruins of the Alejandría plantation aqueduct.

Angerona belonged to a Swiss family, the Souchays, and was visited by many travelers who had heard tell of its beauties and the grandeur of its plantation house. In 1828 the reverend Abiel Abbott recalled it as follows: "One drove up by way of a splendid entrance lined with palms . . . and by the door, on a high pedestal, rose a beautiful marble statue of the goddess Angerona."[131] The house began with an ample, well-appointed drawing room, with waxed wooden parquet; the walls were hung with works of art, and a harp sat in one corner. Next to this was a study, followed by the

Top: El Rosario, the administration building.

Above: El Rosario, view from the roof of the administration building.

library, and finally the bedrooms. The east terrace acted as the dining room, presided over by a marble Venus kneeling over an amphora to pour water into a conch, which served as a handbasin before and after meals. Angerona was supported by 450 slaves, and employed a music teacher to instruct forty of these for the amusement of the master and his guests. The central clearing or *batey* measured several blocks, surrounded by the outbuildings and the slave *bohíos*. The owner confided to Abbot that he had grown so attached to the place that he had made provision to be buried by the gate. According to the research of Jorge Dubouchet, Souchay was married to a black Dominican lady whose energy did much to develop the estate.

The Taoro sugar plantation was founded in 1820, on the land of a former coffee concern belonging to the marquis of Duquesne, in the Guatao region near Santa Fe. It is thought that this property was involved in the sale of slaves brought onto Santa Fe Beach. During the war of 1895, it was burnt down by Lieutenant-General Antonio Maceo, as part of the scorched-earth policy applied by the Mambí (independent) army.

The aqueduct of Alejandría is probably the only remnant of its kind on the island. This intelligent piece of engineering consists of a long row of

arches carrying a deep groove that channeled the waters of the Mayabeque river to irrigate four of the region's sugar giants: Amistad, a gift from the Havana oligarchy to Governor Luis de las Casas; Nueva Holanda, owned by Nicolás Calvo del la Puerta; La Ninfa, belonging to Francisco de Arango y Parreño; and La Alejandría, belonging to Count O'Reilly. The aqueduct was acclaimed as an outstanding piece of hydraulic engineering by nineteenth-century observers, and once the last three plantations were abandoned during the process of centralizing sugar production into new mill units called *centrales*, it continued to ferry water to the surrounding populations for some time.

While the countryside of Havana's outskirts (indeed, of the whole of Cuba) is littered with the derelict vestiges of what had been the fount of its wealth, the villages nevertheless conceal a good deal of anonymous, little-known architecture of indubitable worth. It cannot be adequately reviewed in the brief space available, since it is scattered through a vast geographical region with great historical divergences. Long-standing settlements like Bejucal contain samples of building from the eighteenth to the twentieth centuries; newer ones like Baracoa or Santa Fe reflect the style of early-twentieth-century spa resorts, whereas Guanabacoa was founded as a major urban center—unlike most of the outlying villages, which even today maintain their pastoral atmosphere.

Guanabacoa is obviously a special case. Architecturally speaking it is an outpost of Old Havana: most buildings are one story high, occasionally two, and have no porch, typical of intramural mansions from the eighteenth and nineteenth centuries. There is also a sprinkling of constructions following the lead of other districts in the capital; Guanabacoa's nineteenth-century houses are versions of the *casas quinta* in El Cerro, and twentieth-century examples strive for the chalets of La Víbora and El Vedado. Lifted over all are the towers of imposing eighteenth-century churches.

Other towns in the periphery of Havana present a very different picture. Their buildings have an undeniable affinity with those of the capital, but this is not out of obedience to the authority of given models at a given time. These are houses that are profoundly popular, so to speak, with a history that essentially begins in the nineteenth century, though earlier examples have been identified. Their most widespread common feature is the single story, and this confers a powerful visual unity on the urban panorama, reinforced

Opposite page, top: Wooden house in San Miguel de los Baños.

Opposite page, bottom: Stone house in Varadero.

Left: Typical village church in the hinterlands of Havana.

Right: Gazebo and fountain in the park of Madruga.

Below: The thermal baths of San Miguel de los Baños.

Opposite page: The meeting of river, sea, and sky.

by kinship of design. A range of basic types may be roughly distinguished, in order of chronology.

The first pattern corresponds to houses flush with the street, having flat walls and little adornment, save for the projecting *tejaroz* eaves. Such eaves were prevalent all over the region during the nineteenth century, and reached what some call the "evolved" stage, in which the tiles are arranged in an unusual way: one tile faces down and the next up, producing a zigzag effect that is peculiarly local. The front door is generally, but not always, to one side of the building, and there is no hall. The sloping roofs are scaled-down versions of those in Havana, the doors are *a la española,* and the window bars made of iron. The patio lacks galleries on its longer sides, as was frequently the case in one-story houses in the western part of the country. The presence of a shop below the top corner room, as in Bejucal or Guanabacoa, was the exception. Any such instances date from the colonial period.

The next configuration added porticos to the front, and this became perhaps the most common feature of houses on the outskirts. Any clustering of these consitituted a "porticoed town," and since this was a relatively late nineteenth-century phenomenon, it enables us to date the heyday of these coquettish pueblos. The porticos are not mere decorative appendages to the buildings around the square, but rather cozy verandas that run around all four sides of the block, much frequented by family groups. They come in two versions: with wooden posts and their corresponding socle, or in the form of columns or pillars that support the roof directly. The kind of column, which was most likely born in El Cerro and extended as far as the province of Vuelta Abajo (modern Pinar del Río), also crops up in the most unlikely places: Calabazar, Bauta, or Madruga. In terms of interior distribution and decorative attributes, both this and the previous model are very similar. The walls are built from masonry in both cases.

The wooden house, with or without a portico, is a subdivision that apart from its material of construction presents characteristics closely related to the above. Timber houses in the traditional criollo mold appear all over the territory, but the best surviving examples are in Regla, a coastal town on Havana bay. The different construction material affects the treatment of certain features such as eaves, but the result is fundamentally similar. In the twentieth century the wooden house adopted new ornamental devices such as a lambrequin below the eaves and wooden balustrades, both carved from a template to look almost like lace.

The *casas quinta* used as summer or recreational retreats were erected on the edge of the villages, so as to have large yards; they favored a colonnade running all round the premises, and dispensed with the patio. This is an accurate description of Las Delicias, the O'Farrill summer house in Madruga, which still clings to some of its former charm. The plantation houses, or *casas de vivienda* as they were called, belong to the same category, and went in for prominent porticos and spacious grounds lavishly planted with trees and flowers, as we have seen. A fine example is that of El Rosario in Aguacate, with a teeming garden and lush woods, built by that distinguished *indiano*, the marquis of Valdecillas.

Another well-defined group comprises the frame houses of North American origin (imported in prefabricated parts from the United States), which made their debut in Cuba toward the end of the nineteenth century and remained popular for the first decades of the twentieth. These were compact affairs complete with porch, organized around a central hall or passageway, that could be found all over the region, in Madruga or Catalina de Güines, but especially at seaside resorts like Baracoa, Santa Fe, or Varadero, and health spas like San Miguel de los Baños. It was not unusual to see this type around the *batey* of a plantation, and its shape, techniques, and materials even exerted an influence on industrial buildings, such as the mill at El Rosario. This sugar factory has a wooden facade, with attractive ogival patterns of glass set into the round arches.

As far as resort architecture is concerned, the place with the most complete repertory is undoubtedly Varadero. This corner of the coast was prized early on for its salt deposits, and the town was founded in 1883. The first constructions were of wood, raised on piles, with an all-round veranda. From the 1930s to the 1950s there were some interesting variations on exposed stonework, pitched roofs, and airy porticos. Such designs quoted the basic elements of traditional Cuban architecture within interpretations that ran the gamut from eclecticism to modernism, giving rise to a distinctive Varadero typology that was characterized by the house's adjustment to its habitat. Seen from outside, the Varadero home blends into its idyllic surroundings, and these are conversely integrated inside, where the view is paramount. The house is also well armed against the heat and receptive to the breeze.

During the twentieth century, with the advent of eclecticism, many houses were overhauled and their internal organization transformed: patios disappeared or were shunted to the back. Eclecticism exacerbated the Cuban passion for the porch, but not without its own modifications. The porch was henceforth supported on pillars surmounted by capitals. The main innovation, however, concerned the roof, which was now flat, constructed of posts and beams, and which called for the parapet as a solution to the upper lines of the building. The parapets were molded; when used on public edifices such as those of stores or warehouses, they were built up in the center to provide a space for the name of the establishment or its owners. The decoration of eclectic buildings was as varied as the name suggests, with certain constant motifs: the five-pointed star was a recurrent symbol on the cornices of houses, hospitals, and warehouses, as well as appearing on railings and stained glass. Flowers and garlands, female heads, and medallions were also basic to the repertory. Finally, we cannot close the subject of eclecticism without mentioning the detached chalets—as they were called at the beginning of the Republic—that arose in the city suburbs, in small towns and on the outskirts of these, always with the cherished portico.

Outlying towns are often distinguished by their churches and parks. The first offer some intriguing examples of popular architecture. Almost invariably confined to a single nave, the exterior betrays the date of origin, depending on whether the facade is baroque, neoclassical, or eclectic. Let us not overlook Protestant churches, which tended toward pointed or ogival forms

and became more common after the early twentieth century; they were built either of wood or of masonry. Many parks had quaint bandstands where open-air concerts were played on Sundays and holidays. Under the Republic, military brass bands offered a choice of rousing tunes, from *danzónes* or zarzuelas to fragments of operettas, operas, and symphonies. Musical appreciation was kept alive by such bands in every corner of the country.

Other provincial buildings came to represent a more sophisticated architecture, stretching to more ambitious or culturally aware ornamentation. This group includes masonic lodges—with their single enigmatic eye staring out from the pediment—leisure societies and clubs, schools, hotels, and theaters. Worthy of mention are the social clubs for whites and blacks, respectively, in Santiago de las Vegas, the Palacio Torcedores in San Antonio de los Baños, and the Niagara Hotel in Guanajay. This last is a transitional building with gestures toward a provincial strain of art nouveau, and was originally home to the Longa family before being converted into a hotel. The lights of its arches are embellished with curvaceous patterns of stained glass. Facing the central park and its pert bandstand is the Vicente Mora Theater, a delicious piece of eclectic imagination that dwarfs the elegant neoclassical lodge next door. Further along the same sidewalk is the handsome building sponsored by the Spanish community, and a few blocks down from the park, the art deco seat of the Centro Progresista society.

Outside Matanzas is an astonishing thermal resort, San Miguel de los Baños, emerging amid unspoilt tropical vegetation. This eclectic building is largely based on the turn-of-the-century prototypes of spa houses in Europe, yet with a decidedly Cuban spiciness.

The peaceful, warm-hearted towns of the outskirts seem altogether remote from the hustle and bustle of the capital. The streets are clean, the people friendly, and the shady porch verandas never fail to present an inviting pair of rocking chairs. There is an alluring tranquility about these houses and bungalows with their tended yards and thick fringes of creepers, their banana trees and orchards; and in such modest intimacy is conveyed, too, all the beauty of the Cuban people. A people born from the fusion—over the memory of the indigenous—of the audacity of Spanish adventurers, the endurance and rhythms of African slaves, the tenacity of Chinese immigrants, and the spirit of enterprise of merchants from all over the world, each drawn by a dream of prosperity, a mirage of unspoiled loveliness.

Four centuries after the Discovery, Cuba persisted in the imagination of travelers and in the memories of its sons and daughters as the ideal of the virgin land that suddenly swam into the sights of Christopher Columbus: a paradisiacal island of perennial green, everlasting spring, and abounding fruitfulness, where untold riches might be found at the same time as lost innocence. The image of an idyllic Garden of Eden as the great symbol of *lo cubano* recurs over and over again in popular expressions of Cuban culture: in the names of shops and firms, or cigar brands whose labels rarely omit the image of a voluptuous criolla taking her ease in a garden ablaze with birds, flowers, and fruit. It also suffuses the work of many Cuban landscape painters and poets, especially the exponents of the nineteenth-century Siboneísta school, who have so nostalgically evoked the legendary ingenuousness of our origins.

Epilogue

The root fastens soul to earth as we await the rains. It anchors us to the confines of a
vast expanse where we learn to drink water and salt.

—José Lezama Lima

I love you, city,
though I hear you only as a distant murmur
though I be the invisible isle of your oblivion
Would that I were in your streets tomorrow
as a dim shadow, an object, a star
navigating your hard surface, leaving the sea
the sea I leave to its mirror of moribund forms
where nothing conjures up your existence
and losing myself in you, beloved city . . .

—Gastón Baquero, "Testamento del pez,"
Diez poetas cubanos, *1948*

Beyond the shores of Cuba, in Miami, homesickness has spurred Cubans of different generations to reproduce or integrate into this new environment certain architectural and decorative elements, customs and traditions, which evoke the world that was so abruptly abolished. Yet the Cuban home in Miami is more than a mere nostalgic re-creation. It is a dedicated quest for roots, a work of conservation, the salvaging of the past by a community that has not yet recovered from the ravages wrought by exile, the banishment from the land of one's birth, the loss of cultural heritage, the scattering of family—and most painful of all, perhaps, the impossibility of contributing to the evolution and development of one's own nation. Cubans are determined to preserve the remains of a fragmented identity, inseparable from the memory of land, temperament, traditions, all so deeply missed.

Before the Cubans arrived en masse, the cityscape of Miami was dominated by Mediterranean-style works of masonry. These became embellished as of the 1930s by elements such as arches, wrought iron, and stained glass, while from Cuba antique decorative tiles and roof tiles were imported, often via Trinidad. It was in this atmosphere, already imbued with a taste for colonial architecture, that the Cuban diaspora encountered a natural welcome to found its home in exile.

After 1959, the Cuban flavor of Miami gradually affirmed itself as a conscious, deliberate tendency. Many of the Cuban architects of the 1950s joined United States firms, making valuable contributions to the community's efforts to assert its origins, despite the demand on most of its energies for many years made by the task of survival. Once visits to Cuba became possible in the late 1970s, increased contact between the exiled population and the island-dwellers reinforced the same trend. The impact of the reception of thousands of deportees from the Mariel-Cayo Hueso boatlift kindled a fresh interest in things Cuban, not only as regards architecture but in relation to literature and music as well. This offered, for many people, an experience of rebirth.

In some of their projects in Florida, architects trained in exile have captured the essence of Cuban culture and building traditions. These they express in multiple ways, in designs commissioned by clients and those made for themselves. Willy Borroto, for example, whose work is markedly functionalist yet also inspired by the culture of his roots, fashions shady spaces refreshed by the breeze. The structural simplicity of his designs, enlivened by boldness of form and color, suggests a sensual, Cuban atmosphere. Perhaps the best example of his work is the house of Juan Antonio and Teresita Michelena, facing Biscayne Bay. Inspired by the undulating balconies and high miradors of his native land, and exploiting affinities of light and climate, the architect re-creates a look that underscores the yearning for the island in the graceful curved lines of cascades and verandas sheltered by awnings.

Among the works of Andrés Duany one lovely residence in Key Biscayne stands out, as if to question whether *lo cubano* is a conscious achievement or a seed carried in the blood. One suspects, on contemplating the transparent spaces of this house, that Duany may have had the fluid interiors of his native Santiago mansions in mind. He himself confides that its impulse was born from what the Mediterranean and the Caribbean have in common as two sundered arms of one and the same sea. At any rate, these arcades of sun and shadow and the play of light filtered through a luxuriance of greenery transmit the sense of *lo cubano* in its most authentic form.

Living room at the home of Margarita Cano, in Miami.

Raúl Rodríguez, for his part, reports that he planned his house around a central patio as a way of integrating the world he knew back home into his daily experience here. Rodríguez was familiar with the buildings designed by Romañach for the Noval family, to which he maintains close ties. This is the background to his own house, which adopts the aesthetic values of the modern movement while simultaneously responding to the finest traditions of Cuban architecture. The dining room opens southward onto the central court; to the north it leads into a garden, full of ferns and flowers growing in the shade of oaks and flame trees. The translucence of the whole is effected by an overhanging latticework, offering privacy, fresh air, and shelter from the sun. Details incorporate time-honored materials such as plaster for the walls, ceramic tiles for the floor, and various woods.

But architects are not the only group seeking to reconstruct the welcoming feel of a Cuban home; artists, professionals, and business people have also aspired to it. The well-known painter Julio Larraz spent twenty-six years in New York before moving to Miami precisely because of this longing to recover something; it is what he calls his "obstinacy in tying down the past." In Miami he bought a modest 1940s house with a spacious orchard, to which he added an adjoining building that contains the coveted inner patio complete with fountain. For Larraz this was like putting together a jigsaw puzzle, so as to recuperate a past that, at the same time, his children would have the opportunity to experience in the present.

In terms of interior decoration, no house strikes me as more representative than that belonging to Margarita Cano, one of the most quintessentially Cuban of all the spaces of our exile. Here are found floors covered in Cuban tiles, the *perillita* furniture reminiscent of Cuban colonial pieces, the rockers Cuban women are addicted to, and wicker smoking chairs just like the ones designed in Havana by Ricardo Porro in the late 1950s, based on colonial easy chairs. Bric-a-brac, books, pottery, and paintings abound, almost all of Cuban origin. Nevertheless, the uncannily Cuban nature of the atmosphere does not derive from the mere accumulation of native objects and ornaments so much as from the sensitivity with which Margarita has understood and re-created the special magic of *lo cubano*, managing to suffuse this environment with her memory of the diaphanous Cuban light. Such transparency is what permits the explosive clarity and depth of the colors —elements of contrast, never of transition, as in chiaroscuro—in this femi-nine landscape ruled by serpentine forms. The sensation is reinforced by the aromas wafting in from the small garden: guava and night jasmine. It is an atmosphere that bears witness to the Cuban insistence, the effort to seize the image of who we are, to seal our belonging to a culture—that of Cuba.

Outside of Cuba, moreover, the evocation of "what is Cuban" is not confined to the better off, nor is it expressed solely through the polished works of a group of eminent architects. It is equally to be found in every socioeconomic layer of an immigrant population that strives, within the limitation of its means, to rebuild around itself the physical image of the land that was lost.

Perhaps Cubans of the generations to come will be moved to cherish and defend Havana, the city that by being frozen in time was able to preserve a supremely complete and wide-ranging repertoire of Latin American architecture, from the sixteenth to the mid-twentieth centuries. It is true that the very survival of many monuments is threatened by deterioration, while the dynamic spirit of development tends to ride roughshod over values that should be protected as part of the national heritage. The revival of Havana will be one of the most important tasks facing the Cuban people, in a certain future: a future of healing its wounds, restoring its damaged spaces, feeling it made clean and welcoming again, delivered from the dingy sadness that has obscured its countenance for so long. This is hope, and a legacy to those who live there. A city, in short, that by regaining its true nature in order to step into the new millennium, may preserve and enjoy its centuries-old heritage, the worthy framework of its most authentic everyday life.

In the meantime, south of the Florida straits, encircled by a wall of water, lies the island of Cuba—close yet remote, intimate yet alien, evanescent yet anchored in the memory forever—like a mirage, a muse, a symbol of paradise lost; the island that once seemed to confirm the fantasies of valiant seafarers, and fed the dreams of so many adventurers. Above all it is that romantic, sensual city of Havana, in whose stones the deeds of a people are faithfully recorded and which will forever endure in our memory as legend and longing.

My Cuba, your colors and scents shake me to the depths. I always felt for you with a passion, but how much, much more I felt on losing you. With wounding, piercing force I see you, with sorrow and wistfulness. I sing to you and to what endures, after the hurricane.

Notes

1. From the poem by Eliseo Diego, "Los trenes," in *Por los extraños pueblos*.

2. From the poem by Regino Boti (1878–1958), "Lluvia montañosa," in *El mar y la montaña*.

3. Julio Lobo Olavarría (Caracas, 1898 [Madrid, 1984]), a leading Cuban planter and financier, world-famous in sugar-marketing circles, collector of European and American art, and of Napoleonic objects.

4. The *butifarra* sausages made by El Congo in his small shack in Catalina de Güines, near Havana, were so well known that they found their way into a popular *son* number called "Échale salsita" ("throw on the sauce"). This tune reappears as the main theme of George Gershwin's "Cuban Overture."

5. It may seem surprising that in a country of some 6,700 species of indigenous plants—of which half are found nowhere else—a plant native to Indochina should have been chosen by a congress of botanists to be the national flower. However, it had become widespread and beloved in Cuba, and is the favorite of country women. Legend has it that the Mambises, or independence fighters, used to hide tiny messages within its curled leaves.

6. Cuban tree snail: land mollusk of the species *polymita picta* and its relatives. It is only found around Baracoa, in the province of Oriente, and has a spectacular, colorfully striped shell. "It has been regarded as the most beautiful species of mollusk, not only of Cuba but of the world." Leví Marrero, *Geografía de Cuba*, p. 660.

7. Esteban Chartrand, a Cuban painter born on the sugar estate of Ariadna, in Limonar, Matanzas, on 11 October 1846. His main subject was landscape, characterized by the soft veiled light of his dusks and a muted palette of dark pinks, russets, and mauves. Many critics have judged his work to be derivative from the French, overlooking his melancholic personality, his romanticism, and his Cubanness. He died in New York in January 1883.

8. *Cobo*: species of large sea-snail whose shell is a gorgeous pink inside, ending in a cuneiform shape. The indigenous inhabitants of Cuba used to cut off the tip and blow into the shell to make it a wind instrument, called *guamo*, which is still its name in Oriente province. Elsewhere in Cuba it is called *fotuto*. The mollusk itself is edible.

9. Guido Cantelli was born in Novara, Italy, in 1920. He was more famous as a conductor than as a composer, directing orchestras from a very young age. He died in a plane accident in 1957.

10. Hipólito Hidalgo de Caviedes: painter born in Madrid, 1902. He made his first journey to Cuba in 1936, to paint a large mural in the church of the Bethlehem College, and visited again in 1948, when he did many murals in Havana including the one in my father's office, which depicted the sugar harvest. I was then in my teens, and received a number of painting lessons from the Spanish artist.

11. Alejo Carpentier, "Lo barroco y lo real maravilloso," in *Ensayos*, p. 182.

12. Bernal Díaz del Castillo, *Historia verdadera de la conquista de la Nueva España*, vol.2, p. 18.

13. William H. Hurlbut, *Pictures of Cuba*.

14. The Villa de La Habana was established between the months of April and August 1514, on the south coast, " . . . possibly during May, perchance in April . . . " The date of foundation was commemorated on 25 July, but since this was also the feast of James the Apostle, the Church had it moved to 16 November, the date on which it has been celebrated ever since. See Hortensia Pichardo, *La fundación de las primeras villas de la isla de Cuba*, p. 39.

15. The formula of compliance with royal dispositions appears in the minutes of the Havana town council meeting for 10 October 1550. Juan de Lobera, governor of the fortress, had presented a royal provision in which the king appointed him to the post of alderman. Quoted by Gustavo Eguren, *La fidelísima Habana*, p. 27.

In his monumental history of Cuba, Dr. Leví Marrero argues that the negative phrase was appended for the first time during an October 1551 meeting, which dealt with a royal provision to the effect that in Cuba, the real coin should be assigned the same value as in the kingdoms of Castile, 34 maravedíes to one real. Cuba and other American colonies had been trading it for 44 maravedíes, 10 more than in Spain.

See Leví Marrero, *Cuba: Economía y sociedad*, vol. 2, p. 278.

16. Quoted by Francisco Pérez de la Riva, "La habitación rural en Cuba," Revista de Arqueología y Etnología, 1952, vols. 15–16, pp. 295–392.

17. The *bohío* is still with us, especially at the eastern end of the country around Baracoa. Over and above the conditions of extreme poverty with which it is associated, this dwelling still strikes me as supremely harmonious with the Cuban countryside, and the most appropriate to its needs. On rediscovering it, I reflected on what a boon it would have been had this model been followed for building popular housing here: it is simple, airy, and natural, requiring only the addition of modern comforts such as flooring or bathrooms. Much earlier, during the 1960s, a Scandinavian architect won a prize in Cuba for designing a house based on the *bohío* model. Prejudice prevailed, unfortunately, and the design was rejected, possibly because it perpetuated a discredited folkloric image.

18. Leví Marrero, *op. cit.*, p. 372.

19. See Alicia García Santana, Teresita Angelbello, and Víctor Echenagusía, "Fuentes y antecedentes de la arquitectura tradicional cubana," *Revista de la Biblioteca Nacional José Martí*, 1983, vol. 2, pp. 145–181.

20. Leví Marrero, *op. cit.*, vol. 2, p. 416.

21. *Ibid.* p. 56.

22. José Lezama Lima, *La cantidad hechizada*, p.

23. After the Republic was established, this site was occupied by City Hall.

24. José Luciano Franco, *Armonía y contradicciones cubano-mexicanas (1554–1830)*, p. 10.

25. Leví Marrero, *Cuba: Economía y sociedad*, vol. 2, p. 82.

26. Alexander von Humboldt, *Ensayo político sobre la Isla de Cuba*, p. 39.

27. Leví Marrero, *op. cit.*, p. 409.

28. Jacobo de la Pezuela, *Diccionario geográfico, estadístico, e histórico de la isla de Cuba*, vol. 3, p. 60.

29. Giovanni F. Gemelli Careri, "Giro del Mundo," *Revista de la Biblioteca Nacional José Martí*, 1971, no. 2, p. 76.

30. Quoted by Leví Marrero, *Cuba: Economía y sociedad*, vol. 3, p. 53. The author considers that the demographic growth of Havana was due to the work on the fortresses of El Morro and La Punta, combined with the rise of the sugar industry (established at the end of the previous century) and the cultivation of tobacco.

31. *Ibid.*

32. *Sínodo Diocesano . . .* , 1844, p. 14.

33. Irene A. Wright, "Historia documentada de San Cristóbal de La Habana en la primera mitad del siglo XVII," in Gustavo Eguren, *La fidelísima Habana*, p. 119.

34. Jerónimo Espellosa Ballabriga was born in Huesca, Spain, in 1613. He arrived in Havana in 1644, at the age of 31, and was appointed inspector of weights and measures by Havana City Hall in 1659. His workshop was set up at his home in Calle de los Oficios. Espellosa lived to be 67, and was buried in the monastery church of Santo Domingo on 6 October 1680. Only one of his sons, Francisco, carried on the family trade.

Other silversmiths of the day include Gabriel Villareal, Lázaro García, Manuel Escobar, and Juan Rubio, all of whose workshops were located around the Parroquial Mayor church. Besides the artisans from Havana, Seville, and other parts of Spain, there is documentary evidence of the activity of six more silversmiths originating from leading European centers of this art. From Flanders came Diego de Lara, born in Antwerp, and Pablo de Bruselas, a Havana resident who was commissioned to make a monstrance for the Parroquial Mayor. From Italy, Diego Romano or Román, who settled here to work in both gold and silver, and Ambrosio de Urbino or Urbín, a goldsmith specializing in jewelry and lockets. Portugal sent us Antonio Báez, a native of Lisbon, who owned a shop and also worked in the weights and measures department; finally there was Juan de Chavarría or Chevarría, from Mexico.

See Leandro Romero, "Orfebrería habanera en las Islas Canarias," *Revista de la Universidad de La Habana*, 1984, no. 222, pp. 390–407.

35. Gertrudis Gómez de Avellaneda, "Apuntes biográficos de la Condesa de Merlín," in Condesa de Merlín, *Viaje a La Habana*, p. 13.

36. See Alicia García Santana, "Contradicción entre ideología y realidad en la arquitectura cubana de la etapa colonial," *Arquitectura y Urbanismo*, 1989, no. 3, pp. 2–13.

37. Francisco Prat Puig, *El prebarroco en Cuba: Una escuela criolla de arquitectura morisca*, p. 438.

38. *Ibid.*, p. 201.

39. Quoted in Emil Ludwig, *Biografía de una isla (Cuba)*, p. 112.

40. Papers edited by the Archaeology Department of the City Historian's Office.

41. Manuel Moreno Fraginals, *El ingenio, complejo económico-social cubano del azúcar*, vol. 1, p. 76.

42. See Anita Arroyo, *Las artes industriales en Cuba*, p. 107.

43. Due to the crucial importance of Havana's shipyards, the largest in all the contemporary world, Charles III created a Naval Office in 1763, under the command of Lorenzo Montalvo. This was a distinguished landowner of Havana whose title of Count of Macuriges derived from the name of one of his plantations. Montalvo was, in the words of John D. Harbron, "one of Cuba's first entrepreneurs." See John D. Harbron, *Trafalgar and the Spanish Navy*, p. 56.

44 "Carta anónima enviada al Marqués de la Ensenada," 8 December 1753, in Gustavo Eguren, *La fidelísima Habana*, p. 155.

45. A feast that enjoyed special popularity was Candlemas, on 2 February, when there would normally be a fair. It was traditional for Havana folk to cut their hair on this day, and prune trees and shrubs, in the belief that La Candelaria would favor and embellish whatever was trimmed on or near the day of her feast. In Regla, a village that lay opposite the capital across the bay, the first week of September was devoted to the feast of the Black Virgin of Regla, patroness of Havana port since 1714. Her shrine was loyally maintained by fishermen and sailors. See Zoila Lapique Becali, *Música colonial cubana*, vol. 2 (unpublished manuscript).

46. This active involvement of Havana's foremost ladies in public life dates back to the governorship of Isabel de Bobadilla during the sixteenth century, and constitutes one of the most enduring traditions of Cuban society—right up to the present day, and with brio. One example of this attitude was the contribution made by Havana's leading society women to the cause of the independence of the Thirteen Colonies, a few years after the English occupation of their capital: they raised 1.2 million tournois pounds that reached George Washington's army weeks before the historic Battle of Yorktown that swung the war in favor of the rebel colonists. This incident has been forgotten by many historians, but it makes me proud to think that in eighteenth-century Havana, which already contained people of my blood, the women of the city's first families were able to give priority to a noble cause over their own luxuries, and sell their jewellery in order to make a substantial and decisive contribution to the freedom of a neighboring people that would, in time, become the most powerful nation on earth.

47. The British sought to immortalize their capture of Havana in a series of beautiful prints, engraved and produced in London. Some were based on the drawing of the noted French seascape painter Dominique Serres, others on

works by the military engineer Elias Durnford. The besieged, bombarded city viewed from the sea was shown to the world for the first time as it really was. In the fanciful, fantastic visions purveyed by earlier European engravings, the horizon was almost always dominated by a tower over the sea capped with an onion-dome (purporting to represent the lighthouse of El Morro), and bristling with pinnacles over houses, churches, and convents—something quite inexplicable for eighteenth-century Havana. Shortly after the town fell, Elias Durnford drew a series of everyday scenes from life at key points of the city and its environs. In other pieces he recorded the local flora and the animals peacefully grazing the fields near Jesús de Monte or El Vedado. Now the world would know the true colors of the jewel captured by the English for their crown.

48. *El papel periódico de La Habana*, 29 July 1792.

49. All of Buenaventura Pascual Ferrer's allusions to dancing were published in the form of letters in a Spanish magazine at the end of the eighteenth century. They were later reprinted by Eusebio Valdés Domínguez in his section on Cuban bibliography edited in the *Revista de Cuba*, a Havana magazine directed by José Antonio Cortina since 1877. Pascual y Ferrer also wrote some delightful features about dancing in the early nineteenth century in his satirical journal El regañón de La Habana.

50. *Ibid.*

51. José Martín Félix de Arrate, *Llave del nuevo mundo y antemural de las Indias occidentales*, pp. 94–95.

52. Quoted by Leví Marrero, *Cuba: Economía y sociedad*, vol. 8, p. 223.

53. *La visita eclesiástica*, compiled and introduced by César García del Pino, p. 25.

54 Juan Pérez de la Riva, "Presentación de un censo ignorado: El patrón general de 1778," *Revista de la Biblioteca Nacional José Martí*, 1977, no. 3, pp. 5–16.

55. Jacobo de la Pezuela, *Diccionario geográfico, estadístico, e histórico de la Isla de Cuba*, vol. 3, pp. 88–89.

56. Francisco Pérez de la Riva, "La casa de la obrapía," *Arquitectura*, 1951, no. 228, pp. 331–35.

57. *Ibid.*

58. Arturo G. Lavín, "El palacio de los condes de San Juan de Jaruco, Muralla 109," *Revista de la Biblioteca Nacional José Martí*, no. 3, July–September 1951, pp. 45–70.

59. *Ibid.*

60. Joaquín Weiss, *La arquitectura colonial cubana*, vol. 2, p. 44.

61. *Ibid.*

62. María Sánchez Agustí, *Los edificios públicos en La Habana en el siglo XVIII*, p. 50.

63. *Ibid.*

64. Emilio Roig de Leuchsenring, *Los monumentos nacionales de la República de Cuba: La Plaza de Armas Carlos Manuel de Céspedes de La Habana*, Vol. 1, 1957, pp. 37–38.

65. María Sánchez Agustí, *op. cit.*, p. 50.

66. Condesa de Merlín, *Viaje a La Habana*, p. 7.

67. Graziano Gasparini, *América, barroco y arquitectura*, p. 102.

68. Francisco Prat Puig. "La catedral de La Habana. Bosquejo de un estudio de interpretación del monumento," *Revista Bimestre Cubana*, 1957, no.72, pp. 36–59.

69. Nissa Torrents, *La Habana*, p. 95.

70. Remarks to the Miami press (*El Nuevo Herald*), on the occasion of his designation as cardinal in Cuba at the end of 1994.

71. Graziano Gasparini, *op. cit.*, p. 288.

72. La Merced was the favorite church of both of my grandmothers, María Esperanza and Virginia, and I loved going to Sunday Mass with them in such a mysterious, baroque atmosphere. It was those memories, and the charm of its romantic interior, that led me to choose La Merced for my wedding to John J. Ryan III in 1956. My father, ever the practical man, would have preferred the more accessible cathedral. Besides, he teased, La Merced was "hardly neu-

tral ground" given the quantity of Montalvo ancestors who were buried there. The wedding preparations were almost complete when we decided to elope, and we ended up getting married in an English country church. That church was torn down a few years later, but the Havana temple where I refused to be wed is still standing.

73. Graziano Gasparini, *op. cit.*, p. 288.

74. El papel periódico de La Habana, nºs 55–56, July 1792.

75. According to María Sánchez Agustí, who has researched Vanvitelli's works dossiers, he was born in Rome in 1745, the son of the architect of the Neapolitan Palazzo di Caserta and the brother-in-law of Francisco Sabatini, architect to Charles III. Vanvitelli prospered in Madrid, and in 1787 he was detailed to work in Havana. He was commissioned by Luis de las Casas in 1792 to prepare the Casa de la Beneficiencia. He returned to Spain in 1796, and succeeded Sabatini after he died.

See María Sánchez Agustí, *Edificios públicos de La Habana en el siglo XVIII*.

76 In the fall of 1822, Havana boasted an early lithography workshop installed by a Frenchman, Santiago Lessieur, to make sheet music; it operated until 1829. Another Frenchman, Louis Cayre, carried on this work and produced illustrations for Havana magazines until 1831. During the 1820s and 1830s two noted artists were working in the capital: Hippolyte Garneray, yet another Gaul, elaborating a series of views of the city, and the English James Gay Sawkins, who was expelled from the island in 1837 by Governor Tacón for his own views—this time political, in favor of abolition. The English consul, David Turnbull, was deported with him. In 1839 two new lithographic workshops were founded almost simultaneously: one was French, run by the Royal Economic Society, and sponsored Federico Mialhe, author of an unforgettable album *The Picturesque Island of Cuba*. The other was the Government Lithography, associated with the Costa brothers. They were the authors of a smaller, less inspired series that nevertheless remains invaluable as a document, *Picturesque Walk through the Island of Cuba*. From the 1850s onward, many lithographic workshops became

established in Havana, servicing the press, industry, and commerce, especially the businesses making cigars and cigarettes.

77. According to the inventory of buildings in Old Havana carried out in 1975, there were 3,024 units, of which 144 dated from the sixteenth and seventeenth centuries, 197 from the eighteenth, and 460 from the nineteenth; 1,959 belonged to the period from 1901 to 1935, and 264 had been built from 1936 to 1975.

See *La Habana Vieja: Restauración y Revitalización—Anteproyecto*, pp. 9–124.

78. In such fanlights the tinted glass quarrels were set one by one into the inner groove of a slender rod or flexible strip of wood surrounding the piece; these wooden cames were called *bellotas*. The cames could be bent to a wide range of forms, geometric or floral, radial or curved.

79. Condesa de Merlin, *Viaje a La Habana*, pp. 72–73.

The Tacón's boards were trodden by some of the most acclaimed artists of the day: Fanny Elssler, the Austrian dancer who enthralled the Havana audience with her "Cachucha"; Jenny Lind, the "Swedish nightingale"; Norwegian violinist Ole Bull; the Louisiana pianist Louis Moreau Gottschalk, who played one concert alongside the best Cuban pianists, with Afro-Cuban percussion; soprano Adelina Patti; and countless ballet companies and Italian opera troupes. The house orchestra was manned by European musicians who came with their companies, and reinforced with Spanish instrumentalists from military bands, as well as black, mulatto, and criollo musicians.

80. In 1846 the sugar yield reached 201,650 metric tonnes. See *Cuadro estadístico de la siempre fiel Isla de Cuba correspondiente al año de 1846 . . .*, pp. 60, 61, 63.

81. Cirilo Villaverde, "La Habana en 1841," in Salvador Bueno, *Costumbristas cubanos del siglo XIX*, pp. 167–170.

82. *Cuadro estadístico . . .*, p. 53.

83. Samuel Hazard, *Cuba with Pen and Pencil*, p. 142.

84. J. Milton Mackie, *From Cape Cod to Dixie and the Tropics*, pp. 247, 267.

85. Francisco Pérez de la Riva, "Panoramas de ayer: La casa del marqués de Almendares," *Arquitectura*, 1945, no. 13, pp. 23–24, 38.

86. Quoted by José María Bens Arrarte, "El palacio de Aldama," *Revista de Arqueología y Etnología*, 1946, no.1, pp. 69–77.

87. *Ibid.*

Of Carrerá, whom some scholars claim was Dominican, it should be noted that he was closely involved with all the projects accomplished in Matanzas by the Aldama and Alfonso families, both in town and on the plantations, not excluding railway lines. Along the Calzada de Tirry in Matanzas stands the old Sabanilla train station (1845). The Cárdenas church in the park, facing the statue of Columbus, is also his work.

88. Quoted by Joaquín Weiss, *La arquitectura cubana del siglo XIX*, pp. xv–xvi.

89. Eulalia de Borbón, "Misión en La Habana," a chapter of her memoirs, in *Viajeras al Caribe*, p. 444.

90. Alejo Carpentier, *La ciudad de las columnas*, p. 26.

91. Condesa de Merlin, in her writings on Cuba.

92. Vicente Echerri, "Cuba, de la plantación a la nación: Un viaje de ida y vuelta," lecture delivered in New York, 1994.

93. Later to be named Zulueta and Monserrate.

94. "Ordenanzas de Construcción para la Ciudad de Habana y pueblos de su término municipal," in Jacobo de la Pezuela, *Diccionario geográfico, estadístico, e histórico de la Isla de Cuba*, vol. 3, 1863, pp. 92–116.

95. Ramón Meza, "Las casas habaneras," *La Habana Literaria*, 1893, no, 8, pp. 182–88.

96. Regulations for municipal architects in Havana, 1861.

97. One was Francisco, Count of Pozos Dulces, a noted politician and writer.

98. During the 1880s, the girls who went to the Salón Trotcha to have fun used to dance to demure *danzón* numbers composed by Miguelito Faílde and other musicians of the day, before it came to be considered an Afro-Cuban genre. As years went by, *danzón* became relegated to humbler venues and more popular milieus, but it also evolved as a genre, becoming accepted by the highest echelons of society. During the 1890s, a columnist for *El Fígaro* magazine complained that young *habaneras* remained seated whenever the bands of Enrique Peñes or Papaíto Torroella struck up a *danzón*, whereas he considered it a genuinely Cuban form. At the the very end of the century, in 1898 and '99, as Spanish sovereignty gave way to the threat of the first North American intervention, Ignacio Sarachaga staged an opéra-bouffe in which someone quipped that so long as *danzón* existed, there could be no intervention; and a Cuban magazine of the same date proclaimed that so long as Cuba resounded to the rhythms of *zapateo*, the tunes of *habaneras* and the strains of the *danzón*, there would be national resistance to the penetration of foreign music.

99. The salon was so successful that a hotel of the same name was built next door in 1893. It was all of wood, with the Mudejar penchants that lie at the roots of our architectural tradition, combined with the romantic folklore inherent to the image of a tropical paradise. Not for nothing was the hotel restaurant called Eden. It was a favorite outing for rich families, and newlyweds loved to spend their honeymoon there. The great French actress Sarah Bernhardt conducted a much-publicized romance in this hotel with the Spanish matador José Mazzantini, who was so much the rage in Cuba that even now people use the expression, "Not even Mazantín (*sic*) the bullfighter can do that" to denote the impossibility of doing something.

100 Raimundo Cabrera, *Cuba y sus jueces (rectificaciones oportunas)*, pp. 31–32.

101. Tesifonte Gallego, *Cuba por fuera: Apuntes del natural*, p. 34.

102. During colonial times, the *Mambises* used to cut this patriotic symbol onto their drinking gourds, and women who supported the cause of

independence would pin one to their bodice, headgear, or fan.

103. Leonardo Morales, "La arquitectura en Cuba de 1898 a 1929," *El Arquitecto*, 1929, no.38, pp. 423–(431).

104. This important collector merits a digression. According to his grand-nephew, the antiquarian Juan Portela, Cintas was exposed to the art world since his childhood, when he lived in Sagua la Grande at the home of his maternal grandfather José M. Rodríguez. This character was the representative of the Spanish Crown for the Las Villas province, where he owned a pair of sugar plantations, La Concepción and La Guadalupe. He married Margarita Machado, the daughter of an old Sagua family: *Impressions of the Island of Cuba*, published by Lloyds of London, contains a reference to the Machado household in 1913: "[It] was full of good taste, art works and the center of the literatti of Sagua la Grande."

Cintas was educated in England, and this experience further deepened his love of art, leading him to become a passionate collector. He possessed a superb collection of Ming porcelain, which he purchased from the heirs of J. P. Morgan, the North American magnate. His home was full of eighteenth-century English furniture, with a preference for Sheraton, and some Gainsboroughs hung over the stairwell next to other English portraits of the same period. The passage to the dining room was lined with Roman busts, and framed by two immense columns of lapis lazuli that reached from floor to ceiling: they had been removed from the Tsarskoe-Selo palace and acquired by Cintas during the 1930s, when the Soviet government was selling off a good deal of its objets d'art. From this room the garden could be seen, with a lovely marble statue of a veiled woman.

The Sheraton furniture was arranged around the main drawing-room of the Cintas home. It was an unusual sight in Cuba, where French or reproduction-French was the style of choice in high society; most favored was Louis XV, with few takers for Louis XVI. On top of the Cintas piano stood an exquisite painting by Raphael, and the library, which occupied a separate building, contained thousands of books of which some were extremely valuable, such as a first edition of *Don Quixote*.

Oscar Cintas was married to Graciela Tarafa, whom he met aboard ship on a journey to the United States. Graciela was returning from Paris with her trousseau, preparing for her marriage, which was to take place in Cuba. The passion unleashed between her and Oscar put paid to any such plan and they wed on board the ship before reaching New York, where Graciela's fiancé was to meet her. She died of cancer a few years later, and Oscar preserved her bedroom untouched for the rest of his life as a shrine to this great love.

At the time of his own death at a ripe old age, Oscar B. Cintas made provision for the Cintas Foundation, which grants scholarships in various disciplines to Cuban artists living abroad. These awards of 10,000 dollars apiece still contribute to supporting our culture away from home.

105. These hotels sprang up in response to the growth of American tourism, which was topping 250,000 visitors per year.

106. Pedro Martínez Inclán, "Anverso y reverso," *Arquitectura y artes decorativas*, 1932, nos. 5 and 6, pp. 9–13.

107. Isadora Duncan, *My Life* (New York: Liveright, 1927), pp. 329–30.

108. The National Archaeological Commission was created in 1937, and among its first concerns was to begin restoration of the buildings around the old cathedral squares and Plazas de Armas up and down the island. The third decade of the century saw a general awakening of national consciousness, encouraging the quest for our cultural essence and the study of our roots. One of the leading scholars in this endeavor was Fernando Ortiz, whose untiring research into Cuban culture (emphasizing the contribution of African ethnic groups and that of their criollo descendants) earned him the name of "third discoverer of Cuba"—after Columbus and Humboldt.

109. Despite the fact that this was the work of a North American architect, the painter René Portocarrero once confided to me his feeling that the Hilton was rather Cuban. It was full of fine local hardwoods on shutter doors and other pieces of carpentry, its exterior mosaics were by Amelia Peláez and Cundo Bermúdez, and inside there were murals by cartoonist Juan David and Portocarrero himself, all of which lent a sweetly native air to the complex.

110. In an article about the home of Emilio del Junco and his wife Julieta Abreu, located at 21235 Twenty-nineth Avenue, in the district of La Coronela, Anita Arroyo maintains that it is " . . . in domestic architecture, rather than in civil buildings like churches or government palaces, that Spanish baroque left us its most important legacy. This may be because the home was the core, the redoubt, of criollo culture." (*Diario de la Marina*, 25 October 1958). Emilio del Junco's house is an excellent example of this. Its floor-plan distributes spaces in accordance with our weather and our ways of life, in a reflection, as Arroyo points out, of the principal Cuban contribution to the Spanish baroque: ventilation, filtered light and shade, freshness, and a well-being of the senses and of the spirit. The decor was a splendid collection of the best in contemporary art: paintings by Amelia Peláez, a paravent by Portocarrero, a sort of fragmented mural by Cundo Bermúdez, and works by Eduardo Abella and Raúl Milián. In a central court alive with tropical plants stood the fountain, surmounted by an Alfredo Lozano sculpture whose sinuous forms espoused the lines of the nineteenth-century iron railing.

111. Ricardo Porro, "Cuba y yo," *Escandalar*, 1993, nos. 1–2, p. 26.

112. From a private interview with Frank Martínez.

113. From a personal interview with Manuel Gutiérrez.

114 *Ibid.*

115 Quoted by Darío Carmona, "Una voz bajo las bóvedas," Revista Cuba, October 1964, p. 52.

116. Hortensia Pichardo, *La fundación de las primeras villas de la Isla de Cuba*, p. 8.

117. See Julio Le Riverend, *La Habana: Biografía de una provincia.*

118. Jacobo de la Pezuela, *Diccionario geográfico, estadístico, e histórico de la Isla de Cuba*, vol. 1, p. 177.

119. Hugh Thomas, *Cuba: La lucha por la libertad*, p. 71.

120. The church of Remedios was totally restored by landowner and art-lover Eutimio Falla Bonet, who had a special weakness for architecture. He wanted this church to become a veritable museum of Cuban religious art of the eighteenth century. The restoration of the altars was entrusted to the able hands of Rogelio Atá Zulueta, who had worked for the Havana branch of Jansen's, and on the restoration of Santa María del Rosario. "He had specialized in the French baroque, was a consummate artist and as was later demonstrated, his extraordinary skill made possible the recovery for the church of its marvellous set of altars."

See Aquiles de la Maza, *Eutimio Falla Bonet: Su obra filantrópica y la arquitectura*.

121. Fernández Villaurrutia, "Las artes plásticas hasta el comienzo de la República," in *La Enciclopedia de Cuba*, vol. 7, p. 120.

122. Jacobo de la Pezuela, *op. cit.*, vol. 4, p. 472.

123. *Ibid.*, p. 410.

124. Francisco de Arango y Parreño, *Obras del excemo. señor don Francisco de Arango y Parreño*, vol. 1, pp. 53–126.

125. In 1796, the Royal Commission of Guantánamo was constituted. It was a scientific expedition organized, funded, and led by the Count of Mopox, and buoyed by a notable group of scientific and technical specialists from different fields, all equipped with their instruments and books. Their mission was to make maps and publish papers on natural history, geography, and so on, after the initial period of exploration and study—and this not of the Guantánamo area alone, but of the entire island. Mopox's assistant was his brother-in-law, Juan Montalvo y O'Farrill, in whom he could place every trust; his secretaries were Anastasio Arango and Juan Tirry y Lasy. Among the cartographers were Felix and Francisco Lemaur, José Martínez, Atanasio Echeverría, and others " . . . who fundamentally took care of the plans of the fortifications and cities, and the canal of Güines." The Lemaur brothers remained in Cuba and examined ways of improving the roads. The Güines canal, which was to connect this city with the capital, also serviced the cane plantations in its vicinity, such as La Holanda, Alejandría, Seibabo (belonging to the Count of Mopox, where the first steam appliance was tried out on a mill in 1797), San José de Veitía, Río Hondo, Ingenio de Pedroso, El Navío, Jicotea, and others. The natural history research was assigned to Baltasar José Boldó, who had been on the botanical expedition to New Spain, and was a recognized plant specialist as well as a professional physician. With him worked the noted taxidermist and draftsman José Guío Sánchez, who had been a member of Alejandro Malaspina's expedition, the Mexican draftsman Martín Sessé, and the Cuban naturalist José Estévez. The investigations were prolonged until 1802.

See *Cuba ilustrada: Real Comisión de Guantánamo*, 2 vols.

126. Cirilo Villaverde, *Cecilia Valdés o la Loma del Ángel*, p. 455.

127. Anselmo Suárez y Romero, "Ingenios," in Salvador Bueno, *Costumbristas cubanos del siglo XIX*, p. 524 *passim*.

128. Richard Henry Dana, *To Cuba and Back: A Vacation Voyage*, p. 97 *passim*.

129.. Antón Recio, who competed in power and wealth with Juan de Rojas, was an early citizen and alderman of Havana. During the sixteenth century he founded the first entailed estate in Cuba, with twenty thousand ducats of capital. There was no offspring from his marriage to Catalina Hernández, but his earlier liaison with an indigenous woman had produced two children, Juan and María. They were accepted and adopted by his wife, and later legitimated by the king. Juan, first heir of the entailment, was thus a mestizo criollo, who became very rich and an alderman of Havana in perpetuity.

130. Antonio Bachiller y Morales, *Paseo pintoresco por la Isla de Cuba*, vol. 5.

131. Reverend Abiel Abbott, *Letters Written in the Interior of Cuba*.

Bibliography

Abbott, Rev. Abiel. *Letters Written in the Interior of Cuba.* Boston: Bowles, 1828.

Aguirre, Yolanda. *Vidriería cubana: Lucetas y óculos de La Habana vieja.* Havana: Instituto Cubano del Libro, 1971.

Alonso, Eladio Elso. "La zanja real: Primer acueducto de La Habana." *Revista de la Universidad de La Habana* 222 (1984).

Álvarez-Tabío, Enma. *Vida, mansión, y muerte de la burguesía cubana.* Havana: Editorial Letras Cubanas, 1989.

Angulo Iñigo, Diego. *Historia del arte hispanoamericano.* 3 vols. Barcelona: Salvat, 1956.

———. *Planos de los monumentos arquitectónicos de América: Filipinas existentes en el archivo de Indias.* Seville: Laboratorio de Arte, 1939.

Arango y Parreño, Francisco de. *Obras del excemo: Señor D. Francisco de Arango y Parreño.* 2 vols. Havana: Howson and Heinen, 1888.

Arbolí, Francisco Javier. *De mí para ti, Cuba.* Colombia: AT&T, 1994.

Archaeology Department of the City Historian's Office. Brochure concerning the house at 12 Tacón Street. 1985.

Arignon, Villiet d'. *Voyage du S . . . à la Havane, la Vera-Cruz et le Mexique: Voyages intéressants dans différentes colonies françaises, espagnoles, anglaises, etc.* London and Paris: Jean-Baptiste Bastiev, 1740.

Arrate, José Martín Félix. *Llave del nuevo mundo antemural de las Indias occidentales: La Habana descripta: noticias de su fundación, aumentos y estado.* Vol. 1 of Rafael Cowley and Andrés Pego, *Los tres primeros historiadores de la isla de Cuba.* Havana: Imprenta y Librería de Andrés Pego, 1876 [1760].

Arroyo, Anita. *Las artes industriales en Cuba.* Havana: Cultural, 1943.

Baquero, Gastón. "Testamento del pez." In *Diez poetas cubanos.* Havana: Ediciones Orígenes, 1948.

Barclay, Juliet. *Havana: Portrait of a City.* Photographs by Martin Charles. New York: Cassell, 1993.

Beauvallon, J. B. Rosemond. *L'ile de Cuba.* Paris: Dauvin et Fontaine, 1844.

Bens Arrarte, José María, "El palacio de Aldama." *Revista de Arqueología y Etnología* (November 1946): 69–77.

Berchon, Charles. *A través de Cuba: relato geográfico, descriptivo, y económico.* Sceaux: Charaire Press, 1910.

Bueno, Salvador. *Costumbristas cubanos del siglo XIX.* Caracas: Biblioteca Ayacucho, 1985.

Cabrera, Raimundo. *Cuba y sus jueces (rectificaciones oportunas).* Havana: Imprenta El Retiro, 1887.

Canel, Eva. *Lo que ví en Cuba (a través de la isla).* Havana: Imprenta y Papelería La Universal, 1916.

Carmona, Darío. "Una voz bajo las bóvedas." *Revista Cuba* (October 1964).

Carpentier, Alejo. "Lo barroco y lo real maravilloso." In *Ensayos.* Havana: Editorial Letras Cubanas, 1974.

———. *La ciudad de las columnas.* Havana: Editorial Letras Cubanas, 1982.

———. "La Habana . . . vista por un turista cubano." *Revista Carteles* 41 (October 8, 1939).

Casas, Bartolomé de las. *Historia de las Indias.* 3 vols. Mexico City: Fondo de Cultura Económica, 1951.

Chateloin, Felicia. *La Habana de Tacón.* Havana: Editorial Letras Cubanas, 1989.

Costantino, Gianni. *Cuba.* Introduction by Julio Le Riverend. Havana: Instituto Nacional del Turismo, 1984.

Cuadro estadístico de la siempre fiel isla de Cuba correspondiente al año de 1846, formado bajo la dirección y protección del Excemo. Señor Gobernador y Capitán General Don Leopoldo Donnell por una comisión de oficiales y empleados particulares. Havana: Imprenta del Gobierno y Capitanía General, 1847.

Cuba en 1830: Diario de viaje de un hijo del mariscal Ney. Introduction, notes, and bibliography by Jorge J. Beato Nuñez. Miami: La Universal, 1973.

Cuba ilustrada: Real comisión de Guantánamo, 1796–1802. 2 vols. Madrid: Lunwerg Editores, 1990.

Dana, Richard Henry. *To Cuba and Back: A Vacation Voyage.* Boston: Ticknor and Fields, 1859.

Díaz del Castillo, Bernal. *Historia verdadera de la conquista de la Nueva España.*

Diego, Eliseo. *En la calzada de Jesús del monte.* Havana: UNEAC, 1987.

———. *Por los extraños pueblos.* Havana: Úcar García, 1958.

Echerri, Vicente. "Cuba, de la plantación a la nación: Un viaje de ida y vuelta." Lecture delivered in New York, 1994.

Eguren, Gustavo. *La fidelísima Habana.* Havana: Editorial Letras Cubanas, 1986.

La enciclopedia de Cuba. 15 vols. Madrid, Enciclopedia y Clásicos Cubanos, 1975.

Febure, Roger Le. *The Blue Guide to Cuba: Season of 1935–1936.* Havana: Molina, 1936.

Fernández Santalices, Manuel. *Las calles de La Habana intramuros.* Miami: Saeta, 1989.

Fernández Villa-Urrutia, Rafael. "Las artes plás- ticas hasta el comienzo de la República." In *La Enciclopedia de Cuba.* Madrid: Enciclopedia y Clásicos Cubanos, 1975.

Ferrer, Buenaventura Pascual y. "Viage a la Isla de Cuba." In *Revista de Cuba (1877).*

Franco, José Luciano. *Armonía y contradicciones cubano-mexicanas (1554–1830).* Havana: Casa de las Américas, 1975.

Froude, James Anthony. *The English in the West Indies, or the Bow of Ulysses.* New York, 1888.

Gallego y García, Tesifonte. *Cuba por fuera: Apuntes del natural.* 2 vols. Havana, La Propaganda Literaria, 1890.

García Alvarez, Alejandro. *La gran burguesía comercial en Cuba, 1899–1920.* Havana: Editorial Ciencias Sociales, 1990.

García Santana, Alicia, Teresita Angelbello, and Víctor Echenagusía. "Fuentes y antecedentes de la arquitectura tradicional cubana," *Revista de la Biblioteca Nacional José Martí* 2 (May–August 1983).

———. "Contradicción entre ideología y realidad en la arquitectura cubana de la etapa colo- nial." *Arquitectura y Urbanismo* 3 (1989).

———. *Trinidad de Cuba: Patrimonio de la humanidad-architecture doméstica.* Quito: Ediciones Abya-Yala, 1996.

Gasparini, Graziano. *América: barroco y arquitec- tura.* Caracas: Ernesto Armitano Editor, 1972.

Gemelli Careri, Giovanni Francesco. "Giro del Mondo." In "La Habana de fines del siglo XVIII vista por un italiano." Introduced by Jean-Pierre Berthe. *Revista de la Biblioteca Nacional José Martí* 2 (May- August 1971).

Giraudoux, Jean. *Lettres à Lilita.* Paris: Gallimard, 1989.

Graetz, Rick. *Havana: The City—he People.* Hong Kong: American & World Geographic Publishing, 1991.

Grupo para el desarrollo integral de la capital. *Estrategia.* Havana: Ediciones Plaza Vieja, 1990.

La Habana vieja: Restauración y revitalización-- anteproyecto. *Havana: Dirección de Patrimonio Cultural, 1981.*

Guerra Sánchez, Ramiro. *Historia de Cuba.* 2 vols. Havana: Imprenta El Siglo XX, 1921.

Harbron, John D. *Trafalgar and the Spanish Navy.* London: Naval Institute Press, 1988.

Hazard, Samuel. *Cuba with Pen and Pencil.* London, Sampson, Low, Marston, Low & Searle, 1873.

Humboldt, Alexander von. *Ensayo político sobre la Isla de Cuba.* Havana: Oficina del Historiador de la Ciudad de La Habana, 1959.

Hurlbut, William H. "Noureddin and the Fair Persian." In *Pictures of Cuba.* London: 1855.

Jameson, Francis Robert. "Cartas Habaneras." In Juan Pérez de la Riva, *La Isla de Cuba en el siglo XIX vista por los extranjeros.* Havana: Editorial Ciencias Sociales, 1981.

Jay, W. M. L. *My Winter in Cuba.* New York: E. P. Dutton, 1871.

Jiménez Pastrana, Juan. *Los chinos en las luchas por la liberación cubana (1847–1930).* Havana: Instituto de Historia, 1963.

Kufeld, Adam. *Cuba.* Introduction by Tom Miller. New York and London: Norton, 1994.

Lapique Becali, Zoila. *La litografía en Cuba* (unpublished manuscript).

———. *Música colonial cubana (1812–1902),* vol. 1 Havana: Editorial Letras Cubanas, 1979.

———. *Música colonial cubana.* (unpublished manuscript). 3 vols.

Lavín, Arturo G. *El arquitecto Pedro Hernández de Santiago: Su vida en las escribanías de La Habana.* Havana: Imprenta Belascoaín, 1949.

———. "El palacio de los condes de San Juan de Jaruco: Muralla 109." *Revista de la Biblioteca Nacional José Martí* 3, (July–September 1951): 45–70.

Leal, Eusebio. *La Habana: Ciudad antigua.* Havana: Editorial Letras Cubanas, 1988.

———. *Regresar en el tiempo.* Havana: Editorial Letras Cubanas, 1986.

Lezama Lima, José. *La cantidad hechizada.* Havana: Ediciones Unión, 1969.

———. *La Habana.* Madrid: Editorial Verbum, 1991.

Llanes, Lillian. *Apuntes para una historia sobre los constructores cubanos.* Havana: Editorial Letras Cubanas, 1985.

———. *La transformación de La Habana a través de la arquitectura.* Havana: Editorial Letras Cubanas, 1993.

Loynaz, Dulce María. *Yo fui feliz en Cuba . . . Los días cubanos de la Infanta Eulalia.* Havana: Editorial Letras Cubanas, 1993.

Ludwig, Emil. *Biografía de una isla (Cuba).* Mexico City: Editorial Centauro, 1948.

Machover, Jacobo. *La Habana 1952–1961: El final de un mundo, el principio de una ilusión.* Madrid: Alianza Editorial, 1994.

Mackie, J. Milton. *From Cape Cod to Dixie and the Tropics.* New York: Putnam, 1864.

Marrero, Leví. Cuba: *Economía y sociedad.* 15 vols. Madrid: Editorial Playor, 1971–1985.

———. *Geografía de Cuba.* New York: Minerva Books, 1966.

Martín, María Elena, and Eduardo Luis Rodríguez. *La Habana colonial (1519- 1898): Guía de arquitectura.* Havana: Havana–Seville, 1995.

Martínez Inclán, Pedro. "Anverso y reverso." *Arquitectura y artes decorativas* 5/6 (August–September 1932).

——. *La Habana actual, estudio de la capital de Cuba desde el punto de vista de la arquitectura de ciudades.* Havana: P. Fernández Press, 1925.

Maza, Aquiles de la. *Eutimio Falla Bonet: Su obra filantrópica y la arquitectura.* Geneva: Albert Skira Art Editions, 1971.

Memorias de Doña Eulalia de Borbón, Infanta de España. Barcelona: Editorial Juventud, 1987.

Merlín, Condesa de. *Viaje a La Habana.* Havana: El Siglo XX, 1922.

Meza, Ramón. "Las casas habaneras." *La Habana Literaria* 1:8 (1893): 182–88.

Michener, James A., and John King. *Six Days in Havana.* Austin: University of Texas, 1989.

Montoulieu, Enrique J. "El crecimiento de La Habana y su regularización." In *Evolución de la Cultura Cubana,* vol. 15. Havana: Imprenta Montalvo y Cárdenas, 1928.

Monumentos y sitios históricos de la Ciudad de La Habana. Havana: Ministerio de Cultura, 1983.

Morales, Leonardo. "La arquitectura en Cuba de 1898 a 1929." *El Arquitecto* 38 (May 1929): 423–31.

Morell de Santa Cruz, Pedro Agustín. *La visita eclesiástica.* Compiled and introduced by César García del Pino. Havana: Editorial Ciencias Sociales, 1985.

Moreno Fraginals, Manuel. *El ingenio, complejo económico-social cubano del azúcar.* 3 vols. Havana: Editorial Ciencias Sociales, 1978.

Nieto Cortadellas, Rafael. *Dignidades nobiliarias en Cuba.* Madrid: Eds. Cultura Hispánica, 1954.

——. *Genealogías habaneras.* 4 vols. Madrid: Ediciones de la Revista Hidalguía, 1979, 1995, 1996.

Núñez Jiménez, Antonio, and Carlos Venegas Fornias. *La Habana.* Madrid: Instituto de Cooperación Iberoamericana, 1986.

Ortiz, Fernando. *Nuevo catauro de cubanismos.* Havana: Editorial Ciencias Sociales, 1985.

Otto, Eduard. *Reiseerinnerungen an Cuba, nord und südamérica, 1838, 1841.* Berlin: Verlag der Nauchschen Buchhandlung, 1843.

El papel periódico de La Habana 55/56 (July 1792).

Paseo pintoresco por la Isla de Cuba. Havana: 1841–42.

Pérez Beato, Manuel. *La Habana antigua.* Havana: Seoane Fernández, 1936.

Pérez de Acevedo, Luciano. *La Habana en el siglo XIX descrita por viajeros extranjeros.* Havana: Sociedad Editorial de Cuba Contemporánea, 1919.

Pérez de la Riva, Francisco. "La casa de la Obrapía." *Arquitectura* 19:228 (September 1951): 331–35.

——. "La habitación rural en Cuba." *Revista de Arqueología y Etnología* (December–January 1952): 295–392.

——. "Panoramas de ayer: La casa del marqués de Almendares." *Arquitectura* 13:138 (January 1945): 23–24, 38.

——. "Panoramas de ayer: Una casa cubana del siglo XVII." *Arquitectura* 12:136 (1944).

Pérez de la Riva, Juan. *La isla de Cuba en el siglo XIX vista por los extranjeros.* Havana: Editorial Ciencias Sociales, 1981.

——. "Presentación de un censo ignorado: El padrón general de 1778." *Revista de la Biblioteca Nacional José Martí* 68:3 (September–December 1977): 5–16.

Pezuela, Jacobo de la. *Diccionario geográfico, estadístico, e histórico de la isla de Cuba.* 4 vols. Madrid: Imprenta del Establecimiento de Mellado, 1863–78.

Pichardo, Esteban. *Diccionario provincial cuasi razonado de vozes y frases cubanas.* Havana: Imprenta El Trabajo, 1875.

Pichardo, Hortensia. *Antonio José Valdés, ¿historia de Cuba o historia de La Habana?* Havana: Editorial Ciencias Sociales, 1987.

——. *Documentos para la historia de Cuba.* 2 vols. Havana: Editorial Ciencias Sociales, 1971.

——. *La fundación de las primeras villas de la Isla de Cuba.* Havana: Instituto Cubano del Libro, 1986.

Porro, Ricardo. *Les cinq aspects du contenu.* Paris: Institut Français d'Architecture, 1993.

——. "Cuba y yo," *Escandalar* 1:1–2 (1993).

——. *Œuvres/Obras* 1950–1993. Paris: Institut Français d'Architecture, 1993.

Prat Puig, Francisco. "La catedral de La Habana: Bosquejo de un estudio de interpretación del monumento." *Revista Bimestre Cubana* 72 (January–June 1957): 36–59.

——. *El prebarroco en Cuba: Una escuela criolla de arquitectura morisca.* Havana: Burgay, 1947.

Reglamento para los arquitectos municipales de La Habana. Havana: Imprenta del Gobierno y Capitanía General, 1861.

Riverend, Julio Le. *La Habana: Biografía de una provincia.* Havana: Imprenta El Siglo XX, 1960.

Roberts, Adolphe W. *Havana, the Portrait of a City.* New York: Coward-McCann, 1953.

Rodríguez Jiménez, Fernando L. *Sentir Cuba, gigante del Caribe.* Agualarga Editores, 1995.

Roig de Leuchsenring, Emilio. *La Habana: Apuntes históricos.* Havana, 1931.

——. *Los monumentos nacionales de la República de Cuba: La Plaza de Armas Carlos Manuel de Céspedes de La Habana.* Vol. 1. Havana: Publicaciones de la Junta Nacional de Arqueología y Etnología, 1957.

Romero, Leandro. "Orfebrería habanera en las Islas Canarias." *Revista de la Universidad de La Habana* 222 (1984): 390–407.

Sánchez Agustí, María. *Los edificios públicos en La Habana en el siglo XVIII.* Valladolid, Spain: Universidad de Valladolid, 1984.

Sánchez de Fuentes, Eugenio. *Cuba monumental, estatuaria y epigráfica.* Havana, 1916.

San Juan de Jaruco, Conde de. *Historias de familias cubanas.* 6 vols. Havana: Editorial Hércules, 1940–50.

Sapieha, Nicolas. *Old Havana, Cuba.* Photographs by Francesco Venturi. London: Tauris Parke Books, 1990.

Segre, Roberto. *Arquitectura y urbanismo de la revolución cubana.* Havana: Editorial Pueblo y Educación, 1989.

——. "Significación de Cuba en la evolución tipológica de las fortificaciones coloniales de América." *Revista de la Biblioteca Nacional José Martí* 59:2 (May–August 1968).

——. *La vivienda en Cuba: República y revolución cubana.* Havana: Universidad de La Habana, 1985.

Sínodo Diocesano Havana: Government Imprimatur, 1844.

Smith, Wayne. Cuba. Photographs by Michael Reagan. Turner Publishing, 1991.

Stout, Nancy, and Jorge Rigau. *Havana.* New York: Rizzoli, 1994.

Tanco Armero, Nicolás. *Viaje de Nueva Granada a China y de China a Francia.* Paris: Simon Racon, 1881.

Thomas, Hugh. *Cuba: La lucha por la libertad.* 2 vols. Barcelona and Mexico City: Editorial Grijalbo, 1973–74.

Torre, José María de la. *Lo que fuimos y lo que somos, o La Habana antigua y moderna.* Havana: Imprenta de Spencer, 1857.

Torrents, Nissa. *La Habana.* Barcelona: Ediciones Destino S.A., 1989.

Tylden, Sir John Maxwell. "Diario." *Revista de la Biblioteca Nacional José Martí* 2 (May–August 1972).

Underhill, Edward Bean. *The West Indies: Their Social and Religious Conditions.* London: Jackson, Walford, and Hutter, 1862.

Urrutia y Montoya, Ignacio José de. *Teatro histórico, jurídico y político-militar de la Isla Fernandina de Cuba.* Vol. 2. Havana: A. Pego, 1876.

Vásquez de Espinosa, Antonio. *Compendio y descripción de las Indias Occidentales.* Washington, D.C.: Smithsonian Institution, 1948 [1622].

Venegas, Carlos. *La urbanización de Las Murallas: Dependencia y modernidad.* Havana: Editorial Letras Cubanas, 1990.

Viajeras al Caribe. Selection, prologue, and notes by Nara Araújo. Havana: Casa de las Américas, 1983.

Villaverde, Cirilo. *Cecilia Valdés o la Loma del Ángel.* Havana: Editorial Arte y Literatura, 1977.

Vocabulario arquitectónico ilustrado. Mexico City: Secretaría de Asentamientos Humanos y Obras Públicas, 1980.

Weiss, Joaquín. *Arquitectura cubana contemporánea.* Havana: Cultural, 1947.

——. *La arquitectura cubana del siglo XIX.* Havana: Publicaciones de la Junta Nacional de Arqueología y Etnología, 1960.

——. "La nueva arquitectura y nosotros." *Revista de la Universidad de La Habana* 3 (May–June 1934).

Wright, Irene A. *Historia documentada de San Cristóbal de La Habana en el siglo XVI, basada en los documentos originales existentes en el Archivo General de Indias en Sevilla.* Havana, 1927.

——. *Historia documentada de San Cristóbal de La Habana en la primera mitad del siglo XVI, basada en los documentos originales existentes en el Archivo General de Indias en Sevilla.* Havana: Imprenta El Siglo XX, 1930.

Wurdermann, J. G. F. *Notes on Cuba.* Boston, 1844.

Maps

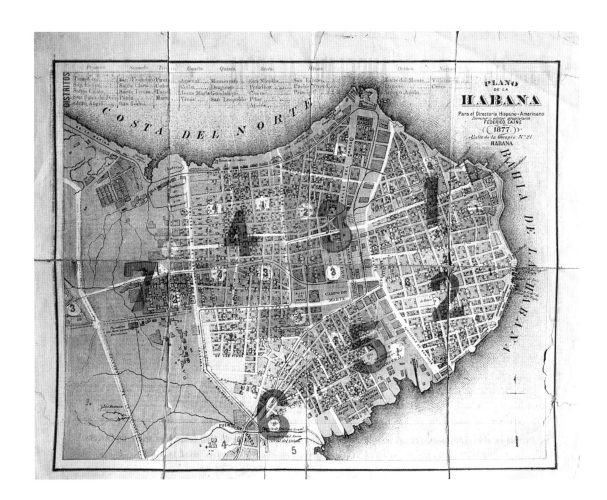

Right: *Map of Havana.*

Below: *Map of Cuba.*

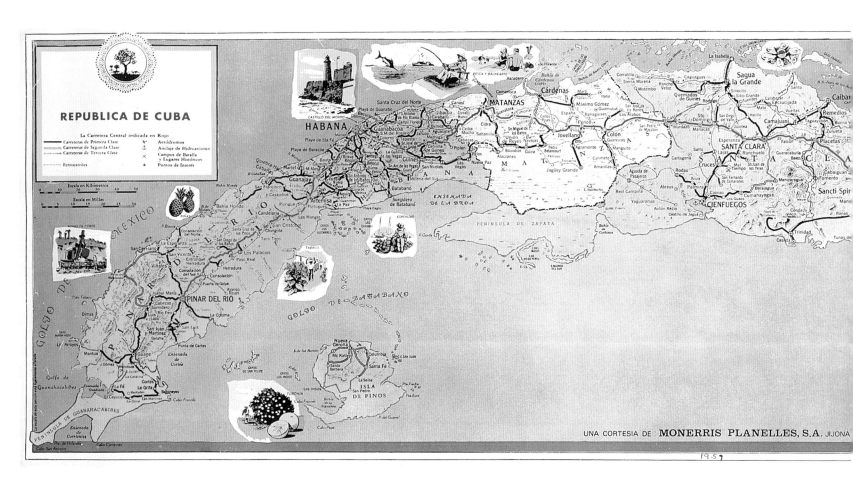

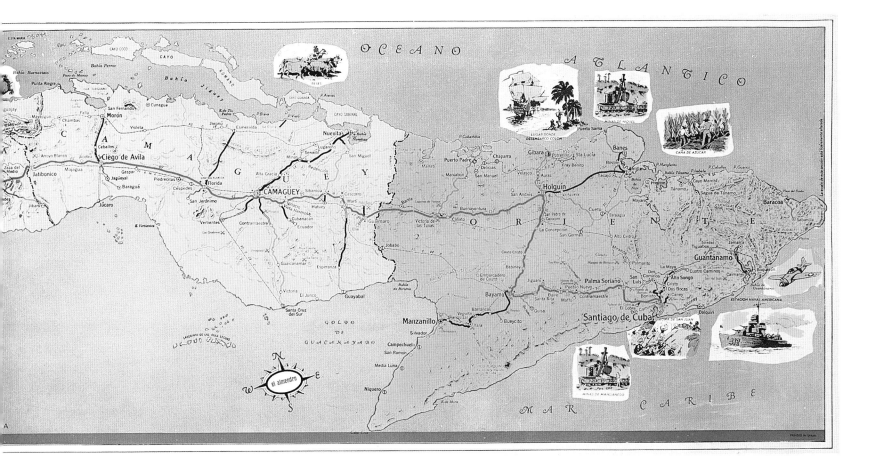

Index